T0339814

Roots of Cataclysm

Roots of Cataclysm

Geopulsation and the Atlantis Supervolcano in History

Richard W. Welch

Algora Publishing
New York

Library of Congress Cataloging-in-Publication Data —

Welch, Richard W., 1929-
    Roots of cataclysm: geopulsation and the Atlantis supervolcano / Richard W.
Welch.
      p. cm.
    Includes bibliographical references and index.
    ISBN 978-0-87586-732-8 (soft cover: alk. paper) — ISBN 978-0-87586-733-5 (hard
cover: alk. paper) 1. Atlantis (Legendary place) I. Title.
    GN751.W39 2009
    398.23'4—dc22
                                    2009020932

Printed in the United States

To Susan and Barbara

TABLE OF CONTENTS

Introduction

The unwritten past does not decipher easily. Sir Arthur Conan Doyle himself could not have conjured up a detective story more intriguing than the prehistory of human kind on planet Earth. Or one with a more devious plot line. It is a tale of paradoxes, shifting premises, missing clues and false trails, of vanishing victims and mysterious strangers who intrude unannounced.

The initial prehistoric settlement of the New World, for instance, only grows murkier and more controversial as our "enlightened" era progresses. Taking on the question, it soon comes clear that no resolution is likely without first descrambling the quandaries still surrounding the geography and climatology of the last Ice Age. It is our lack of understanding of the real Pleistocene environment that has, more than anything else, befogged the problem of the First Americans.

Once these geo-climatic factors are brought into focus, the whole knot begins to unravel — not only the tangle of Native American origins but a number of associated enigmas as well, including one of the oldest and most baffling of all: the legend of the Lost Atlantis.

The questions of how we humans came to be where we are, and what we are, has a natural fascination for most of us. But the trail grows rapidly faint. Following the historical footsteps back to the Nile and Euphrates valleys soon leads us to the barrier of universal illiteracy, a time when no one on Earth could read or write. Yet beyond this barrier is more than 99 percent of the human experience. In this wordless realm, where only stones and bones are left to speak, the difficulties in deciphering the human adventure are compounded a hundred times. Yet because of this, because there is more mystery and uncertainty, prehistory is, in ways, more fascinating than written history. Moreover, what happened in this veiled arena of remote antiquity is much more basic to our destiny than the campaigns of ancient Mediterranean kings.

Mankind has only recently become conscious of the fact that there is something of import behind the curtain of non-literacy. Only lately have we been driven to probe behind it and devise ingenious techniques to aid in the probes. But the effort so far has produced as many questions as answers. First we were confronted with incomprehensible but undeniable evidence that a quarter of our world was not very long ago covered with masses of ice a mile thick. Hardly had we begun to accept this incredibility than we encountered others even more baffling.

Of late, within the past few decades, geologists have accepted the stunning notion that the continents are not permanently fixed but actually migrate about the surface of the earth — a concept that seemed almost laughable within the memory of many of us. Worst of all, no explanation for this enigmatic phenomenon really works. Once confident that we could easily explain the peopling of the New World, we now find aspects of this settlement that cannot be made to jibe with the accepted Bering Straits theory of approach. Recent finds in both North and South America virtually vaporize current dogma on this issue.

The genesis of the pre-Columbian American civilizations has become a matter of increasing uncertainty as new discoveries suggest exotic influences from unknown directions. More consternation is produced by strange myths and legends from the dim dawn of history: stories such as that of Atlantis, which seem at once to demand and defy explanation. We are further bemused by the fact that some of these tales — those of Troy and of the Minoan kings, for example — have been found to contain more truth than fantasy. Meanwhile, geologists have lately established that planet Earth is periodically afflicted by violent geological events exponentially beyond the intensity of anything in our written records. With the discovery of supervolcanoes — so vast that they are only perceptible from the air — the sudden destruction of large areas, a la Atlantis, is much less far-fetched than we thought. Our planet is nowhere near as stable as has been assumed.

Confronted by all this confounding testimony about our own antiquity, we may be excused the suspicion that some factor of key consequence has been omitted from the equation, that some touchstone of prehistory has gone undiscovered. This, in fact, turns out to be just the case. The key to prehistory is the driving mechanism behind the great glaciers of the Pleistocene era — the same force, it happens, that underlies continental drift.

The mechanism is deductible from recently developed data showing that Earth's core rotates with a degree of independence, causing the velocity of planetary rotation to vary slightly, plus or minus, over the millennia. The import of this revelation has not yet been imagined. But as we unravel the implications we are able to lift some of the darkest curtains of antiquity. As those curtains rise, they reveal a stage setting and a plot line quite different from what has been supposed.

CHAPTER 1. PORTENTS OF ATLANTICA

In November of 1963, off the southern coast of Iceland, a cauldron beneath the sea began to boil. Fishermen drawn by what they assumed to be smoke from a burning ship found the sea water seething. By nightfall, a black volcanic cone oozing lava had thrust itself into the Arctic atmosphere. As super-heated rock and steam spewed skyward, flashes of lightning crackled through the pillar of smoke that marked the event for eyes leagues away. It was a piece out of Genesis: the birth of Surtsey.

The islet grew steadily through the next few years to nearly two square miles in area. As parts of it cooled, life found it. First bacteria and molds, then algae and seaweed grasped this new offering of sustaining earth.

Less than a decade after the eruption of Surtsey, and not many miles away, a sudden fissure split open the island of Heimaey. Lava boiled out and a new volcanic cone began to build. Much of the isle's only town was buried in volcanic debris and molten lava. More lava poured into the sea and increased the area of the small island by more than a half a square mile.

Surtsey and Heimaey are only the latest of the contortions by fire and ice that have shaped the geography of the North Atlantic and the history of much of our world. For Iceland itself is a creation of Vulcan, formed of thousands of Surtseys over many millions of years. And Iceland is but a part of a huge lava plateau that sprawls above and beneath the surface of the sea from Britain to northern North America.

The plateau has been building since some catastrophic rift split the continents of Europe and North America from their former union more than a hundred million years ago. As the tectonic plates migrated the thousands of miles that now separate them, basaltic magma welled out of the ocean floor fissures from the inferno beneath, building an epical land — albeit one with no name. Call it "Atlantica."

In this Atlantica are buried many of the keys to secrets of the Pleistocene, or Ice Age, the past two million years that have made mankind something apart from the rest of nature. Here, written in geological esoterica, are missing chapters from our past. When deciphered, they speak of human migrations, creeping continents, massive glaciations, and also of lost lands. Woven through these intertwined tales we will find clues to a surprising number of associated enigmas in Earth's history and our own.

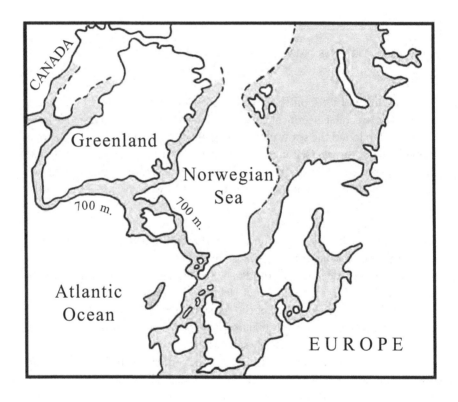

Fig. 1: Sketch map of the North Atlantic showing the 700 meter isobath. Waters shallower than 700 meters are shaded. The map shows the land bridge that would emerge in the North Atlantic with a 700 meter alteration of land-sea relationships. Since the sea floor has not, of course, been mapped as accurately as land surfaces, there is some disagreement in the submarine charts. Some indicate a 600 meter fall in sea level would be sufficient to establish the bridge.

Some supposedly exotic views will be found to contain more truth than some accepted doctrines. For example, evidence exists for the presence in Pleistocene time of a traversable link intermittently connecting the continents of Europe and North America. This link — Atlantica — not only emerges as a main avenue for Stone Age migration to America, it also leads us to the forcing mechanism behind the Ice Ages and ultimately to a resolution of the Atlantis Legend.

A lot of this is going to sound like heresy. But it is all demonstrable.

A Troublous Link

Scanning the faunal populations of North America, it is hard to avoid a nagging feeling that something is not quite right. The standard story of how the animals that inhabit the continent got here fails to hold together.

Of one thing there is no question: Eurasia must have been tied by a land connection to the Americas in Pleistocene time. The point is beyond dispute because of the high similarity between Palearctic and Nearctic fauna. The assumption is that the necessary link could have only been at the Bering Strait during glacial episodes.

The now submerged plain between Alaska and Siberia was above sea level at time during the Pliocene Epoch but then sank to about its present station. Later, during the Ice Age, seas dropped periodically to again lay bare the ancient tie. It is estimated that ocean levels fell about 125 meters (ca. 400 ft.), perhaps a good deal more, during the glacial maxima due to the immense amount of the world's water locked in the ice. A drop of about half that magnitude would be enough to permit land passage from Siberia to Nome.

Thus is provided the solid earth between the two great world islands needed to explain the close affinity between the animal life of the Old World and the New.

Superficially, it all seems feasible enough. But there are flaws in the scenario to which even those who accept it are not blind. The catch is most evident in the types of creatures known to have migrated to the Americas during the Ice Age. Among them were mastodons, bison, elk (wapiti), mountain sheep and goats, foxes, bears, wolves and horses (the horse later died out and had to be reintroduced).

Oddly, these are not tundra animals. Yet they are alleged to have made the journey from Siberia to Alaska during periods of heavy glaciation when Beringia had an even more severe climate than it does today. Even now, there are hundreds of miles of frozen, barren tundra between the woodlands and grasslands of Alaska and those of northeast Asia. In glacial times the tundra gap must have been much wider. How curious the tale that we are asked to accept at the hands of zoologists.

Writing on this point, William Haag says, "It must be admitted that the Bering Strait land bridge of the geologist, appearing as it does only intermittently above sea level, does not fully serve the purposes of the zoologist and the botanist. Most zoologists...argue for a broad bridge available throughout nearly all of the Pleistocene. What is more, the animals that came across the bridge were not typically cold-climate animals (none of the true cold-climate animals such as the woolly rhinoceros ever reached America). On the contrary, the animals were the ones that would have preferred the warmer interglacial times for their spread."[1]

As tenuous as the Bering Strait route seems in light of Haag's comments, it becomes even more so when another aspect is considered. The uncomfortable fact is that even when the Siberia–Alaska bridge was open to traffic, there was another barricade not far down the road: a mile-high wall of ice.

When the glaciers lowered the sea to expose the Beringian plain, they almost simultaneously blocked the route from Alaska to the American heartland with continental ice sheets. These glacial masses covered virtually all of Canada and, at times parts of the northern United States. The best that conventional theory can offer us here is the hypothesis of the "ice free corridor," i.e., that there must have been a gap between the continental ice sheets through which the animals passed. But it is an onerous, frigid, and extremely sporadic route, this, and one that, even when open, must usually have been flooded by glacial lakes and bogs.

Present doctrine, then, can most kindly be classed as "inadequate." Plainly, it does not provide any broad avenue accessible to cool temperate animals for protracted periods of time.

Aside from the geographic difficulties involved in the Bering Strait route, there are certain peculiarities in faunal relationships that do not square with the usual explications of animal distribution.

There is a distinctive small, white breed of Rangifer, called the "Peary caribou" in America and the "Svalbard reindeer" in Europe, that inhabits only the Svalbard Islands north of Norway and the Ellesmere–Queen Elizabeth Isles of northern Canada.[2] Some of the species were still in northern Greenland in historical times. This exotic geographic distribution is completely inexplicable by way of current concepts. Indeed, since the Svalbards are isolated by broad waters nearly 300 meters deep, one can only wonder how the reindeer ever got there at all — unless the Arctic Ocean waters fell far more than is presumed.

Many naturalists consider the reindeer of Greenland to be more similar to their cousins in Europe than to the American caribou. And what of the early Pleistocene vole, *Mimomys*, which left its bones in North America and Europe but not in Asia?

---

1 W. Haag, "The Bering Strait Land Bridge," *Scientific American*, Jan 1962, p. 123

2 Russell, H. John, *The World of Caribou*, Sierra Club Books, San Francisco, 1998, p. 9

On the east coast of Greenland live colonies of ermine completely isolated by the Greenland ice cap and the sea from others of their kind, as distant from the ermine of North America as from those of Scotland. How did they get to Greenland?

Some faunal anomalies are glaring. That industrious carpenter of the animal world, the beaver, could hardly thrive on the treeless tundra, yet it inhabits the forests of both Europe and America. How did it get across the huge Ice Age tundra gap? And the red deer (C. elephas), though absent from Alaska and northeast Siberia, nonetheless roams the American and Eurasian woodlands.

Whatever the explanation for these incongruities, one thing is plain: They do not fit the conventional doctrine. Altogether, there are enough of these ragged edges to compel the question: Is something awry in the accepted story of animal migrations to America? Is there a piece of the puzzle missing?

MANKIND IN THE NEW WORLD

With all of this talk of animals, yet to be mentioned is the most intriguing of all the creatures that arrived in the Americas during the Pleistocene: Man.

Anthropologists are 99.9% certain that genus Homo originated in the warm zone of the Afro-Eurasia island and did not reach the new World until relatively recent millennia. Just when is a subject of some debate. In fact, it is fair to say that no archeological issue has generated so much heat for so long a time as the question of when the ancestors of the Native Americans first arrived in the New World.

Oddly, the settlement of America was not regarded as much of a problem a few decades ago. It had all been neatly settled through the good offices of Professor Ales Hrdlicka, to wit: The Paleo-Americans arrived from Asia by crossing the Bering Strait in post-Pleistocene times, i.e., since the end of the last Ice Age. This "fact" Hrdlicka established by demolishing all evidence to the contrary. No American fossils alleged to be of Pleistocene age could withstand his withering analysis. But nothing fails like success. Soon the good professor convinced himself that no ancient American could ever be unearthed because none had been. Worse, he convinced everybody else. The Hrdlicka doctrine became one of the most unchallengeable in anthropology. Even to question it was to hazard one's academic reputation.

Alas for Ales, the Folsom find in the southwestern United States suddenly came to light. This was the discovery of a well-crafted projectile point imbedded in the bones of an extinct species of bison — extinct for at least 8,000 years. The Folsom culture turned out to date from the last millennium of the Wisconsin glacial that ended almost 10,000 C14 years before the present — more than 11,000 calendar years BP.[1] Folsom sparked an overdue resurgence of interest in American prehistory, soon rewarded by abundant evidence of far greater Paleo-Indian antiquity.

Projectile points of an earlier vintage than Folsom, of the Clovis and Sandia types, were uncovered in the southwestern US and elsewhere. The Clovis points approach 12,000 C14 years in age; the Sandia points are even older (the Sandia complex preceded the Folsom layer by at least two or three millennia). The Clovis material is both voluminous and well documented, but for many years pre-Clovis finds were few and often challengeable. So it was at the 12,000 year horizon that the conservatives choose to make their last stand. No American, they ruled, could be older than that.

But since the 60s, new finds have sprouted almost yearly, so many and so nearly irrefutable that the disciples of the 12,000 year limit are now backed against their goal line. There are more than a score of Paleo-Indian sites carbon-dated to prior to 12,000 BP. Not everyone is ironclad, but it is near impossible that all are erroneous. There is no need to recite every scrap of the data; a few examples suffice:

A recent blow to the conventional wisdom, and one of the more devastating, comes from southern Chile. There, Tom Dillehay carefully excavated an ancient living site that dates to 12,500 BP. His team found the remains of wooden structures, the bones of butchered Ice Age animals, stone tools and clay-lined hearths. Though the chronology goes only slightly beyond 12,000 year pale, the site presents seemingly insoluble problems for two reasons: its enormous distance from the Bering Strait and the fact that its dating is as sure as anything in the lexicon.

Skeptical experts visited Monte Verde in 1997 and came away admitting that the site is beyond refutation.[2] The fact that the locale is about 9,000 miles from Beringia means that humans must have penetrated North America well before 13,000 years ago. There was a brief but sharp interstadial (warming) phase — usually termed the Bolling — circa 12,300 carbon years BP. However, for tens of thousands of years before that, North America was so heavily glaciated that no access to the heartland from Beringia could have been available. In short, there is no way people could have been in Chile 12,500 years ago, but there they were.

Monte Verde is only one of many archeological outposts that testify to an inexplicably early human presence in the western hemisphere:

At Wilson Butte in Idaho, stone tools and a projectile point were recovered from a layer of earth 14,500 years old. A similar date was obtained at the Alice Boer site in southeastern Brazil where stone points and blades were found. Sup-

---

1 Carbon dates from the Paleo-Indian era are about 1,500 years too recent due to variable atmospheric carbon, but still dominate the literature. Accordingly, dates in this text are the usual carbon dates unless otherwise specified.

2 Meltzer, D.J., et al., "On the Pleistocene Antiquity of Monte Verde, Southern Chile," *American Antiquity*, October 1997

porting this chronology is a date from Taima Taima in Venezuela where an El Jobo point was pulled from the pelvis of a butchered mammoth. Several carbon dates from the site range around 14,000 years BP. More evidence of human habitation in the same timeframe comes from Peru where stone tools and a child's jawbone were uncovered at the 14,000 year level of Pikimachay Cave.

Two sites in Nebraska, La Sena and Jensen, offer nearly incontrovertible proof that man was butchering mammoths on these high plains long before twelve millennia ago. La Sena is at least 18,000 years old, Jensen about 14,000. The bones show the same butchery patterns that have been observed at other well confirmed Paleo-Indian sites.

One of the most formidable pre-Clovis finds surfaced at the Meadowcroft rock shelter in Pennsylvania. The carbon dates from the oldest occupation level, firmly associated with stonework, average about 17,000 years.[1] All are in perfect sequence with the stratigraphy, meaning they are almost surely accurate. (The field work here, under James Adovasio, may be the most meticulous ever done in the Americas.) Critics like to argue that some of the flora samples from Meadowcroft are too climate-temperate to have thrived so close to the edge of the ice sheet, but we know the ice front vacillated considerably during the time in question. It should be noted too, that the locale is only a few miles north of the Mason-Dixon line, i.e., too far south to be turned to tundra despite glacial proximity.

Kindred dates emerged during the late 1990s from eastern Virginia. At Cactus Hill, a layer 15–18,000 years old, bearing blade tools was found directly beneath a Clovis occupation level — at several neighboring dig sites. The tools bear a clear resemblance to those of comparable age from Meadowcroft, strongly reinforcing the chronological validity of both sites. Thus, the combined evidence from Cactus Hill and Meadowcroft, of and by itself, is enough to demolish the long-held "Clovis first" dictum.

The dates get older. What was clearly the remnant of an Ice Age campsite was found decades ago at Scripps Campus on the California coast. Containing burned earth, charred shell and bone, and small stone flakes, the site was carbon-dated at ca. 21,500 years. In Mexico's Pueblo state, C. Irwin-Williams found proof that Paleo-Indians were butchering game animals around the time of the Wisconsin glacial maximum of ca. 20,000 years ago. Nearby at Tlapacoya, other searchers uncovered two hearths in association with the bones of extinct animals, along with stone and obsidian tools.[2] The hearths were dated at 22,000 and 24,000 years. Inscribed animal bones, reminiscent of similar art work from the European Upper Paleolithic, have been found in his same region. Though not precisely dated, the engravings figure on stratigraphic grounds to be about 22,000 years

---

1 For an apt analysis of this key site, see Brian Fagan's *The Great Journey*, Thames & Hudson, New York, NY, 1987, pp. 150-152
2 Mirabell, L. "Tlapacoya: A Late Pleistocene Site in Central Mexico." In *Early Man in America*, A.L. Bryan, ed., 1978, pp. 221-230

old. Another piece of art, an animal head carved from the pelvic bone of an extinct llama species, was discovered at a depth of forty feet near Mexico City. Overlying beds, well above specimen (hence younger) have been dated at 16,000 years.

We have not cited a number of carbon dates obtained from fossil human bones in the Americas, some of which go back to 17–23,000 years, because the highly refined techniques for accurately dating ancient bone were still unperfected when these dates were obtained. (The oldest was the Los Angeles skull, found 13 feet down in Pleistocene strata in 1938, dates at 23,600 BP) Recent progress has made bone-dating more reliable, but for now, the great bulk of our useful dates are from C14 dated charcoal or wood (reasonably accurate back to ca. 40,000 BP).

The common sense conclusion from all this is that humans must have entered the Americas well before the late Wisconsin maximum, indeed before the end of the mid-Wisconsin which is customarily set at 23,000 carbon years ago. We shall find momentarily that even this estimate of Amerindian antiquity is too limited, but it can already be seen that the 12,000 year horizon still defended by some is untenable. It is only by the most tortured arguments and the most improbable suppositions that the case for mid-Wisconsin settlement of the Americas can be assailed.

There is no question that a systematic effort has been made over the past several decades to undermine any archeological discovery that appeared to challenge the primacy of Clovis. The basic assumption of those wryly termed was "the Clovis Police" has been that any such site simply had to be erroneous — therefore any means was justified to discredit it. In reality, these pre-Clovis finds are like archeological discoveries in general; some are perfectly valid, some have questionable aspects.

Into the Mid-Wisconsin

The Clovis police have known for a long time they were in trouble. Back in 1986, Guidon and Delibrias of France investigated a large painted rock shelter at Boqueirado do Sitio da Pedra Furada in Brazil. They found stunningly early evidence of human occupation, including fragments of painted rock in a level carbon dated at circa 32,000 years.[1] The stone tools recovered from this level could conceivably be geofacts but there can be little doubt that some from Pedra Furada III, dated at 21,000 years, are the work of human hands. Further, the French team found a rock fragment with two distinct paint stripes on it at the 17,000 year level. Since few animals but man make and use paint, the pre-Clovis antiquity of the site can scarcely be questioned.

While most archeologists are reluctant to accept the 32,000-year-old date from Pedra Furada without more conclusive evidence, that date is supported by another very ancient find from the deep level of Chile's Monte Verde site. There,

---

1 N. Guidon and G. Delibras, "Carbon 14 Dates Point to Man in the Americas 32,000 Years Ago," *Nature*, 19 June 1986, p. 769

six feet down, Dillehay uncovered remnants of three hearths, carbon dated to 33,000 BP. About two dozen fractured pebbles were found with the hearths, stones that show percussion scars and evidence of use. There is no chance that the material is intrusive; the overlying strata were entirely undisturbed.[1] Monte Verde does not provide the long occupation continuum of Pedra Furada but it does put a crowning cap on it. The two sites together, with their closely comple-mentary dates and similar stone work, are very nearly conclusive.

THE NEWS FROM NORTH AMERICA

If there were humans in South America 33,000 years ago, then other people necessarily lived in the more northerly reaches of the New World in the same timeframe. And, in fact, there is evidence both fresh and hoary confirming similar antiquity in the United States.

Hearths and the remains of slaughtered dwarf mammoths have been found on Santa Rosa Island off the coast of California. The carbon dates range in age from 11,000 to over 40,000 years. While some of the hearths may be remnants of lighting fires, certainly not all of them are. Some of the butchered bones have been dated at 27,000 years.

Turning to the mainland: In the early 90s, Richard MacNeish of the Andover Foundation for Archeological Research, announced a find at Pendejo Cave near Orogrande, New Mexico that testifies to human activity more than 30 millennia ago. Some of the animal bones found in the cave were clearly modified by the hand of man in marrowing activities. There was also an Equus phalange with a pointed stone fragment imbedded in it, dated 32,000 BP, and a worked bone pendant perhaps a few thousand years older than that.[2]

Some of the stone implements from Orogrande, though primitive, are geologi-cally distinct from the cave interior and so must have been transported inside by humans. (The cavern is well stratified so it is not likely that burrowing animals disturbed the evidence as some skeptics have contended.)

The Orogrande cave is by no means the only indicator of extreme human an-tiquity in North America. There is older, more celebrated, and more controversial evidence. Near Lewisville, Texas, a number of hearths were unearthed decades ago by an excavating operation. Some primitive tools — and one not so primitive — were discovered. The UCLA labs determined a carbon dating for one of the hearths of 38,000 BP., a startling date that was nonetheless supported by a piece of charred bone and other charcoal almost as old.

---

1 Dixon, E. James, *Quest for the Origins of the First Americas*, University of New Mexico Press, Albuquerque, 1993, p. 101
2 MacNeish, R.S. Chrisman, D & Cunnar, G., "Human Modification of Animal Bones in Pre-Clovis Zones of Pendejo Cave," *University of Massachusetts Amherst, Dept. of Anthropology* website

The glitch that made Lewisville a controversial case was a Clovis projectile point which was found at the site, an implement that could not be more than about 12,000 years old because the Clovis technology was strictly confined around that era. The consternation and argument that followed this paradoxical discovery strained many a scholarly friendship. The Lewisville site became — and remains to this day — one of the most disputed in the history of American archeology. And since the site is now under water it is unlikely that any absolutely conclusive determination of the contention will come about.

In a way, it is unfortunate that the Lewisville site was found when it was. With today's more careful and more sophisticated excavation techniques it is possible the case might never have become as confused as it has.

There are a couple feasible explanations for the Clovis Point anachronism. One is that some misguided Hrdlickan planted the point with the specific purpose of discrediting Lewisville's antiquity. Many archeologists and visitors stopped by the site during the original excavation, and without a doubt someone had the motive, opportunity and expertise to make the plant. The point did not turn up until it was clear that Lewisville threatened accepted doctrine. Such skullduggery is fortunately rare in archeology but by no means unknown, e.g., the Piltdown hoax.

If we wish to be more charitable, we might postulate that the Lewisville site was disturbed by Clovis era Paleo-Americans. The locale is a river bank which could have been a popular camp site over many millennia. A good deal of casual digging goes on at camp sites.

Whatever happened, there is little reason to doubt that Lewisville far antedates the Clovis era: Except for the single projectile point, there is nothing in any way inconsistent with a mid-Wisconsin dating. All the other tools and the fauna fit that timeframe and the site was widely accepted as mid-Wisconsin until the Clovis point so abruptly surfaced.[1]

In the early 1980s the argument over Lewisville became somewhat academic when seven ancient hearths were uncovered at El Cedral in north central Mexico. The hearths, surrounded by burned animal bones, were carbon dated from 21,000–37,000 years BP.[2] A circular quartz scraper was recovered from a stratum dated at 33,000 BP. Still more data of the same ilk has come from the Burnham site in Oklahoma where retouched flakes and artifacts, associated with extinct bison bones, were recovered from a deposit dated at 28,000–32,000 years BP.

---

1 It has been argued that some old lignite found in the area was burned by Paleo-Indians contaminating the carbon dates. But, if so, it is curious that all the several dates were so consistent — 35,000 to 38,000 BP. Contamination, if it occurred, must have been slight.

2 Lorenzo, Jose L., and Lorena Mirabell, "The Inhabitants of Mexico during the Upper Pleistocene" in *The Ice Age People of North America*, Oregon State University Press, Corvallis OR, 1999.

Even this is not the end: A footprint in volcanic ash in Mexico has recently been carbon dated at around 40,000 years BP, give or take a few millennia.

One important indicator of Paleo-Indian antiquity has been all but forgotten. In the mid 1960s, a crude stone implement was uncovered in Altonian age stratum, ca. 30,000–40,000 years old, in Illinois.[1] It has been argued that the artifact might possibly be a product of natural processes; yet had it been found anywhere except America it would be accepted without hesitation as manmade.

Going back to the 1930s, we have the stone images from the Malakoff gravel pit, not far from Lewisville. Twenty-six feet deep in the pit, excavators found three large stones crudely carved to represent human faces.[2] The associated fauna was mid-Wisconsin. The carvings must be around 30,000 years old.

We may not yet have reached the stage where we can confidently pinpoint the exact time of the Paleo-Indian arrival in the New World. However, the cumulative weight of the evidence from both North and South America makes the period around 35,000 BP, give or take a millennium or so, far the most likely timeframe.

It is not just archeology and anthropology that testify to so early an arrival. The etymologists and the geneticists, using entirely different lines of evidence, have come to the same conclusion.

The languages of the Native Americans present a confounding verbal array — over a hundred mutually unintelligible tongues. In the view of most experts, it would be impossible for such a linguistic mélange to evolve in less than 25,000–40,000 years. Another telling point has been made by Richard Rogers (University of Kansas): The huge formerly-glaciated area of North America is dominated by the varied Amerindian tongues also found south of the glaciation zone, not the few arctic languages to the north.[3] The clear implication is that the area vacated by the melting ice caps was settled from the south. Ergo, the Paleo-Indians were already in the American heartland when the glaciers began their final meltdown.

The discovery that mitochondrial DNA evolves at a measured rate has allowed geneticists to estimate humanity's evolutionary timeframe. While the method cannot produce precise dates, the studies of Native American mitochondria all indicate a racial antiquity far exceeding 12,000 years. Nearly all geneticists agree that the Paleo-Indians must have occupied the New World 20–40,000 years ago.

The net impact of the accumulated new evidence all but demolishes the old paradigm. So insurmountable are the contradictions involved in the conventional view that we are obliged to reconsider the migratory route of the First Americans.

1 Munson, Patrick & Frye, John C., "Artifact from Deposits of Mid-Wisconsin Age in Illinois," *Science*, 150: 1722-23, 1965.
2 Wormington, H.M., *Ancient Man in North America*, Denver Museum of Natural History, 1957, p. 154-155.
3 Fagan, Brian M., *The Great Journey*, Thames & Hudson, New York NY, 1987, p. 186

CHAPTER 2. DIFFICULTIES WITH DOGMA

Before probing more deeply into the genesis of the Native Americans, a brief overview of the chronology of the last glaciation could help to set the stage. This glacial episode, the "Wisconsin" in America, is called the "Weichsel" or the "Wurm" in Europe; it was approximately contemporaneous on both continents. Expansion of the ice began about 120,000 years ago in both Europe and North America, maxing out around 20,000 years ago. Along the way, there were a number of oscillations of the glacial masses, expansions and contractions, until the end of the glacial period about 8000 BC. The occasional limited moderations of climate during glaciation, known as interstadials, were more or less simultaneous in the Old World and the New, though their precise datings are not always crystal clear.

Most important though: While the early stages of the last Ice Age were relatively mild, there occurred, about 70,000 years ago, a sharp intensification of glacial conditions. It was at this stage that the Keewatin and Cordilleran ice sheers must have merged, cutting off access to the New World from Asia. And, as figure 2 illustrates, the situation did not materially change for a very long time. In short, the migration gate slammed shut 70,000 years ago and, in any realistic assessment, did not reopen until about 12,500 carbon years ago (ca. 14,500 calendar years) during the Bolling interstadial.

The situation plainly presents horrendous — actually, insoluble — difficulties for the traditional migration theory. There is no way it can handle the many firm Paleo-Indian dates exceeding 13,000 C14 years since no "ice free corridor" could then have existed. This is the main reason defenders of the conservative view so vigorously contest the earlier sites. Once the settlement of America is pushed back beyond 12,000 years, the whole conventional line of approach disintegrates:

Its adherents would have to hypothesize a migration through "the corridor" during some earlier Wisconsin interstadial. Few are willing to do so since the tack so obviously amounts to a convenient fiction. As can be seen from the SPECMAP data, it is next to impossible that the corridor existed at any time during the main Wisconsin, or even during the mid-Wisconsin (ca. 53,000–23,000 BP).

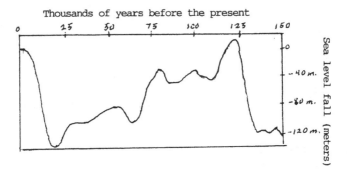

Fig. 2: The above SPECMAP[1] data, calculated from planktonic Oxygen 18 is the most generally accepted estimate of the total amount of glacial ice on the planet during the last glaciation. The fall in sea level is, of course, directly proportional to the amount of glaciation at any particular time. Note that sea levels were very low and glaciers particularly massive in the last half of the glacial cycle, making any ice free corridor through Canada at that time extremely unlikely. (The data are somewhat generalized and cannot show minor, short-term variations.) A graph of North American glaciation — not yet been entirely worked out — would vary slightly, but not significantly, from SPECMAP's delineation.

Possibly, a labored case might be made for a corridor during the Port Talbot II interstadial ca. 45,000 calendar years ago when extensive deglaciation is documented in the Great Lakes region. Or, less likely, during the Plum Point interstadial around 34,000 years BP. But even these extremities fail — on a number of counts.

Most obviously, there is not a wisp of evidence that Beringia (or any part of Alaska) was occupied so early. The oldest bit of occupational evidence from the Alaska-Yukon region comes from the Bluefish Caves where the butchered bones of the Ice Age mammals have been dated at circa 13 to 15-thousand years. Still, in spite of steady progress on bone-dating, the process remains a bit dicey. The oldest well-established culture in Alaska is the Nenana, carbon dated at almost 12,000 years — little, if any, older than Clovis.

Turning to east Siberia, things do not improve for the Bering Strait advocates. One of their key sites, Ushki Lake on the Kamchatka Peninsula, has recently

---

1 The SPECMAP date was developed by the NOAA National Geophysical Data Center

been found to be a good deal younger than was thought. Reinvestigation of a human grave there has revealed that the original dating was too old by more than three thousand years and the site is not even as ancient as the Nenana complex in Alaska.[1]

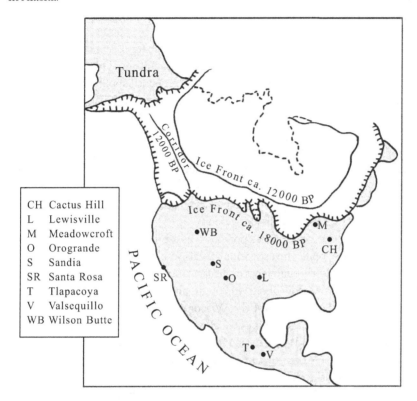

Fig. 3: Map of Ice Age North America showing the ice-free corridor that formed about 12,000 C14 years ago after being closed since the Port Talbot II interstadial of 45,000 years BP, or before. Also shown are major Paleo-Indian sites older than ca. 13,000 years that the corridor migration hypothesis cannot explain.

Bottom line, then: Despite intensive searching for decades, there is not a stick, stone, or bone anywhere along the Beringian migratory route that supports a human presence prior to the Wisconsin glacial peak around 19-20,000 years ago — much less at the time of the Plum Point or Port Talbot interstadials. Archeology, then, supports what common sense would suppose: that Beringia was not occupied by humans until the meltdown of the Wisconsin glaciers was well under way.

---

1 "Late Date for Siberian Site Challenges Bering Pathway," *Science*, 25 July 2003

Even if the ice-free corridor nation is pushed to its theoretical limits, it still cannot account for the earliest evidence of humanity in the Americas. If we hypothesize — with no proof — that some dauntless race of people managed to cling to life in south Beringia ca. 30-40,000 years ago, it is still fantastical to suppose they could have trekked through any conjectural corridor to the heartland since they lacked Upper Paleolithic technology.

Bad as conditions then were in Beringia, the climate of any corridor had to be far worse, and we know the Upper Paleolithic culture, with its sewn clothing, did not reach Japan (much less eastern Siberia) until about 29,000 BP. So, if any Asians trod a Yukon corridor before then they must have had a superhuman resistance to cold — especially since the supposed corridor would have been a treeless tundra without a stick of firewood for warmth. They could have clad themselves only in loosely wrapped skins, with scraped hides around their feet as they plodded through the ice and snow looking for some trace of food. The bizarre prospect of such primitives wending their tortuous way through a blizzard-swept, subzero alleyway between glacial masses in the midst of an Ice Age strains credulity far past the breaking point.

Though Beringia is sometimes portrayed as a broad Ice Age grassland, teeming with big game, pollen investigation reveals something else: The region was a desolate polar desert through most of the last third of the Wisconsin glacial. The climate hardened markedly about 40,000 BP and the area remained bitter cold, dry tundra until near the end of the Wisconsin, ca. 15,000 years ago.[1] The era around 20-35,000 years ago looks especially inhospitable since very few mammal remains have been found there dating from that time. If the hunting was sparse, there was no motive to venture into such foreboding territory. Thus if, by some miracle, a corridor through Canada had opened, there would have been nobody to traverse it — not that they could have made it through anyway.

The discomfort of the traditionalists with the idea of a mid-Wisconsin migration to America, then, is easily understood. There is just no way they can handle it since the "ice free corridor" flat fails. Actually, the main appeal of their position is that it is easier to just deny the Paleo-Indian presence before 12,000 years ago than to explain it. Yet the evidence for it has grown massive and mounts with nearly every passing year.

To get around the mile-thick blockade of the continental ice cap during the main Wisconsin, some researchers have hypothesized that the first Americans might have been able to make their way down the north Pacific coast by boat, hopping from once ice-free enclave to another. This suggestion, though, does not materially change the basic picture. During have glacial phases such enclaves must have been few and far between on this notoriously rugged and stormy shore.

1 Colinvaux, P.A. & West, F.H., "The Beringia Ecosystem," *Quarterly Review of Archeology*, 5 (3) pp. 10-16, 1984

At the same time, massive ice sheets based on the Aleutian and south Alaska mountain ranges had completely cut off Beringia from the Canadian littoral, so the coastal enclaves would have been virtually inaccessible anyway. The route could only have been available during the most acute interstadials, i.e., about the same times as the inland corridor. Investigation of the coastal zone so far has uncovered no trace of human bones or tools prior to about 9,000 years ago — far too late to figure in the case.

The Impossible Scheme

The crux problem of America's initial settlement can be summarized simply: There is now irrefutable proof that humans spread through the New World long before 13,000 carbon years BP, yet entry to the American heartland from Asia before that date is practically out of the question. The Beringian approach, whether coastal or corridor, cannot be made to work.

We are not the first to notice the blatant inadequacy of current theory on the settlement of the Americas. Indeed, at times, the situation has driven responsible scholars close to the brink of desperation. More than three decades ago, Charles Hunt of Johns Hopkins expressed his frustrations this way in a book review in "Science":

"It is doctrine in archeology that man came to North America by way of the Bering land bridge, although neither this book nor the rest of archeological literature records any supporting evidence. The problem has overtones suggestive of those still undiscovered Tertiary land bridges that enabled North American fauna to mix intermittently with European ones.

Constant reiteration does not make man's use of the land bridge a fact, and what little evidence there is suggests that he may have used another route...There is no need to labor the point about the bridge developing because of lowered sea level; the bridge was there, but it was not used (according to doctrine) until the last glacial maximum.[1] At that time, the area must have been bleak frozen ground and immigration across it would have been the original ice folly. To this observer, it would seem that one of the archeological doctrines will have to go — either man reached North America by a route other than the Bering land bridge, or George Carter is right in saying that man arrived on this continent before the last glacial maximum"[2]

Carter maintained that the ancestral Americans made their way to the New World — presumably by boat — during the last interglacial, more than 100,000 years ago and prior to the Weichsel/Wisconsin altogether. In his book, *Pleistocene Man at San Diego*, Carter builds a tenuous case for the existence of an early Wisconsin North American stone culture. Flakes, cobble cores, and plano-convex

1 Hunt refers here to the whole span of heavy Wisconsin glaciation, not just to the peak of the Main Wisconsin, ca. 20,000 years ago.
2 Hunt, Charles, "Quaternary Geology Reviewed," *Science*, October 1, 1965, p. 49

stone tools from La Jolla and Point Loma, which Carter labels the "La Jolla Culture," come from alluvium just overlying what appear to be interglacial beaches.

Carter also tries to establish the presence of a "Third Interglacial" culture. He rests his case on what seem to be hearths and very primitive stone tools — so primitive that they could easily be the result of natural breakage. The hearths might be remnants of lightning fires.

Carter's evidence failed to convince any sizable segment of the scientific community, and the few supporting voices he once enjoyed have now all but faded away. A marine crossing of the stormy Bering Strait 100,000-plus years ago is widely seen to be implausible, even assuming the area was settled. And a putative early Wisconsin migratory trek brings us right back to the problem of getting very primitive migrants through a frostbitten climatic zone. The Carter hypothesis, obviously, has even more trouble than the standard theory with the lack of any very early occupation sites in Beringia.

Are we afoot in a maze with no exit?

There looks to be no workable scenario for the settlement of the New World. A late Wisconsin arrival fails because of the overwhelming evidence for a mid-Wisconsin occupation while there is no credible proof for any early Wisconsin debut. A mid-Wisconsin entry from Asia falls apart in the face of the near certainty that Beringia was settled only after the glacial peak of ca. 20,000 years ago, with no chance of any ice free corridor then, or for about 15,000 years prior.

All this, though, represents merely the first phase of the difficulties for the accepted wisdom. We have yet to deal with the fact that the Native Americans are not, and never have been typical of what anthropologists classify as the Mongoloid or East Asian race.

Tribal Roots

"We are here to give thanks to the elements of the universe that protected this individual that the world calls Kennewick Man." The bearded speaker of these words was presiding over a ritual gathering of the Asatru Folk Assembly at Columbia Park, Washington State in late August of 1997. With a "Hammer of Thor" before him on a makeshift altar, this blue-cloaked leader of a small band of mystics was speaking of a 9,300-year-old fossil skeleton found on the banks of the Columbia River a year before.

The Asatru Folk are followers of the pre-Christian deities of ancient western Europe. What brought them to the site was the anthropological analysis of Kennewick Man as Caucasoid, or at least mostly so. One facial reconstruction showed him to be a dead-ringer for Captain Piccard of the starship Enterprise (though there is an obvious subjective element in these endeavors that makes them all approximations). Despite its great age, the remarkably preserved and complete skeleton is unlikely to be entirely of Asian descent. Mysticism aside, the fossil delivers one more body blow to the conventional concepts of Amerindian origins.

Kennewick Man is not unique. A Nevada skeleton of similar age from Spirit Cave does not fit the conventional model, either. The facial reconstruction looks more Caucasoid than anything else — and in this case it is not just a matter of the bones. Preserved bits of skin are parchment colored and the hair is no straight black Asian variety, but soft and brown, i.e., European. Douglas Owsley of National Museum of National History, who did an exhaustive cranial analysis of Spirit Cave Man and two Minnesota skulls of similar age, observed, "we were impressed with how different the older skulls are from any of the modern-day (Native American) groups. They do not have the broad faces, they do not have the big, prominent cheekbones that you think of as the more traditional features of the Chinese and American Indians."[1]

The oldest firmly dated South American Paleo-Indian fossil, from southeastern Brazil, has a non-Asiatic skull and teeth. Recently, five skulls found in Mexico in 1959, were carbon-dated at 2,000 years before Clovis and all are long and narrow, "very unlike those of modern native Americans."[2] To most anthropologists it has come clear that there are pronounced differences between the morphologies of modern and Ice Age American natives.

Even aside from these ancient bones, the view that the origin of the Americoids was Asia, and Asia alone, has a very hard time contending with a huge mass of anthropological data. Comparative racial characteristics offer compelling testimony against an exclusively Asian heritage. Whereas substantial Asiatic infusion can be seen nearly in all tribes, the typical Amerindian is clearly something other than a transplanted Manchurian.

Most American natives are noted for their prominent profiles, a very un-Mongoloid feature. In fact, hawkish profiles are typically and almost exclusively Caucasoid — and just as racially diagnostic as pigmentation, if not more so (many Caucasians are as dark-complected as some American Indians). The natives of the New World simply do not exhibit the relative facial flatness typical of most East Asian peoples. Neither do they display the characteristic almond eye. Skin color is similar but by no means the same.

To quote from the article "Human Populations" by the eminent (if occasionally controversial) anthropologist Carleton Coon in the 1974 *Britannica*:

> Skin pigmentation (of native Americans) ranges from almost Caucasoid brunet white in northwestern Canada through various shades of reddish brown in Central American and the Andes to a pale yellow in the shady atmosphere of the equatorial forests to almost white among the Alakalufs.

The description continues with this thought-provoking paragraph:

1 Wright, Karen, "First Americans," *Discover*, Feb. 1999, p. 55
2 "Vintage Skulls," *Archaeology*, March/April 2003, p. 15

Despite this essentially Mongoloid anatomy, many Indians have a Caucasoid appearance, especially in facial features and particularly among the New England Indians. Prehistoric Indian skulls from this region have narrow faces and noses that are hard to fit into the Mongoloid pattern, and the same has been found among the skulls of the Ona of Tierra del Fuego. Whether the Caucasoid morphology is of genetic origin or due to parallelism is not known.

Coon's analysis is underscored by a less scientific but nonetheless noteworthy observation: When casting "westerns," motion picture moguls often use Caucasians to portray "Indians" but very rarely utilize Asians in such roles. John Ford may not have been much of an anthropologist, but he knew what people were supposed to look like. Another non-scientific observer, William Penn, in a letter describing the American natives, noted their European features and described their complexions as "Italian." (He thought they might be one of the lost tribes of Israel.) Anyone who has perused frontier-era photo albums of the Amerindians cannot fail to be struck by the European faces of many of the subjects. In some cases, the faces are not just predominantly European, but are entirely so, without the faintest trace of any Asiatic influence.

Comparing stature, we find the American natives to be far taller than Asians. In fact, the range of Amerindian stature is an almost precise match for the Caucasoid range.

Even with all this, perhaps the most inexplicable discrepancy between East Asian peoples and Native Americans can be found in a comparison of blood types. While the Asiatics have a very high proportion of type B blood, the Amerindians have almost none, except in the far north of North America. The blood type ratios of the Amerindians are actually much more similar to those of west European populations, and nearly identical to those of the Basques, an ancient ethnicity surviving in the Pyrenees Mountains.

While Mongoloid hair tends to be relatively coarse, fine hair is common among Amerindian tribes. A study of the Zunis, for example, showed fully 40% had fine hair. And many American natives, from California to Tierra del Fuego, grew beards a Viking might envy, not all had sparse Asian-type beards. Depictions of bearded and mustachioed males are fairly common in pre-Columbian Mexic art and statuary, particularly among Toltecs.

It has been demonstrated that dry ear wax, strange to say, is a racial indicator, largely confined to Asiatics who typically show it to a proportion of around 90%. The trait is uncommon among both Whites and Blacks. Some Indian tribes show a high percentage of dry ear wax but many others do not. Among the Sioux and the Maya, for example, the ratio is very low[1] — within the Caucasoid range.

---

1 Petrakis, Nicholas L., et al., "Cerumen in American Indians: Genetic Implications," *Science*, Dec. 1, 1967, pp. 1192-93

Light coloring, though rare, is not unknown among the American Indians. George Catlin, a reliable first-hand chronicler of the frontier, was struck by the curiously light pigmentation of the Mandans of the Dakotas, and he was by no means the only one to make that observation.

Other explorers made similar reports about the Menominees of Wisconsin and some tribes in the St. Lawrence Valley. A tribe of "white Indians" reportedly still survives in the back-country of Columbia. Old timers remarked on the oddly light coloring of chief Crazy Horse, a pure-blood Sioux.

Head form is another feature that does not check with the assumption that the Native Americans are just an Asian offshoot. Paleo-Indian skulls tend everywhere to be long-headed whereas Mongoloids are not, and according to the fossil evidence never have been. (A long-headed skull has a width less than 75% of its length; e.g., Kennewick Man has a cephalic index of 73.8.)

It is not just obvious physical traits that attest to the insolvency of the official story about the Amerindian heritage. Studies of mitochondrial DNA show that one of the four common Americoid DNA lineages, the so-called "B" line, does not even occur among any supposed Siberian ancestors. Where then, did the B line come from? Even more telling, there is an "X" lineage in the American natives which is found in Europe but nowhere in Asia east of Turkey![1] Are we to believe then, that some ancient Europeans traipsed across all of Asia to Beringia, but left not a trace of their passage?

A GNASHING OF TEETH

Despite the many indicators that the American Natives' genetic heritage is not entirely Asian, most anthropologists still decline to acknowledge any Caucasoid contribution. Habitually, they cite the so-called Mongoloid or "sinodent" tooth patterns found in most Amerindians — especially shoveled incisors (a concave form of the backs of the incisor teeth). The two most obvious oversights in their argument are both methodological. First, they fail to distinguish between modern and Paleolithic samples. Sinodent teeth, while common in the former are much scarcer in the latter (Kennewick, Spirit Cave, etc.). In fact, of the seven oldest Paleo-Indian specimens, not one has sinodent teeth — showing that the trait was greatly accentuated by relatively later entries from Asia. Secondly, very little of the dental research has been done in eastern North America, the zone most affected by any early Caucasoid gene flow. Nearly all studies are of natives farther west where Asian influence would be maximized. As is usually the case, investigators found what they went looking for.

These procedural flaws, of and by themselves, are enough to invalidate the whole "sinodent" argument. But even if such dentition were found in a very ancient American fossil, it would prove little since sinodent teeth are not exclu-

---

1 Morell, Virginia, Research News: Human Genetics, *Science*, April 24, 1998

sively Asiatic. They are not unusual in some north European populations, e.g., the Lapps, and were fairly common in Upper Paleolithic Europeans — very common in their cold-adapted Neanderthal neighbors with whom some interbreeding was likely. It is now known that there were cultural interchanges between Cro Magnons and the Neanderthals, and some fossils look very much like hybrids of the two types. The latest to surface are the bones of a child from Portugal showing a mix of sapiens and Neanderthal characteristics. Meanwhile, Neanderthal remains from Spain have been found to contain a version of the FOXPZ gene identical to that in modern humans (and involved in the development of language and speech.) The gene is a near certain sign of cross-breeding.

While initial work with mitochondrial DNA shows no Neanderthal genes in modern humans, it is naive to suppose that mtDNA can settle the interbreeding question. In those unenlightened days of yore, the capture/rape of sapiens women must have been a common diversion among Neanderthal males. Because it is inherited only through the female line, the mtDNA would show no trace of such Neanderthal input. It is easily feasible then, that a good many early Caucasoids carried the genetic potential for "sinodent" teeth.

While conventional anthropologists are fond of talking about shoveled incisors, they are much less likely to mention Carabelli's cusp, a Caucasian dental trait that is rare among Asiatics but very widespread among Native Americans. For example, a survey of the Queckchis of Guatemala shows that about half the tribe has the feature, and among the Sioux, more than half. Some tribes such as the Pima of the United States and the Lengua of interior Bolivia are actually within the Caucasoid range (70–90%).[1]

So, the teeth of ancient and modern Native Americans are a good deal less "mongoloid" than advertised. Eying the whole constellation of racial indicators, we can only conclude that Caucasians as well as Asians must have been involved in the evolution of the Americoid race.

DISSENTING VOICES

Not all the big names in anthropology have fallen compliantly into line with the official gospel on Americoid origins. One of the most prominent, Carleton Coon, eventually came to the conclusion that the Native Americans are mostly of Caucasoid extraction (though he could only suggest the Neanderthals as a possible genetic source).[2]

Another notable anthropologist of some decades ago, E.A. Hooten, admitted being more than a little puzzled by a series of oil portraits of American Indians in the Peabody Museum:

1 Hassanali, J., "The Incidence of Carabelli's Trait in Kenyan Africans and Asians," *The American Journal of Physical Anthropology*, Nov. 1982, p. 319 (Table 2)
2 Coon, Carleton, *Racial Adaptations*, Nelson-Hall Inc., Chicago, IL, 1982, pp. 163-165

Plate I: Randomly selected photos from the Smithsonian Institution illustrating typical North American Indian types. Note that Caucasoid facial characteristics clearly predominate over Mongoloid in nearly all cases.

> The majority of these [portraits] represent eastern and southern United States Indians and, although the portraits are the work of an excellent painter, the subjects look very European. The features of most are very un-Mongoloid, with prominent noses and oval faces. Mongoloid cheek bones are rarely portrayed. The skin color is reddish-brown rather than yellow-brown. However, some Plains Indians are included in the series, and these seem to be accurate representations of types familiar today. I am, therefore, disposed to think that the European-like types are not the result of an artistic convention, but actually did exist. These portraits, and old photographs of Eastern Indians, convey the impression that the eastern dolichocephals [longheads] were by no means as Mongoloid as are the Plains and Southwestern Indians. Many of the photographs of Indians (supposedly full-blooded) from eastern Canada appear similarly non-Mongoloid.[1]

Hooten saw the Plains and Southwest Indians as an amalgam of this same Euro-looking type, "washed over with dominant Mongoloid characteristics." To him, the Mayas of Central America with their typically convex noses seemed "even farther removed from the ideal Mongoloid type than are the Plains and Southwestern tribes." Though too old-school to win any popularity contests with modern-day academicians, Hooten had one overriding virtue: He called the evidence just the way he saw it, regardless of whether it fitted in with the prevailing vogue.

Clearly, the American deviations from the East Asian phenotype are far too widespread and variable to be ascribed to genetic drift, or to the romantic prowess of the pre-Columbian Vikings. There is no way the orthodox view of Amerindian ancestry can account for the physical types found in the New World. Not only is there a definite Caucasian element but it is earlier than the Asiatic. That much is apparent from the fact that the most marginal American natives are the least Mongoloid. Ergo, the Caucasoids must have arrived first.

THE TESTIMONY OF THE TOOLS

While climate, fauna, and the ethnology all offer formidable objections to the current theory of American beginnings, there are still other points of disparity. If we survey the comparative technologies, the wobbly Bering Strait bridge crumbles entirely. It happens that the stone tool traditions of the Old World divide into two distinct zones: an eastern one covering most of Asia and a western one found in Europe and Africa. This division persists for most of a million years.

If all Amerindians came to the Americas from the Asiatic realm, we should expect that their tool cultures and techniques all would bear the stamp of the Oriental tradition. Not the case.

In Early Man in the New World, McGowan wrote:

> Of all the bits of stone that bear on the existence of early man in American, perhaps the most puzzling and certainly the most neglected are the

---

1 Hooten, E.A., *Apes, Men and Morons*, F.P. Putnam's Sons, New York, NY, 1937, pp. 178-179

artifacts which E.G. Reynaud has found in countless numbers in south-western Wyoming. Here at 105 sites on the arid surface of Black Fork Valley, he had picked up by 1940 some 6,000 chipped stones, many of them like the rude hand axes which suggest a parallel with the industries of Paleolithic man in the Old World. European authorities have stated that Reynaud's finds agree in type with hand axes, choppers, and blades of the Abbevillian., Acheulian, Mousterian, and Clactonian cultures of Europe.[1]

The cited cultures are all alien to Asia; none ever penetrated within thousands of miles of the Bering Strait. As far back as 1933, N.C. Nelson was writing of New World spear throwers of Magdalenian affinity, of Solutrean chipped blades and Aurignacian end scrapers, all European types.

There is a singular bone tool, shaped like a donut with a handle, found in Clovis era America that is identical with what the French call a *baton de commandement*. This highly diagnostic tool, a kind of Ice Age wrench, is found in Europe and North America, but not in Asia.

Despite strenuous efforts by archeologists, it has not been possible to establish convincing parallels between the Paleolithic hunter technologies of America and those of northeast Asia. Further, the North American tool sites seem to be more recent as one moves northward, arguing against the theory of migration from Beringia southward. Remarkably, the closest matches to early American projectile points are found not in Asia but in western Europe. The likeness in design and workmanship is so striking that some experts, such as Dennis Stanford of the Smithsonian, have roiled the archeological waters by suggesting that an Ice Age connection is likely.[2]

Stanford and a few like-minded cohorts have not been able to rock the boat much, so far, because there seems no way to account for such protean journeys across the Atlantic in such remote times. The proposal, for instance, that the migrants followed the edge of the Atlantic ice sheet 3,000 miles from Europe to America looks to most analysts like a hundred-to-one shot.

Nevertheless, some of the pre-Clovis, unfluted projectile points from Virginia (18,000–15,000 BP) are amazingly similar to some of the Solutrean points of Europe of 16,000–24,000 years ago. In a few cases, as at Sandia, American points even exemplify the peculiar shouldered design seen in some Solutrean spearheads. Nothing like the bifacially pressure-flaked Sandia points has ever been uncovered in Asia.

Stanford is by no means the first investigator to remark on the Solutrean–Clovis–Sandia affinity. Nearly half a century ago, René Malaise summed it up well in a forgotten treatise titled "Oceanic Bottom Investigations and their Bearing on Geology":

---

1 Kenneth MacGowen, *Early Man in the New World*, New York, Macmillan, 1950, p. 131
2 Wright, Karen, "First Americans," *Discover*, February 1999 p.62

The flint points of these two people [Solutrean and Sandia man] that lived separated by the Atlantic Ocean at approximately the same time during the Wisconsin [Wurm] glacial stage, are mutually extremely similar, but otherwise most singular in their general shape. This similarity has already been noticed by archeologists, but nobody has dared to advance that they should belong to the same culture source. The Atlantic Ocean has been regarded as impossible for hunting people to cross at that time. The similarity has been regarded as an indisputable example of parallel development. Had it only been a question of a similar general shape, one would nevertheless have been justified in speaking of a parallel develop, ment, but when both of these peoples also were the first to introduce the superior, "pressure flaking" technique in shaping their flint points, the co-incidence begins to be astonishing, not to say doubtful.[1] (See Fig. 4.)

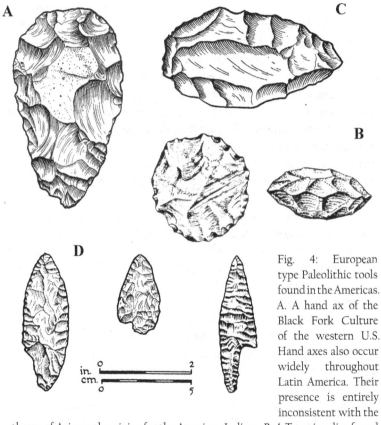

Fig. 4: European type Paleolithic tools found in the Americas. A. A hand ax of the Black Fork Culture of the western U.S. Hand axes also occur widely throughout Latin America. Their presence is entirely inconsistent with the theory of Asian-only origins for the American Indians. B. A Tayacian disc found in southwestern USA. "C" is a spear point with Mousterian affinities discovered near Trenton, New Jersey. The drawings are not on a uniform scale. (From Early Man in the New World). D Flint point from Sandia Cave (left) compared with two Solutrean points from Morocco and France.

1 R. Malaise, *Geologiska Foreningens I Stockholm Forhandlingar*, Mars-Apr., 1957

The triple coincidence of time, design, and technique becomes a quadruple "coincidence" when the geographic distribution of the Solutrean and the Sandia/Clovis flintwork is considered. The Solutrean exists only in western Europe; the Sandia/Clovis only in North America, mainly in the eastern and southern United States. In other words, if a trans-Atlantic connection is postulated between Labrador and the British Isles, it joins the eastern and western wings of the Solutrean/Sandia/Clovis complex. Remarkable.

The Solutrean age in Europe occurs shortly before the dawn of the Mesolithic period. No less than an authority than J. Grahame Clark was struck by the comparison between the culture of the Mesolithic Indians of eastern North America and that of the Mesolithic Europeans. He notes these similarities (but draws no conclusions): the domestication of the dog; the absence of pottery; the polishing of stone for axes, bowls and plummets; the use of red ochre to cover the dead; head-dresses of native copper which recall ones made of natural antlers in Europe.[1]

Even in the area of language, there are suspicious hints of some pre-historic contacts between the New World and Europe. The Basque tongue, an ancient pre-Aryan linguistic relic surviving in the Pyrenees, seems more closely related to some North American Indian tongues than any other. There are even legends, persistent legends, from the early American frontier of "Welsh-speaking" Indian tribes in the eastern and central United States. More of these strange tales later.

There are still other false notes in the psalms of orthodoxy. What of the swastika symbol which was common to the ancient Celts in Europe and to the American aborigines? What of the macabre custom of scalping the vanquished enemy? Again, an ancient Celtic and Native American practice. What of the Irish myth telling of a contest among the birds to determine which could fly highest? — a tale duplicated almost word for word by an American Indian story. What of those persistent traditions among many American tribes about ancestors who came from the direction of the rising sun, the direction of Europe?

Over the past few decades, scores of odd and inconvenient anomalies have been uncovered that do not mesh with accepted theory. One by one, as they have appeared, these annoying little archeological dust bunnies have not been too difficult to sweep under the doctrinal carpet. But taken altogether, they have accumulated into an awkward, unsightly bulge now impossible to ignore. Despite the conventionalists' frenetic efforts (sometimes bordering on desperation) to discredit this evidence, the truth that is the facts point in just one direction: prehistoric contacts between the American and European continents.

---

1 Grahame Clark, *World Prehistory*, Cambridge U. Press, 1961, pp. 277-78

CHAPTER 3. A BRIDGE BETWEEN WORLDS

The host of affinities between eastern North America and western Europe is rationally explicable only in terms of a traversable land bridge, or near-bridge, over the North Atlantic during some period or periods of the Pleistocene.

The empirical evidence for such a bridge is by no means indistinct. A look at the map shows the remnants of what could have constituted such a connection. Some of these are obvious: Iceland, Greenland, the Faeroes. If our map shows the ocean floor as well as sub-aerial land, it can be seen that these islands are joined to each other and to the continental masses of Europe and America by a submarine ledge at shallow depth (Fig. 1). In fact, were the level of the Atlantic to subside only 700 meters, a sufficiently enthusiastic hiker could walk from London to Labrador. If such a condition existed in the Pleistocene it would provide the direct connection we suspect between the first Americans and the early sapiens of Europe.

But as already observed, sea level (based on the extent and thickness of the ice caps) is calculated to have dropped only 120–130 meters during the Wurm-Wisconsin. Presumably, the drop during the other glacial phases was on the same order — maybe more during the great Mindel glaciation.

Fact is, there is little question that a North Atlantic connection once joined the two great world islands of eastern and western hemisphere. During the Pliocene — the geological period preceding the Pleistocene — the similarity between European and North American fauna is so marked that there is no argument: zoologists, botanists, and geologists all agree there had to be a traversable land bridge.

Moreover, careful analysis of the continental shelf around Iceland plainly shows that in past times the island must have been at least 400 meters higher above sea level that it now is — for a protracted time, i.e., some millions of years.

The fact that a bridge existed during the Pliocene, an epoch of relatively high sea level, makes it almost certain that during the low sea level phases of the Pleistocene a bridge, or something close to it, would have reappeared. (It is unlikely that the geoidal level of the entire ledge just dropped abruptly some hundreds of meters at the end of the Pliocene).

What is more, there are to this day Ice Age animals on the remnants of North Atlantic bridge. Consider the presence of indigenous foxes on the isle of Iceland. These are not flying foxes, nor a web-footed variety. The dubious explanation is that they must have drifted to the island on ice floes. There are old-time reports that the European elk (moose) was once native to Iceland but this is doubted by most zoologists who can conceive of no way the beasts could have reached the isle. There are also various rodents on the island — all, we must presume, introduced by man. Turning to another Atlantican locale, there is a curious distribution of fauna on Greenland. The animal life on the Island's southern end is quite different from that on the northern end, a situation suggestive of different sources for the fauna of the two sectors. Indeed, since a huge ice cap isolates the southern part of Greenland from any other land region, one might wonder how the various Ice Age animals of the south reached their habitat at all.

These peculiar faunal situations on the North Atlantic isles, plus similar incongruities noted earlier (p. 7), almost mandate the conclusion that Ice Age Atlantica did at times constitute a traversable passageway between the hemispheres. These animal migrations, of course, could have been made before the Wisconsin glaciations; in fact, the fossil evidence suggests most were.

Still, the fact that a traversable Atlantic bridge was extant in early Pleistocene times suggests that something close to it may well have been there in Wisconsin time. Happily, we are not without data on the geographic situation in the North Atlantic during the last glaciations. Cores taken from the North Atlantic sea bed by Soviet scientists strongly imply that the Atlantic bridge was continuous, or nearly so, at the time of humanity's American debut. The Russian investigators — Saks, Belov, and Lapina — reported:

> It seems that during the period in question [the last 50,000 years], a considerable part of the Arctic shelf was dry; there was no, or almost no, communication with the Atlantic. The climate was cold.[1]

In the same report, a somewhat less chilly period in the Arctic is noted, beginning about 30,000 years ago:

---

1 "Our Present Concepts of Geology in the Central Atlantic," *Priroda*, Defense Scientific Information Service, Ottawa, Canada, Oct. 4, 1955

The luxuriant development of foraminiferal fauna of a North Atlantic type testifies that during this period warm Atlantic waters were invading the Arctic Basin on a broad front; that is, communications between the Arctic Basin and the Atlantic Ocean, which apparently had been interrupted in the previous period were re-established. The duration of the warm period has been set at about 10,000 to 12,000 years.

More recent work by German and Norwegian scientists supports the Soviet findings but cuts the span of the warmer water intrusion about in half, placing it between 27,000 and 33,000 years ago.[1] The following three thousand years were marked by renewed isolation of the Arctic from the Atlantic (a point we will revisit later).

What the accumulation of data says is simply this: that on one or more occasion during the Pleistocene there must have been a land bridge joining the British shelf with North America. And during the most recent glaciation (the Weichsel/Wisconsin), if there was not such a bridge, there was something tantalizingly close to it.

The evidence grows bulky for a traversable Euro-American connection during the last Ice Age, but a final hurdle remains. The main reason orthodox science rejects the notion of an Atlantic bridge lies in the tenets of basic geology, tenets which have thwarted the divination of any feasible mechanism for the creation and submergence of such a feature.

Donnelly tried to build a link between the Old World and the New out of myths and legends centered around the lost continent of Atlantis. His semi-scientific efforts have plagued all subsequent advocates of such prehistoric contacts with a kind of guilt-by-association. In fact, it is fair to say the whole subject is frowned upon in a polite academic company.

Nevertheless, professors Malaise and Kolbe of Sweden braved the suggestion in the 1950s that such a bridge did in fact exist in late Pleistocene time. Their theory, which offered some formidable arguments, failed acceptance because it defied a firm geological principle — the principle of isostacy. On this point we must side, somewhat regretfully, with the critics. The concept of isostacy is almost beyond assault. Applied to geology, it holds that the lithosphere of the earth (which includes the crust) "floats" on a denser layer of slightly plastic rock known as the asthenosphere. As a rough analogy, the crust might be compared to an ice floe on the surface of the sea. An iceberg floats only because it is lighter than water. The thicker an ice floe, the higher it pushes above the surface (since one-tenth of any body of ice must stay above the water line). Isostatic doctrine requires that the continents must be thicker or lighter than the sea floor because they float higher on the asthenosphere. It has been established, through seismic

---

1 D. Hebbein, T. Dokken, et al, "Moisture supply for northern ice-sheet growth during the last Glacial Maximum," *Nature*, August 4, 1994, p.357

wave analysis and study of the rock components, that the continental blocs are actually *both* thicker and lighter.

Additional weight is lent to the isostatic concept by the fact that the great Pleistocene glaciers depressed the earth on which they stood, sometimes by hundreds of meters. The rebound of the earth's crust after glacial melt has been observed and measured. Raised beaches are found around the former glacial cen-ters of Hudson Bay and the Baltic Sea. The bones of whales have been uncovered hundreds of feet above sea level in the St. Lawrence River Valley. This depres-sion-and-rebound phenomenon is a near irrefutable argument for the validity if isostatic doctrine, even though there are minor deviations from isostatic balance and the principle cannot be rigidly applied to small areas.

Obviously, under the principle of isostacy, it is no more possible for a large land mass to sink suddenly into the ocean than it is possible for an iceberg to plunge to the bottom of the sea. Conversely, the ocean floor cannot rise above the sea surface except in cases of volcanic eruption involving quite limited areas.

Or so it has been generally presumed.

Major changes in land/sea relationships do take place, of course, but suppos-edly only over very long periods — millions of years. These changes are achieved by gradual erosion, sedimentary deposition, extrusions of volcanic rock and the imperceptible lateral movements of the earth's crust that build mountains. Su-perimposed on these slow changes are relatively rapid but not very dramatic os-cillations of sea level caused by variations in the size of the polar caps. Or so we are advised.

The argument against the Atlantic bridge, then, is simply that it could not have existed in relatively recent geological time because parts of it are now over 600 meters below sea level. There is no known force that could sink the ledge so quickly to such a depth. So, the principle of isostacy seems to bar us from elevating (or lowering) the trans-Atlantic ledge with anywhere near the speed required. At the same time, we are told that sea level changes were insufficient to bare the ledge to travel.

But what if there were a force, conformal with isostacy, affecting sea level to a greater degree than is now imagined? A sea change in spades, as it were.

How Deep the Ocean?

If a North Atlantic land bridge/archipelago existed in Pleistocene times, it must surely have resulted from a spectacular reduction in sea level, much greater than the 120–130 meters attributed to the formation of the great continental gla-ciers. That is, some presently unrecognized phenomenon must have been affect-ing the level of the world ocean.

Signally, a number of earth scientists have noted a peculiar pattern of oceanic inundations and regressions throughout Earth's history. In fact, this alternating rise and fall of the sea waters is a widely accepted phenomenon in geology, even though most geologists admit to being baffled by it.

Umgrove says, "the most important question concerns the depth to which the level was depressed in distinct periods of intense regression. In other words, the extent of the change to which the distance between the surface of the continents and the ocean floors were subjected during the pulsating rhythm of the subcrustal processes. Joly was the only one who approached this question from the geological side, and he arrived at an order of *one thousand meters*."[1]

Schuchert calculated that North America has been extensively inundated no fewer than seventeen times. Amadeus Grabau (Columbia University) observed, "This rhythmic succession and essential simultaneousness of the transgressions, as well as the regressions in all the continents, indicates a periodic rise and fall of sea level, a slow pulsatory movement..."[2]

It is clear that these sporadic fluctuations are not just a result of ice caps melting and reforming because they occur in periods of geological history when there were no significant ice caps.

Joly's notion of large cyclical variations in sea level may seem improbable at first consideration. One might be tempted to say that he must have made some mistake; after all, he worked long ago. We are often inclined to dismiss the conclusions of yesteryear with a wave of the hand simply on the grounds that the investigator could not have been as enlightened as ourselves. Quite recently, though, investigations carried out at Rice University in Texas, in conjunction with petroleum exploration techniques, have confirmed Joly's contention. The new data, known as the Exxon Sea Level Curves, have scientists scratching their heads and in some cases simply refusing to accept the evidence because it seems to have no possible explanation. (See analysis of the Exxon Sea Level Curves in Chapter 4.)

There are other independent lines of evidence that suggest that Joly was on the right track. Particularly powerful testimony is supplied by the existence of deep submarine canyons at the edge of the continental shelves, considered one of the more baffling geological phenomena.

At the mouths of many rivers throughout the world, there are submerged canyons extending far from shore beneath the sea. They are frequently V-shaped and carved through solid rock, strongly indicating sub-aerial erosion. Yet most scientific opinion rejects sub-aerial erosion on the grounds that there is no accounting for a sea level reduction of the magnitude required — several hundred meters in some cases. Faced with this paradox, orthodoxy has fallen back on this dubious theory of turbidity currents, that is, monster mudslides beneath the sea. Doubt-

1 Umgrove, J.H.F. *The pulse of the Earth*, 2nd ed., Martinus Nijhof, The Hague, Netherlands, 1947, p. 9
2 A.W. Grabau, *The Rhythm of the Ages: Earth History in Light of the Pulsation and Polar Control Theories*, Peking, Vetch, 1940

less, some such slides do occur and the theory may be adequate in some instances, but it is near ridiculous in the cases of submarine canyons cut through solid rock. Such canyons had to be carved sub-aerially, at least in their upper reaches.

Aside from the submarine canyons, there are plenty of other data testifying that sea levels have been much lower than is customarily postulated for the glacial epochs.

For example, the islands of Corsica and Sardinia have a rich Pleistocene fauna. The animals must have walked, or swum very narrow channels, to reach these islands. Yet, the isles are separated from the mainland by broad waters over 200 meters deep.[1]

The Arctic hares and indigenous reindeer on the Svalbard Islands (Spitsbergen) are separated from the mainland by great expanses of sea at least 250 meters deep. And the presence of the Svalbard reindeer in northern Canada and Greenland suggests a drop in arctic sea levels on the order 500 meters or more. Then, there are those nagging foxes on Iceland, plus at least one variety of field mouse that is probably indigenous.

The Aleutian Island chain is instructive too. There are red foxes on the Fox Island group. And these foxes were once indigenous to the Rat Island group which is divorced from the mainland by wide waters over 400 meters in depth. The ice flow hypothesis does not work at all well in this situation; the prevailing currents are heavily against it.

Again, there are too many false notes in the orthodox tune. Pleistocene seas subsided more than we have been told. We are pushed inexorably to the conclusion that the conventional figure of minus 120–130 meters is way too conservative.

SIBERIAN BONES

Some of the more intriguing evidence of near catastrophic changes in sea level during the Ice Age comes from the New Siberian and Liakof Islands in the Arctic Ocean. These islands are littered with the bones of mammoths and other Pleistocene animals. The isles are on the continental shelf, so there's no trouble explaining how the beasts got there. What is significant is the incalculable number of bones. They must represent the remains of thousands of animals that were somehow trapped to die on these islands.

The only reasonable interpretation of the facts is that a much larger area than the present isles was cut off and quite rapidly inundated. The rising waters must have driven great numbers of animals to the small segments of high ground which now constitute the islands. These unfortunate creatures were packed into

---

1 It does no good to argue that the fauna might have reached Sardo-Corsica at a time when the Strait of Gibraltar was closed and the Mediterranean Sea level reduced. Sea level would have to drop 320 meters to close the strait.

a living space far too limited to support their numbers and they died by the thousands from starvation.

Here is yet another implication that the post-glacial surges in Arctic seas were sometimes faster and greater than current concepts can easily accommodate.

It can be seen, then, that our notion of dramatic ups and downs in relative sea level during the Pleistocene can explain numerous oddities: the enigmatic distribution of some Ice Age fauna, the puzzle of the submarine canyons, extensive oceanic transgressions, even the curious caches of Siberian bones.

But the most portentous impact of these larger-than-imagined sea level fluctuations lies in their capacity to supply the causality for the Ice Age itself.

CHAPTER 4. THE ICE AGE AND ROTATIONAL VARIATION

The planet spins, blue and white, through the black of space. But sometimes there is much more white — not the whiteness of clouds but of ice sheets. Periodically, massive expanses of glacial ice begin to build and spread over the face of the planet, incredible in their extent, inexorable in their progress. Relentlessly, the ice plows its ponderous way over millions of square miles of landscape, crushing the largest trees, carrying away the most massive boulders. Everything alive flees before it or dies.

It has happened many times before — since the isthmus of Panama emerged above sea level about two million years ago, radically altering the world's ocean currents and triggering the Pleistocene epoch. It almost certainly will happen again.

As we have seen, the movement of the glaciers is not a simple matter of their coming and going. Sometimes they pause in their progress, even retreat temporarily before resuming their onward push. The maximum sway of the white mantle seems to be reached when it covers about a quarter of the earth's land surface.

The chronology of the Ice Ages was a subject of debate for most of the 20th century. Gradually though, a reasonably reliable time table for the great glacial advances was worked out. It is now clear that the main glacial cycle during the Pleistocene has been about 100,000 years long. Geologists can identify five major ice onslaughts in the past half million years.

The key step in settling the chronology was the discovery that the ocean waters contain more of the oxygen isotope, O18, during heavy glaciation. The presence of this isotope in the seas is easily traceable in ocean sediments, i.e., by drilling core samples from the sea floor. By measuring the oxygen 18 in the marine sediments, oceanographers can tell how much land ice there was at a given time.

The glaciations tend to peak late in the cycle, that is, the ice builds up gradually and fades fast. The Weichsel/Wisconsin was entirely typical, with a 100,000 year expansion reaching a peak about 20,000 years ago and melting away in a mere ten thousand years.

The planet spins, blue and white, through the spatial void. But what of that spin? Is it steady and unvarying as we have always assumed? Or does it, perchance, alter in its pace? And if it does alter, what are the consequences?

An Unilluminating Litany

All attempts so far to account for the waxing and waning of the continental ice and the associated mountain glaciers (in the Alps, Andes, etc.) have fallen well short of full success. Typically, sequential theories attain a passing fashion only to dissolve in the light of closer examination.

To recount the myriad hypotheses devised to explain the Ice Ages would be largely a waste of time. The suggestions can be broken down into two basic categories, astronomical and terrestrial — with only a single viable entry in each group.

The most popular of the astronomical theories is based on minor variations in the earth's orbit and tilt. Originated by the early 20th century astronomer Milutin Milankovitch, the theory, in addition to other difficulties,[1] requires at least one gigantic leap of faith.

Basically, summer insolation in the northern hemisphere is supposed to be the key to the Ice Age cycles. The insolation varies somewhat with three cycles — the obliquity cycle, the precession cycle, and the orbital eccentricity cycle of 93,000 years. While some climatic correlations with the first two cycles appear fairly convincing, the theory collapses at the critical point. In order to cope with the main glacial cycle of ca. 100,000 years, Milankovitch falls back on a miniscule eccentricity in the earth's orbit, a swing of about one tenth of one percent![2] It is baldly obvious that this factor could not alter our planet's temperatures by more than a fraction of one degree. Yet this is supposed to account for the basic glaciation pattern. (Hardly anyone, in or out of academe, really believes this.)

Other hypotheses try to trace the cause of the Ice Ages to radical changes on the earth: sliding crusts, wandering poles, unexplained volcanic catastrophes, etc. Suffice it to say that these propositions, besides offending common sense, are in fatal conflict with firm geological principles or observed facts, or do not even approximate the required timeframes in their supposed effects.

One terrestrial theory, while not sufficient unto itself, deserves some discussion since it could feasibly figure in some aspects of glaciation phenomena. The

1 For the latest, see D.B. Karen and R.A. Muller, "A Causality Problem for Milankovitch," *Science*, June 23, 2000

2 J.D. Hays, John Imbrie, N.J. Shackleton, "Variations in the Earth's Orbit: Pacemaker of the Ice Ages," *Science*, Dec. 10 1976, p.1125

thought that some sort of blockage or deflection of the Gulf Stream may have fig-ured in the Pleistocene weather pattern has occurred to more than one investiga-tor. The Gulf Stream, a monstrous "River in the Sea," constantly pours megatons of warm water into the northern latitudes. The flow is far greater than all the rivers on earth combined. It is the Gulf Stream that is responsible for the fact that all of northern Europe, even to the northern-most tip of Norway, enjoys a much more moderate climate than comparable latitudes elsewhere.

The isothermic map of the Atlantic graphically illustrates the effects of the Gulf Stream and the North Atlantic Drift: Nowhere on earth but in the Nor-wegian Sea do such moderate winter temperatures extend north of the Arctic Circle. Were this influx of warm water into the Arctic and Norwegian Seas to be allayed in some fashion, there can be no question that temperatures in North Europe would fall sharply. The Arctic Ocean, which now trades massive volumes of water with the Atlantic, would become isolated from temporizing influences. This would create a huge cold cell at the top of the world, adversely affecting temperatures over northern Canada and Eurasia.

There are a couple of hitches which undermine any easy Gulf Stream explica-tion of the Ice Ages. Most obviously, the glaciations were worldwide. Any deflec-tion of the Gulf Stream would have a measurable effect only on Northern Eurasia and upper Canada. There might be slight ancillary effects in other parts of the world, but the impact would not be sufficient to produce the extensive glacia-tions that occurred in the Andes, the Himalayas, the Caucasus and Australia.

The other difficulty with the Gulf Stream hypothesis has to do with how the current could have been repeatedly blocked and unblocked over the past two million years. Coincident with this question is a broader and more fundamental consideration: Realistically, it would be almost impossible for the Scandian Ice Cap to develop unless the Gulf Stream was allayed or diverted in some way. But how?

THE GEOPULSATION SOLUTION

Like the Gordian knot of old, the causality of the Ice Age seems to defy every effort to unravel it. The Alexandrian sword in this case is simply a reversal of perspective, i.e., major reductions in arctic sea level seen as a cause rather than merely an effect of glaciation. In short, the paleoclimatologists seem to have been peering through the wrong end of the telescope.

A substantial elevation of any continental bloc relative to the surface of the sea would have drastic climatic effects. It is well known that temperatures tend to decrease at least one degree (F.) for every one hundred meters of increased altitude above sea level. We have seen that sea level fell some hundreds of meters at various times and places during the Pleistocene, even though drops of that magnitude could not be due to glacial water storage alone.

A sea fall of, say, 500 meters would be just the same in its climatic effects as an elevation of the land by 500 meters. In other words, land temperatures would drop about five degrees from this effect alone, so such a reduction would have profound climatic repercussions. But the key to the whole Pleistocene mystery is the latitudinal orientation of the temperature fall during the Ice Age, i.e., the higher the latitude, the more severe was the temperature drop. In arctic areas, temperature reductions were several times what they were in the tropics.[1] The significance of this latitudinal bias has been overlooked. It tells us that the fall in sea level was more marked in the high latitudes, a prospect supported by the faunal evidence that the sharpest drops occurred in the high latitudes (the foxes on Iceland and in the Aleutians).

But what earthly cause could produce a sea level reduction on the scale required, while accentuating that fall in the polar regions? The only possible answer is *centrifugal force*.

Our earth is not a perfect sphere, but rather an oblate spheroid: a sphere somewhat flattened at the poles and bulging at the equator. The globe assumes this shape because it is rotating and so is pushed slightly out of shape by centrifugal force, making the polar diameter about 27 miles shorter than the equatorial diameter. The earth takes almost exactly the same shape as the ocean surface because the planet was formed in a plastic state and remains plastic in its interior.

The point is that the shapes of the earth and the sea surface are determined by the combined effects of gravity and rotational velocity. The earth is in the shape it's in because we have a 24 hour day. But to think outside of the box for a moment, suppose the length of that day should vary a bit. What would be the impact of a shift in the planet's spin velocity?

Obviously, an increase in rotational velocity would accentuate the ellipsoidal form of the planet. The most pronounced immediate effect would be manifested in the surface of the fluid oceans. Sea waters would flow toward the equator and away from the poles. In other words, sea level in the polar areas would fall, producing a relative elevation of the arctic (and Antarctic) lands. The snowline would drop in these areas and glaciers would start to build. And there would be a kind of snowball effect. That is, the more sea level fell, the more glaciation would increase; the more the glaciations increased, the more sea level would drop.

The earth itself, being extremely viscous in its interior, would react to the change in centrifugal force far slower than the fluid oceans. Theoretically, over a period of tens of thousands or years, Earth would eventually assume the same geoidal shape as the surface seas and "normalcy" would be reestablished. That is, assuming the increased rotational velocity held constant for a sufficient time.

---

1 Sutcliffe, Anthony, *On the Track of the Ice Age Mammals*, Harvard University Press, Cambridge, MA, 1985, p. 69

But alternatively — and this is what actually happens — an Ice Age would be ended by a reduction in the rotational speed, that is, a return to the "normal" (slower) spin velocity that raises polar sea levels again.

The effects of such polar sea level reductions would be accentuated in the northern hemisphere by the emergence of the North Atlantic ledge. The relative elevation of the ledge would constrict Gulf Stream flow, and its powerful moderating influence would be curtailed in the Norwegian Sea and the Arctic Ocean, producing a particularly icy climate in the higher latitudes of the northern hemisphere.

The Climap Project of a few years ago, an extensive probe into ancient climatic conditions, provides a striking bit of supportive data on the emergence of the Atlantic Ledge. Researchers found that the main current of the Gulf Stream shifted southward during the last glacial episode, flowing towards Iberia instead of Britain and seldom penetrating north of the latitude of New York.

Such a shift is just what would result from emergence of the North Atlantic ledge. With normal Gulf Stream flow into the Norwegian Sea impeded, the full power of the stream would be deflected southward along Europe's coast toward Iberia. So the Climap work reinforces the conclusions reached by Saks, Belov, and Lapina. It is difficult to conjure up any other explanation for this Gulf Stream diversion.

The idea of rotational change as the instigator of the Ice Ages offers the bonus advantage of maintaining world precipitation levels. A weakness inherent in the solar radiation theories is that they imply a reduction in the precipitation needed to feed the expanding ice sheets. What we postulate, on the other hand, only shifts the climatic belts somewhat towards the equator, leaving ample snowfall available for glacial growth.

CRACKING THE CODE

Pressing questions remain. This notion that shifting rotational velocity is behind the Ice Ages immediately raises some points of inquiry. What we have at this stage is a hypothesis. To pursue it to advantage we have to determine whether it is fundamentally feasible. Is there actual evidence that Earth's spin speed changes, plus and minus? If so, what mechanism could produce such a phenomenon? And if there is a cycle of velocity variation, where are we, chronologically, in that cycle?

Though the Earth seems constant enough beneath our feet, the fact is that its spin speed is more than a little erratic.

Short-term fluctuations are small but quite perceptible with modern measurement systems. The variation in the length of the day may amount to several milliseconds in a typical decade, as much as four milliseconds in a single year. These minor variations are superimposed on a very long-term trend towards slower rotation of the planet caused by tidal friction — the effect of the moon's gravity on our oceans.

But the slowing has some curious aspects.

One of the most careful studies of the long term slow-down in spin speed was done by Stephenson in the early 1980s.[1] By analyzing historical data on eclipses, he was able to compute that the day has grown longer, on average, by about 1.5 milliseconds per century over the past 2,700 years. (The cumulative effect of these small quantities is not trivial because they increase with the square of the time: In the last 2,000 years, the accumulated clock error comes to over 5 hours.)

But Stephenson's calculations show Earth's rotation is not slowing nearly as much as it should. Tidal friction ought to decelerate spin speed by 2.5 ms per century, but the actual rate, as we see, is much less — and lessening. The earth's slowing rotation, it seems, is not a straight line process: The deceleration rate, especially in recent centuries, has been slackening off noticeably — a curious, and significant, phenomenon. In fact, despite some 20th century blips, the planet's rotation speed today is *exactly the same* as it was 300 years ago. In other words, the slowing of the spin has essentially ceased. Clearly, some "X" factor is at work, tending to speed rotation even as tidal friction works in the opposite direction. This mystery force is getting stronger with time and is now overcoming the deceleration tendency entirely. The inference is clear: There exists a force that can actually tend to increase our planet's spin velocity.

The implications of this surprising fact are, as we'll see, earthshaking in their portent.

DAYS LONG GONE

While the variations in Earth's rotation in our era have been small, there is ample evidence that more dramatic disturbances occurred in the distant past. There is nothing consistent, nothing straight line, about this phenomenon.

The pioneer in Earth rotation studies, John Wells, managed to calculate that a Devonian year had about 400 days: That is, the earth was revolving about 10 percent faster in Devonian times than it is now.[2] The determination was made by an ingenious technique he introduced in 1962. Wells discovered that the number of days in ancient years could be calculated by counting the daily growth lines in fossil corals and bivalves.[3] But the most remarkable outgrowth of this method

---

1 Stephenson, F.R., "Historical Eclipses," *Scientific American*, Oct. 1982. See also: www. ucolick.org/~sla/leapsecs/dutc.html

2 Wells, John West, "Coral Growth and Geochronometry," *Nature*, 197: 948-50

3 The daily growth lines are arranged in a pattern of annual or monthly (lunar) series, depending on the species being examined, so it is possible to tell how many days constituted a year or a lunar month by optical and/or chemical count of the growth lines. There is a high degree of correlation in these counts, indicating strong reliability in the process.

lies in the evidence that the spin speed of the planet has increased significantly from time to time (Fig. 6).

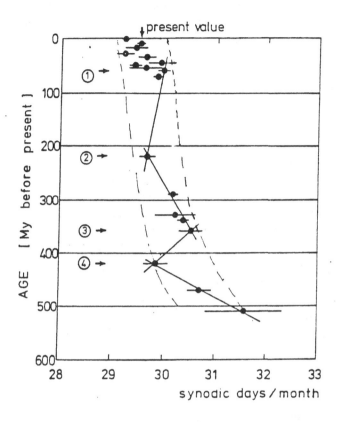

Fig. 7: The above graph illustrates variations in the length of the day over the past several hundred million years. Despite the long-term lengthening of the day, at times the day's length has actually decreased, i.e., the speed of the Earth's rotation increased. The data for the past 70 million years, which is more detailed, presents a picture of frequent acceleration and deceleration though there are plainly too few data points to show all fluctuations in rotational velocity. This study correlates generally with other independent investigations. Realistically though, it probably contains slight measurement errors which would tend to exaggerate the degree of rotational variation. The range indicated by the dashed lines, suggesting variations on the order of 3%, is likely to be overstated. Some indicators suggest the actual range is probably less than 2%.

The long term trend is towards rotational deceleration, *but* with intermittent periods of *acceleration*. Moreover, the variations in spin speed, in any given segment or geological time, have been pronounced enough to produce significant effects on the earth's surface.

Actually (since centrifugal force increases with the square of rotational velocity), it would take only about a one percent acceleration of planetary spin speed to produce the sea level changes needed to trigger the glaciations — ignoring asthenospheric flow in the earth's interior. But in an Ice Age timeframe, some such flow must occur by which the shape of the earth itself tends to slowly follow the changing shape of the hydrosphere, slightly attenuating the surface effects of oceanic flow towards the equator. This factor suggests a range of cyclical spin speed somewhat over one percent.

Also to be considered in the calculation are certain random components impacting rotational velocity, such as haphazard churn in the earth's liquid core, and variations in the magnetic field which could alter the rotation of earth's solid shell vis-à-vis its core by way of magnetic torque.

All in all, then, we might expect eccentricities in planetary rotation approaching two percent in a given segment of geological time — a range that tracks almost exactly with the variations indicated by data from a series of Pleistocene mollusk fossils from California sandstone.[1] The two percent estimate also checks out well enough with the long term historical data graphed in Figure 6.

It is plain from the available data that these variations are, in a geological sense, relatively rapid. Even in the past 75 million years, where we have many data points, there are no cases where consecutive data points show the same rotational velocity (Figure 6). So we have, in this factor of spin variation, something which could easily operate in the same timeframe as the Ice Age glaciations.

RECENT CONFIRMATIONS

Our preceding chapter cited the conclusions of Joly, Umgrove, and Grabau that some sort rhythmic, pulsatory force has been effecting global sea level fluctuations over geological time.

Besides these venerable authorities, we mentioned some more contemporary evidence. Data accumulated by Exxon Corporation, some if it still proprietary, confirms that large, rapid and inexplicable alterations of sea level have been occurring on a global basis for millions of years. These fluctuations, the Exxon Sea Level Curves, rest on a vast accumulation by independent researchers.[2] Changes in oceanic levels have been so great at times that whole sedimentary layers of the continental shelves have been washed away by subaerial erosion in geologically brief periods. Conversely, sedimentary layers have been deposited far inland in intervals much too brief to be accounted for by the slow rise and fall of land forms. It is impossible to lay the Exxon variations at the door of glaciations because

---

1 Cited in "The slowing Spin Speed of Earth," www.creation-answers.com/
2 See "Ancient Sea-Level Swings Confirmed." Research News, *Science*, May 14 1996, p. 1097

they are too large and because they occur in periods when there were no great glaciers.

Since they are based on the study of sediment deposits, the Exxon Curve data cannot accurately reflect all the relatively short term deviations in sea level that are involved in the glaciation cycle. But the main message is clear enough: There have been large, comparatively rapid fluctuations in world sea levels that cannot be accommodated by current geological theory. These fluctuations clearly comport with the expected effects of rotational variation.

CHAPTER 5. THE MECHANISM OF GEOPULSATION

Copious data support the idea that significant alterations in Earth's spin speed have occurred, and in a timeframe commensurate with the glaciations cycles. But to nail things down, we need to identify some theoretical basis for how such changes occur. There has to be some cryptic geophysical mechanism that can intermittently slow and accelerate the earth's rotational velocity.

The clues lead to the planet's core. Certainly, the fact that Earth's magnetic field varies constantly in intensity and direction demonstrates considerable commotion in the outer (liquid) core. Even in historical times, the location of magnetic north has been anything but stable. Records at London show magnetic declination there has swung from 12 degrees East to 24 degrees West, and part way back again, since 1576.[1] And there is evidence for far greater eccentricity in the geological record. We now know that the whole magnetic field has actually reversed a number of times through history, north becoming south and vice versa. These reversals are so far an utter enigma. But clearly, the molten flow in the outer core, which must be the genesis of the magnetic field, is subject to changes in direction that could easily add to, or detract from, the speed of planetary spin.

Actually, the mechanism producing long-term alternations in Earth's rotational velocity is fairly obvious. The variations hinge on the fact that core of our planet tends not to spin at the same speed, or even on the same plane, as the solid outer shell (mantle/crust). There are, in other words, rotational differences between the interior and exterior of the planet.

To quote a long-ago observation by geophysicist F.D. Stacy: "There is a relative motion of its [Earth's] parts. Although slow by comparison with human ac-

---

1   Takeuchi, H. Uyeda, S. & Kanmori, H., *Debate About the Earth*, Freeman Cooper & Co., San Francisco CA, 1970, p. 103

tivity, it is a million times faster than large-scale geological change."[1] He adds this prescient note, "We have not yet explored all the consequences of this discovery" — a masterpiece of understatement as it turns out.

It came as something of a jolt to geophysicists when Song and Richards showed in 1996 that the inner core is rotating faster than the rest of the planet.[2] But their much talked about paper should have been less of a surprise than it was.

Ordinary logic imputes that the earth's core must rotate slightly faster than the mantle/crust. Part of the reason lies in the way our planet was formed — from small particles whirling into a gravitational center. Aside from that, the outer shell must rotate more slowly because of the moon's gravitational drag, clearly greater on the solid segment that is closer to the moon and has more mass than either the solid or liquid core.

Song and Richards calculated the differential rotation of the solid core as very slight, about one degree per year, but that figure is still far from settled due to some sparseness in the data and our dim understanding of certain core characteristics. (See appendix I.) The calculation also makes what we will find to be a questionable assumption: that all portions of the planet always rotate around exactly the same axis.

Using an entirely different approach, Raymond Jeanloz, of Cal–Berkeley, has estimated that the core is rotating at about the spin speed of the whole earth of 100,000 years ago, a far bigger divergence — about what John Wells' data would lead us to expect, and one with potential to markedly impact Earth's overall rotation.

It would be only fair to mention that Song and Richards do pose a "new question" near the end of their pioneering paper, i.e., "Does the inner core rotation track the north-south spin axis in the precession of the equinoxes?" Apparently not. Recently, other scientists looking into the differential rotation problem, found evidence that the rotational axis of the inner core does indeed differ from the Earth's main axis.[3]

THE POWER OF PRECESSION

To get to our point, it is the differences in core/mantle spin speeds and angles that provide the motive power for the curious sporadic hikes in our globe's rotational velocity. The phenomenon might seem abstruse at first, but is plain once we consider all the geological effects of the earth's astronomical cycle of precession. As those who stayed awake in Astronomy 101 well know, the axis of plan-

---

1 Stacy, F.D., "The Main Field," *Global Geophysics*, RAW, Tucker, et al; American Elsevier Publishing Co., New York, NY, 1970, p. 152

2 Song, Xiaodong, & Richards, Paul G., "Seismological Evidence for Differential Rotation of the Earth's Inner Core," *Nature*, July 18, 1996, p. 221

3 Henri-Claude Natif, "Inner Core Takes Another Turn," *Nature*, May 25, 2000, p. 411

etary rotation does not consistently point to any fixed star. That is, the axis has no constant directional orientation, but instead wanders, describing a cone in space over the millennia (Figure 6).

The reader will no doubt recall that the Earth's axis is tilted by 23.5 degrees relative to the plane of its orbit around the sun, an inclination that causes the four seasons. But though this angle of inclination remains fairly steady, the direction that the axis points does not. Due to the equatorial bulge, there is a constant solar and lunar gravitational force trying to pull the axis of the earth into a line perpendicular with the plane of the ecliptic (the plane of our rotation about the sun). But, because the planet is spinning, this alignment is never achieved. Instead, precession occurs. That is, the earth's axis wanders around the way the axis of a spinning top (or gyroscope) does if it is not spinning straight up. Hence, our planet's

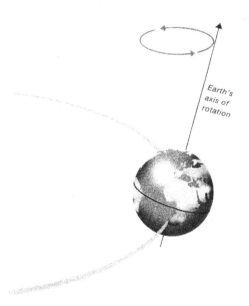

axis does not always point to the North Star.

Fig. 6: Presently, the earth's axis of rotation points at the North Star, Polaris. However, the direction that the axis points slowly changes with time as the planet precesses (wobbles). Over 26,000 years, Earth's axis will describe a complete circle, changing the apparent position of the "fixed stars."

This precession is quite slow in human terms. It takes almost 26,000 years for the axis to describe its cone in space, so navigators need not worry. But, in the geological sense, this movement is rapid, easily rapid enough to figure in the phenomenon of cyclical glaciations.

When considering the precession process, habitualized thinking tends to picture the earth as a solid sphere, which of course, it is not. The subterranean planet is more like a three layer cake — actually a two layer cake with a liquid layer in between. Beneath the solid mantle is the liquid core, and at the center of that is a solid iron core only about 1,500 miles in diameter but of extreme density and colossal mass.

The crucial point is that the natural precession rate of the solid outer earth must differ from that of the solid core. It is clearly impossible that precessional forces affect the two components just the same way due to mass/distance and gravitational factors. There is a vast difference between the size and mass of the solid core and the outer shell of the planet and the distances vis-à-vis the sun and moon are not the same. Hence, the precession tendencies cannot be identical.

Plainly, there is a lot more going on in the interior of the earth than has been assumed, phenomena that have portentous effects on our planet. Since the inner core tends to precess at a different rate, obviously the spin axis of the core must change relative to the spin axis of the mantle/crust. The intermediate liquid core may be visualized as a kind of hydraulic coupling between the solid core and the mantle, whereby the differential changes in the precession of the solid core impact the rotation of the mantle/crust. (The hydraulic couple is a powerful factor tending to attenuate the potential misalignment between the solid core and the mantle, but is not strong enough to completely cancel out the effects of the precession differences.)

Strangely enough, there has been unperceived evidence of this core/mantle misalignment for well over a century — since the discovery of the Chandler wobble. Seth Chandler detected in 1891 a slight circular variation in position of the poles, amounting to about .7 arc seconds over a period of about 14 months. This wobble should theoretically dampen out in a few decades, but it does not. A number of explanations have been offered, none very convincing. Yet just such a wobble is to be expected if the solid core's rotation is not quite aligned with that of the mantle/crust.

More recent evidence that the inner core is rotating on a different plane and axis came in the mid-90s with the discovery that the core's crystalline grain is canted about 10 degrees off the axis of Earth's rotation. This grain, or anisotropy, almost surely indicates the approximate directional axis of the core's rotation.

The ten degree misalignment (probably fairly near the max) accounts for the fact that the velocity of Earth's spin right now is very nearly steady. The degree of misalignment is just barely overcoming the effect of the core's higher rotation speed. This stability of our own era, however, is a phantasm. It cannot last because the degree of the misalignment is slowly but constantly changing.

When, as now, the rotational axis of the core is significantly out of line with the axis of the outer earth, there has to be a directional drag that tends to slow Earth's rotation to its minimum. But during periods when the rotational plane of core is in sync with that of the mantle/crust, planetary spin regains the lost velocity — rotation speeds up, especially since the core's spin outpaces that of the outer shell.[1]

---

1 Readers interested in more detail may wish to refer to Appendix I.

This idea of differential precession is not just theoretical: It is required by basic laws of physics and mechanics. And, in conjunction with continental drift, it helps explain the mysterious wide wanderings of the magnetic poles through geological time.[1]

The fact that the earth's precessional cycle is 26,000 years does not imply that the glacial cycle covers that same period. It is the *difference* between the precession pace of the core and that of the overall earth that modulates the planet's spin and produces the great glaciations. So the issue is, how long does it take the mantle/crust precession to lap that of the core? — an easier question than it seems. We already know the answer because studies of the glaciations, as noted earlier, have established a main cycle of about 100,000 years — which means the precessions of the earth's outer shell must be lapping those of the core in the length of time.

Back-up evidence is added by sediment cores that reveal a 100,000 year periodicity in the inclination and intensity of the earth's magnetic field. Scientists have no convincing explanation of this phenomenon, but just such a cycle would be expected from the variations in core-mantle alignments postulated by Geopulsation Theory.

WHERE ARE WE?

Since the earth is now slowing almost imperceptibly in its rotation, the planet plainly must be in a phase of the main cycle near a stabilization point, i.e., a point where there is minimal change in spin velocity. Clearly, there are two such spots in every 100,000 year cycle: at the peak rotational velocity and at the nadir (fig.8).

Because we have only lately emerged from the Weichsel/Wisconsin era (and so are in an interglacial phase) the earth cannot be turning at its peak velocity. A key premise of our theory is that heightened rotation speed is the motor of glaciation. It is the reduction of spin velocity that raises the polar sea levels and vanquishes the great continental ice caps. Ergo, the planet must be close to its lowest rotational velocity, following the end phase of the previous glaciation cycle.

This conclusion is confirmed by measurements which show the pace of deceleration is currently being attenuated almost to the vanishing point. In the not-very-distant future any decline in spin speed is due to cease entirely; the low ebb of planetary whirl will be passed and the stage set for a new glacial onslaught.

The fact that we are living near a stabilization point in Earth's spin cycle accounts for our failure to realize the magnitude of the changes that can and do occur in the planet's rotation. While spin velocity appears virtually steady right now, that only means the past deceleration is about over, and the onset of acceleration is imminent — if not already dawning.

---

1 Yamazaki, T. & Oda, H., "Orbital Influence on Earth's Magnetic Field: 100,000 Year Periodicity in Inclination," *Science*, Mar. 29 2002, p. 2435

Consider recent data coming to light through satellite monitoring of the shape of the Earth. In 1998, for the first time since the start of these observations in 1979, the planet stopped becoming steadily more spherical (as might be expected with a declining spin speed) and even took a tiny bounce towards a more oblate shape.[1] The phenomenon jibes well with Rotational Pulsation Theory — and with the shorter term spin data that suggest a tentative trend toward accelerated rotation since 1970, a tendency that has brought Earth's spin into almost exact synchrony with atomic time. (It has been necessary to add only two leap seconds since 1998 to achieve coordination.) It is too soon to say that 1970s marked the nadir of the earth's spin velocity in the current cycle, but such is a clear possibility. Meanwhile, measurements show the magnetic north pole has been moving noticeably closer to the geographic north pole in recent decades, another indicator that the rotational axes of the core and the mantle-crust are edging toward alignment. Our planet's form has reached virtual stabilization and the next phase, the upward spin trend, may already be in the process of materializing.

As that phase takes hold, oceanic flow will again head back towards the tropics, effectively elevating the higher latitude lands. Slowly, the glaciers will begin to re-form and start to push their way over Scandinavia and Canada. The cold white mantle will spread again over millions of square miles of our home planet. It is very unlikely that the warming impact of human activity will be able to materially offset these massive impending natural trends. (Earth's climate, if anything, has shown a cooling tendency since the year 2000.)

THE VOLCANO AGE

Towering columns of black smoke and the reverberating roar of volcanic eruptions were common features of the Pleistocene environment — much more than is the case today. The reason can be found in a corollary of Geopulsation Theory, a side implication that affects both the glaciation cycle and its secondary variations (such as the interstadial phases). The plastic flow produced in Earth's interior by rotational changes necessarily produces violent episodes of volcanism. The effect, of course, is most pronounced during the periods of more rapid change in planetary spin speed. Chronologically, these peaks would be about a quarter of the way through the glacial cycle and again about three quarters of the way — in the last Ice Age, about 25-30,000 and 75-to-80,000 years ago.

Nowadays, the magnitude of plastic flow below the solid lithosphere is limited by the relative stability of present day rotation. But even in this period of comparative quietude, volcanism continues sporadically, especially along the trenches and ridge–rift systems that mark the edges of the tectonic plates. The movement of the asthensophere (a plastic layer about 100 kilometers below us)

---

1 Cazenave, Anny, & Nerum, R.S., "Redistributing Earth's Mass," *Science*, 2 August 2002.

never halts entirely. The plastic flow is always chasing the changes in rotational speed but, because of it extreme viscosity, never quite catches up.

Our present day volcanism, such as the eruptions at Surtsey and Heimaey on the Atlantic ridge, is only an aftertaste of the colossal volcanic activity that must have been generated during periods in which Earth's spin speed was changing more rapidly. Spin deceleration creates enormous compressional pressure and heat at the tectonic plate margins with resultant seismic eruptions. Spin acceleration splits the rift system open, producing volcanism on an unimaginable scale of magnitude and frequency.[1] (The planetary-scale geological implications of these disruptions of the rift systems are reviewed in our section on continental drift, Chapters 8 and 9.)

The stepped up volcanic activity during glacial phases had dramatic and pervasive impacts. It was a substantial factor in creating the glaciation itself. Volcanic eruptions, of course, fill the air with ash and dust, blocking out some of the sun's rays. Studies of the climatological effects of volcanic dust show than even relatively small amounts can seriously cut the intensity of solar radiation at the earth's surface. The blow-up of Krakatoa in the 1889 produced a noticeable temperature drop over most of the world, lasting for many months. So did the eruption of Alaska's Mount Katmai in 1912.

There is no doubt that volcanic activity was much more general during the Wisconsin glaciation than now, with cataclysmic lava flows in the American West, violent eruptions along the Cascade range, also in Arizona and Alaska. And there are huge lava flows in central and southeast Asia dating from the last glacial period. Layers of volcanic ash cover the ocean floor east of the North Atlantic ridge, attesting to extreme volcanism along the rift system during the late Wisconsin. The intensity of the activity was dramatic enough to convince Hibben that volcanoes were the prime cause of the mass extinctions of Pleistocene animals at the end of the Wisconsin glacial phase.[2]

The evidence of Pleistocene eruptions is so ubiquitous, in fact, that some theorists have actually laid the whole responsibility for the Ice Ages on volcanism. They overstate their case, but are partly correct. Volcanic activity was doubtless a strong contributing factor. Geopulsation provides the theoretical basis for the Pleistocene paroxysms, otherwise a mystery.

---

1 The reason for the splitting of the rifts is rooted in the natural characteristics of the sphere. Any deviation from a perfect sphere requires an increase in surface area to retain a given volume. As Earth's spin accelerates in glacial epochs, the form of the planet becomes more ellipsoidal, less and less spherical, so surface area has to increase. It increases mainly at the plate boundaries as mantle material wells up to fill the widening gaps between the plates. This process, and its obverse — compression of the plate junctions during spin slowing — had to be accompanied by a degree of volcanism unknown in recorded history.

2 Hibben, Frank C., *The Lost Americans*, Thomas Crowell, New York NY, 1946, pp. 176-178.

Obviously, these volcanic spasms were no uniform affair, but varied greatly from time to time and place to place. Different parts of Earth in different latitudes came under strain from the moving asthenosphere at varying times. Hence, the amount and the geographic distribution of volcanic dust must have been erratic. This variable dust pattern is part of the reason that the climatic character of the Pleistocene was so mercurial, as demonstrated by the Greenland ice cores (figure 8).

The amount of dust in the Ice Age atmosphere would be easily enough to induce apoplexy in a modern day environmentalist: about 30 times what we find today, judging from the cores drilled into the Greenland ice cap — though Greenland might not be an entirely typical case due to its proximity to the volcanoes of Iceland.

It might be mentioned in passing that Geopulsation Theory dissolves one more nagging geological curiosity. That is the great depression of the lands under the ice caps — even such secondary ones as covered the Andes. The difficulty here only became evident after the realization that the crust of the earth, the solid lithosphere, is much thicker than previously thought — about 60 miles thick. It's hard to see the weight of even a mile-thick ice layer having any substantial depressing effect on so thick a surface layer. Unless, that is, we introduce the concept of asthenospheric flow produced by variable rotation. When this force is added in with the weight of the glaciers, the equation becomes intelligible.

The asthenosphere was forced to move by centrifugal forces associated with the increase in rotational velocity during glacial phases. It moved most easily, obviously, in areas where there was an excess weight factor in the form an ice load on the crust. So, it was not only the weight of the ice, but the force of increased rotation that set the asthenosphere to moving under the ice caps.

CHECK THE TEMPERATURE

It can be no accident that the temperature record of the Pleistocene meshes exactly with the Geopulsation Theory. While the average fall in land temperatures in the mid-latitudes was around 10–15°F, the drop was much more in the high latitudes where the thermometer skidded to around 30 degrees below today's norms. Meanwhile, in the tropics the cooling amounted to as little as 5–6 degrees.[1] This latitudinal scaling of Ice Age cooling reflects the geopulsation process, which is keyed to the centrifugal force of rotation. Increasing this force clearly produces the most dramatic sea level fall in the arctic, the effect decreasing with latitude. In the tropics, seas would actually rise were it not for the fall overall sea level due to glacial water storage.

The sea drop is not responsible for all the temperature decline in the arctic. And, of course, the relatively steady sea levels in the tropics do not account the

---

1 Sutcliffe, Anthony, *On the Track of Ice Age Animals*, Harvard University Press, Cambridge MA, 1985, p. 69.

slight fall of the mercury there. But we have already seen the substantial roles played by volcanism and other miscellaneous perturbations.

There is another ingredient in the mix that is worth noting: the reflective effect of the continental glaciations themselves. This massive expanse of ice, about ten million square miles of it, had inherent repercussions on the amount of solar radiation reaching Earth's surface. To a degree, continental glaciers tend to "make their own climate." Their very formation robs the earth of substantial heat as the ice sheets reflect solar radiation back into space, reducing the radiant energy trapped by the atmosphere. Though most marked in the vicinity of the ice sheets, the effect is actually worldwide.

The combination of secondary factors — volcanism, the Milankovitch variations, glacial reflection, etc., could account for up to half the temperature drop during the Pleistocene. Nonetheless, the fundamental triggering mechanism was the alteration of land/sea relationships brought on by variations in the planet's rotational velocity.

A Footnote on the Future

The summary lesson conveyed by Geopulsation Theory is this: that while we now live on a comparatively stable Earth, that stability is not permanent. The present period of relatively constant planetary rotation must inevitably be followed by a period of acceleration which will bring with it portentous changes as the hydrosphere, then the asthenosphere, shift towards the equatorial zone.

There will be marked alterations in the land and sea levels, though these will be gradual in nature, developing over thousands of years. Imperceptibly, sea level will fall in the polar and higher latitudes, with less dramatic changes approaching the equator. So slow will be these trends though, that they will have limited impact on the conduct of everyday affairs. Our northern wharves and quays will crumble with age before they are left high and dry by receding seas.

We might characterize that as the good news. There is some bad news.

The distortion of the geoid will split the great rifts and warp the land surfaces, multiplying the frequency and intensity of volcanism and earthquakes. As the planet's equatorial bulge enlarges, our distant descendents will experience earth shocks and fiery eruptions far beyond anything in our own experience. The onset of this heightened seismic activity will be gradual, but it will become apparent within the next several centuries.

A broad philosophic effect of the rotational variation concept is to revive an element of catastrophism — the idea that violent changes of more than customary magnitude can overtake our earth. Recent revelations about massive meteor impacts have already made it clear that the uniformitarians much overstated their case. The world does *not* go on indefinitely just the way it does today. Geopulsation Theory adds even more evidence that what is happening in our time is not necessarily typical of distant yesteryears. Aside from the meteors and comets, there is a cyclical tide in the planet's internal affairs that involves periods of quietude — such as we enjoy today — and other, less benign phases of wrenching readjustment. At best, then, uniformitarianism is a half truth.

Despite the geologists' long insistence on uniformitarian principles, most of the world's people have retained a kind of intuitive belief in catastrophism, in the chance of unprecedented cataclysm. This ingrained adherence to (and subconscious dread of) catastrophic prospects may relate to actual experiences of the human race in the last periods of planetary expansion and contraction many millennia ago. The lore and legends spawned by the experience, and the world view produced thereby, have simply refused to die. It seems almost as though some subtle genetic memory compels us to a belief in impending chaos because our progenitors actually lived through it. It is true after all, that our grandest edifices will tumble and our great cities will be cast down — just as we have always feared.

* * *

In this chapter, we have unearthed the root causes of the great Pleistocene glaciations. The process is involved enough that a brief recap of the main points might be useful:

1. Due to differential precession of the earth and its core, the spin speed of the planet varies slightly, both plus and minus, with the solid crust and the liquid oceans reacting to the changes at different rates and magnitudes.

2. When the velocity of rotation increases, the ocean waters are driven towards the equator, lowering sea level in the polar regions. The lowering of the polar seas drops land temperatures in the high latitudes, spawning glaciation. Eventually, as planetary spin speed slows, the oceanic flow reverses and the ice caps melt away,

3. The distortions of the geoid caused by spin-speed variations produce violent volcanism, itself a sizable factor in promoting glaciation. Volcanism peaks during episodes of rapid rotational change, often reinforcing the climatic impact of sea level change.

4. The constant variations in glacial expanse are partly due to the vagaries of volcanic dust clouds but are influenced also by the Milankovitch variations superimposed on the main glacial cycle of 100,000 years.

CHAPTER 6. DOWN TO EARTH

Some key points have been established. There is a variable velocity cycle involved in Earth's rotation, and the mechanism producing it has been identified. We have seen that the planet must now be near the nadir of the velocity cycle, i.e., the reduction of Earth's spin speed has virtually ceased. The crucial question for us now is the magnitude of the changes in relative sea/land levels effected by these spin variations. More precisely, what was the effective decline in sea level in the vicinity of the Atlantic ledge during the last (Wisconsin/Weichsel) glaciation? Was it enough to establish a traversable land-bridge between northwestern Europe and North America?

Before trying to estimate the total reduction in sea level in the ledge area, we have to come up with a usable figure for the effect of glacial storage on sea level during the last glacial episode — something more definite than the customary guestimate of "around about 125 meters."[1]

Happily, there is some direct evidence on this question. Some of the best of it comes from terraces near the Mississippi River delta and from measurements on the Atlantic island of Bermuda. These locales happen to be in the very latitudes (circa 35° North) where the geoidal swings in sea level were minimal; that is, where the sea level fall was due essentially to the glacial storage factor. The rotational acceleration which produced glaciation tended to lower sea level above the 35th parallel(s) and raise it by a lesser amount in the tropic zone (ignoring glacial water storage).[2] But there would be negligible geoidal change circa 35° latitude —

---

1 Recently, a few geologists have been backing away from the traditional estimate, saying that the seas may have dropped about 500 feet, or circa 150 meters.
2 Under the geopulsation concept, the geoidal decrease in the level of the polar oceans would mean a compensating increase throughout the tropic zone (ignoring glacial

virtually all the sea level drop thereabouts would result from glacial storage. The data from both Bermuda and the Mississippi terraces indicate a sea level drop of at least 140 meters.[1] This is already on the high side of the common estimates but still well short of the limits of the envelope. That the river terraces represent the absolute nadir of marine depression during the last glacial phase is most unlikely: There must have been extremes of which no traces have been found. The fact that Ice Age fauna reached Corsica and Santa Rosa Island (both near the 35th parallel) mandates a non-geoidal (glacial storage) sea fall of a good 200 meters. This figure, while larger than usually contemplated, is actually not much more than the "high estimate" of 165 meters issued by the famed Climap Project of the 1960s.

But to get a better handle on total sea fall at the latitude of the Atlantic ledge we could use more data. In this case we are rescued by a fortunate happenstance. On the north coast of the equatorial isle of New Guinea lies a succession of elevated limestone reefs, five in all, extending back more than 130,000 years.

In other words, we have here ancient sea strands that have been elevated out of the ocean waters by isostatic uplift and preserved for our convenient study today. By calculating the average rate of uplift, we can tell the approximate height of the seas through the entire Weichsel/Wisconsin glaciation — even though the levels were lower than they are today.

A study of these Huon Peninsula reefs (in Papua New Guinea) reveals what is to conventional geologist a startling circumstance: a period of transgression, relatively high sea level, occurred in the mid-Wisconsin about 55,000 years ago (fig. 9). Yet this was a period of very heavy glaciation that should have been marked by sharply depressed seas. How could sea level have been almost the same as it is today when massive continental glaciers were holding fast millions of cubic miles of the planet's water? There is no answer in the conventional lexicon, but the case fits exactly with Geopulsation Theory since the geoidal decrease in the polar ocean levels means a compensating rise throughout the tropics.

If centrifugal force, for example, lowered sea level at the pole by 400 meters, the compensatory sea level increase at the equator would be about 200m[2] — just about offsetting the glacial storage factor. The data from New Guinea suggest a shift of a shade less than this magnitude since the strands show the sea was still about 15–20 meters below the present level during the maximum planetary spin of the mid-Wisconsin.

---

storage). The potential rise in equatorial seas would be much less than the drop in polar waters, obviously, since the sea water lost from the polar regions is spread around the entire tropic belt.

1 Haag W.G., "The Bering Strait Land Bridge," *Scientific American*, January 1962, p. 120.
2 The oceanic geoid, like the earth itself, tends to assume the form of an oblate spheroid due to planetary rotation. The volume of a spheroid = 4 abc/3. Hence, shortening the "a" (polar) axis requires lengthening the b and c axes only slightly to retain the same volume.

Of course, the situation was constantly altering with time. During the period with which we are most concerned, ca. 37,000 years BP — when the First
Americans were traversing the Atlantic Archipelago — indications are the Arctic
Ocean was down about 390 meters from today's level (-240 geoidal and -150 in
glacial storage, fig. 9). At the latitude of the Atlantic ledge, the drop would have
been less, circa 350 meters (-200 geoidal and -150 glacial storage).

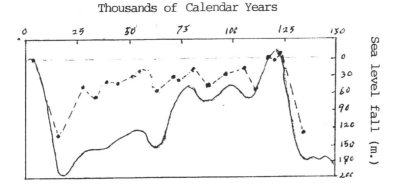

Fig 7. The graph compares the fall in sea level near the equator (dashed line)
during the last glaciation to the average sea level drop, worldwide, as calculated
from SPECMAP data (solid line). The dated points showing equatorial levels
are calculated from raised reefs on New Guinea's Huon peninsula. Around
the middle of the Wisconsin era (ca. 55,000 BP), a period of heavy glaciation,
equatorial seas were only about 20 meters below present sea levels — completely
inexplicable in the context of conventional theory.
In the era yielding the earliest evidence of New World occupation, ca. 36,000
years ago, there is a difference of about 120 meters between SPECMAP and the
New Guinea levels. This indicates a 240 m. geoidal ocean fall at the North Pole
(plus 150 meters more from the effect of glacial storage.)
Note that even in the tropics, sea level fell dramatically late in the glaciation
cycles (in conformance with geopulsation theory), allowing Pleistocene fauna
to reach most Indonesian islands. (The data should be viewed as closely
approximate rather than exact since there is a small estimation factor in the
New Guinea calculations.)

Certain peripheral factors also impact the relative elevation of parts of Atlantica during the Ice Age. Massive ice caps have an influence in their marginal
zones: The weight of the ice forces an asthenospheric flow out from under the
glacial mass, pushing up the adjacent lands. This effect would drive an elevation
of the eastern and western ends of the Atlantic ledge, proximate to the continen-

tal glaciers. The same phenomenon would elevate the margins of the Icelandic cap, helping to create three sizable islands east of Iceland on the Iceland–Faroes shelf. Even though this vertical component is not spectacular — probably less than 100 meters — the effect would materially shorten some of the wider water gaps.

The net effective rise of the ledge vis-à-vis the ocean surface, then, would be the practical equivalent of at least 400 meters in the mid-Wisconsin era — enough to create a near-bridge, an Atlantic archipelago with only modest intermittent gaps — too modest to negate the strong prospect of human transit.

(The -400 m. figure correlates well with analysis of the continental shelf around Iceland which shows the island must have been that much higher above sea level for extended periods in the past.)

Thus we see the trans-Atlantic stepping stones begin to rise from the oceanic foam.

CHAPTER 7. INTIMATIONS OF TRAVERSABILITY

Though we have explored all the geophysical forces acting on the North Atlantic ledge, there remains an equally germane consideration that goes beyond the physical environment. That is the resourcefulness, the inventiveness of the human species — and our boundless wanderlust. What exactly, were the capabilities of Stone Age humans for exploration? Until that question is answered there can be no clear closure to the enigmatic case of the First Americans.

If, 35,000 calendar years ago, the Atlantic ledge did not quite constitute a complete bridge, in the sense that people could simply hike from one end to the other, we must still ponder its potential as an avenue of human migration. The evidence is that people have able to navigate moderate distances over water for a very long time — at least since the dawn of the Upper Paleolithic era 40,000 years ago, and probably well before that. One of the most egregious oversights of archeological science has been its failure to comprehend the maritime abilities of Stone Age man — though in recent years some light has begun belatedly to dawn. So if we are, in fact, dealing with an Atlantic archipelago, rather than a complete land bridge, there are still real prospects for traversability.

THE AMERINDIAN ADAM

Our stand on humanity's debut in the New World is at once both novel and prosaic. Throwing orthodoxy aside, we will simply opt here to espouse the uncommon view that the evidence means just what it seems to mean. In short, we will disabuse ourselves of the notion that what does not fit the official prescription simply cannot be so.

It is easy enough to challenge almost any archeological find. There is usually some alternative explanation if one cares to reach far enough for it. But it so happens that with the concept of geopulsation in hand, it is not necessary to spend time trying to undermine what the archeological record tells us. There is persuasive evidence that humans walked the fields and woods of the New World during the mid-Wisconsin, and with our new insights there is no reason to presume the evidence to be erroneous.

The data from Monte Verde, Orogrande, Lewisville, etc., combine with genetic and linguistic proofs to make a solid case for a human presence in the Americas over 30,000 years ago. From that point, there is a reasonably continuous line of material evidence through the Main Wisconsin connecting to the Clovis horizon.

True enough, the *volume* of the evidence is not overwhelming. It is this matter of volume, rather than just the presence or absence of credible data, that lies, almost subconsciously, at the root of the skepticism about early Paleo-Indian origins.

The real hang-up many archeologists have with a mid-Wisconsin settlement of the New World is a perceived thinness in the evidence, in particular the scarcity of stone tools. In the view of most experts, there is just not *enough* evidence of human occupation. So they presume there must be something wrong with what proofs there are.

They are used to thinking in European terms — and this is much of the problem. Europe was amply populated during the mid-Wisconsin and plenty of data are available to support the fact. It has to be realized that the Americas then held only an extremely sparse population. A handful of adventurous wanderers had found their way over the Atlantic archipelago and their not-very-numerous descendents were scattered over two gigantic continents. In Pleistocene times, the infant — and adult—mortality rates were so high that population increase must have been exceedingly slow. In all the Americas, there may have been no more than a few thousand people.

Anthropologists are prone to assume that America's original settlement was driven by population pressures, but this ignores one of the most basic human drives: the curiosity about what lies on the other side of the river or beyond the next ridge. The exploratory impulse was actually much more important than population pressure in the initial spread of the Paleo-Indians through the vast expanse of the New World. Hence, they must have been very sparsely distributed over the Americas for a great many millennia.

There is no parallel case in recorded history of humans spreading through a vacant continent. Consider, though, the European settlement of the Americas as an example of exploratory drive. Barely two centuries after the Pilgrims anchored at Plymouth Rock, pioneer immigrants were pushing into Oregon on the opposite side of continent — despite an almost complete lack of population pressure and the often fierce resistance of the American natives.

One more factor, surely, in the sparseness of mid-Wisconsin material was the heavy Paleo-American reliance on bone and antler rather than stone as a raw material for tools. Stone tools last forever. Bone and antler seldom do. Little wonder, then, that there is no great plethora of archeological artifacts. But, though the confirming proof may seem spare to some, it *is* there.

And what is there is nearly impossible to discount.

At present, we have to side with the nay-sayers so far as any occupation pre-dating 40,000 BP is concerned. Carter's "early Wisconsin" material from San Diego is not securely dated. The Calico Hills site in California, alleged by a few to date back 100,000 years or more, has a serious weakness: The "tools" there are so primitive they might easily be the result of natural breakage. Other scraps of data suggesting dates beyond 40,000 years are all flawed in one way or another.

There is an intriguing bit of evidence from the Catskill Mountains of New York: tools virtually identical with pre-Wurm implements of western Europe. Raemsch and Vernon thought some of these to be 70,000 years old.[1] But others maintain the finds are much younger. Regardless of age, though, the similarity of these tools to European types is significant.

It would be rash to absolutely rule out any chance of migration to America prior to 40,000 BP, but there is, for now, no very credible evidence (though the Atlantic bridge concept could easily handle considerably older dates).

MARITIME MAN AND THE ATLANTIC ARCHIPELAGO

But it is time to deal with two key points. While there is a good deal of proof that humans were in the New World circa 35,000 years ago, there remains the fact that the Atlantic bridge was incomplete at the time. It was interrupted in three or four places by the ocean seas. In winter, the front-line of the ice pack would have connected the not-very-distant isles of the Atlantic ledge. Ice Age hunters, on the prowl for their favorite game, fur seals (as well as fish), could have followed this line either by foot or boat from one island to another. Even if this was not accomplished, a transit over the summer water gaps by small boat would have been a virtual certainty. (There is no question that Ice Age Britain was occupied at this time: Stone implements dating from 35,000–40,000 years ago have been recovered from the Pin Hole, Robin Hood's Cave and Soldier's Hole in England.[2])

It is easy enough to picture how the Ice Age transit of the Atlantic began:

On the Faeroes Islands, a small group of Paleolithic hunter–fishers pull their canoes ashore after a profitless summer day. The fishing, usually good, has been poor for several days. They made a spear shot at a fur seal but missed and it got

1 "Some Paleolithic Tools, from Northeastern North America," *Current Anthropology*, March 1977, pp. 97-99.
2 *The Emergence of Modern Humans*, Paul Mellars, Ed., Cornell University Press, Ithaca NY, 1990, pp. 207-210.

away. Actually, no one in the clan has bagged a seal for over a week. As they sit on the rocky shore mulling the bleakness of it all, our tired nimrods unbutton their neatly sewn fur jackets and throw back their hoods. The temperature is over 50 degrees and the wind has died down. The one interesting event of the day was a Hillingar, a high-latitude mirage that allows one to actually see far beyond the horizon. This one had revealed an image of Iceland to the west. As they discuss it, one of the group abruptly pipes up with an odd notion: "Why don't we try to reach that place, whatever it is, tomorrow. After all, it has never been fished or hunted and the coast is probably swarming with seals and fish." The others almost laugh, but the food situation is getting ominous. Eventually, they decide to give it a go if the weather allows. The next day dawns clear with only a slight wind rippling the Atlantic surface. With some trepidation, they start paddling westward. For hours the boatsmen see only horizon, but just when they are ready to turn back, one of them spots the peak of an outlying isle of the Icelandic shelf. There are still a couple hours of light left in the 20-hour day, so, revitalized, they make for it. After a good night's sleep, they arise to see that they have found a bonanza: There are scores of unwary fur seals and the fishing is fabulous. (Even today, Icelandic waters are prodigious producers of cod and halibut.) Our adventurers return home in triumph with enough food for weeks.

The word spreads rapidly. Soon others are working Iceland and its waters. Then a few families decide to move to the island. They do not know it, but they are half way across the Atlantic. And in a few generations, their descendents will be all the way across.

The Hillingar, it should be said, is far from rare, occurring more than half the days of some months.[1] At times, this optical diffraction reveals a view of Greenland from Iceland. The phenomenon was surely instrumental in luring the Norsemen across the Atlantic a thousand years ago.

We are accustomed to thinking of civilized man as the only possessor of maritime prowess but the assumption is entirely baseless. We know, for example, that 50,000–60,000 years ago the ancestors of the Australian aborigines first reached their island continent by sea — because sea levels never fell anywhere near the degree needed to establish a land bridge to Australia. Plainly then, Stone Age people were capable of point-to-point navigation. That is, they could reach any land they could see, using rafts or primitive boats.

The Papuans, though still in the Old Stone Age when first encountered by the Europeans, nonetheless were accomplished boat builders. One of their craft was the "lakatoi," composed of several dugouts lashed together and covered with decking. Even the now-extinct Tasmanians, the most primitive people encoun-

---

1 Sawatsky, H.L. & W.H., "The Arctic Mirage and the Early North Atlantic," *Science* (magazine), June 25, 1976.

tered in the Age of Discovery, had three-log rafts — similar, no doubt to those used to reach Australia over 50 millennia ago.

Without question, the Europeans of the 36th millennium BC were far more advanced than the ancestral Australian aborigines ever were. The stone work of Upper Paleolithic Europe is ages ahead of anything produced by the Australians right up to their discovery by the Dutch in the 17th century. It is impossible, then, to argue that mid-Wurm Europeans did not have point-to-point navigational abilities. We are dealing with people whose brains were fully equal in mental potential to our own. They could easily have rafted over any break in the Atlantic bridge of up to about 60 miles. These primitive mariners would not have voluntarily ventured out of sight of land, but if they could see it, they could reach it. And, given human inquisitiveness, they would have.

With sea level effectively 400 meters lower, the longest sea leg of a trans-Atlantic journey would have been between the Faeroes and an emerged isle east of the Icelandic shelf — a distance of maybe 50 miles. Significantly, this is the same distance the ancestors of the Australian natives must have navigated to cross Wallace's Line at a comparable time. So any argument that such a voyage would have been impossible just collapses of its own weight.

The peaks of the mountainous Faeroe Islands rise 3,000 feet above the sea today and would have been well over 4,000 feet above the surface circa 35,000 years ago. A Stone Age explorer could have ventured far enough out to sea to espy the outlying isles of Iceland without even losing sight of home. And with 20 hours of sun in the summer, there would have been enough light to keep one's bearings around the clock, no worries about being overtaken by darkness. In these circumstances, the discovery of greater Iceland, and then Greenland, and Labrador, was not only likely, it was practically inevitable.

Our projected occupation time for the New World is in striking harmony with what we know of cultural evolution. The huge leap forward represented by the Upper Paleolithic technology emerged in Europe about 40,000 years ago. It was an advance that gave the first anatomically modern humans the ability to cope with almost any environment on earth. It was, in fact, one of the most spectacular breakthroughs in all human history. These early sapiens people were sharp as tacks and tough as nails. And they were at least as courageous and adventurous as ourselves. Beyond any question, they possessed point-to-point navigation ability and the resourcefulness to exploit it to their advantage.

Once the maritime element is introduced into the puzzle of America's settlement, the mid-Wisconsin era becomes the most likely time for it to occur. There is a saying among prehistorians that "whatever can happen, will happen." And the exploration of Atlantica by Upper Paleolithic rafters and boaters is more than just a possibility; in any rational assessment it is an overwhelming probability.

WEATHERWISE?

We have scrutinized the Ice Age geography of the North Atlantic and found that it does lend itself to human migration. But what of the other elements of the North Atlantic environment at the time in question. Would not the harsh Pleistocene climate be a daunting impediment to our erstwhile travelers?

In the broad context of the climatic milieu, it is clear the ledge–archipelago would only have emerged above sea level during periods of substantial glaciation, the times of arctic sea level subsidence. It seems then, at first look, that we are describing a hard route — almost as hard as the Bering Strait-corridor route from Asia. Not so, though.

We have to remember that the Ice Age, in our construction, did not produce a universal fall in temperature in quite the manner that is commonly assumed. Basically, there was a reduction in temperatures according to effective changes in altitude. The point is that a coastal region at a given latitude was not necessarily much colder than it would be today. So the southern coast of Iceland during the Pleistocene was not significantly more arduous than is the case right now; the coast was merely shifted slightly southward as the old coastline was elevated relative to sea level. The climate of the littoral zone, dominated by oceanic influences, would have changed but little

Few people realize it, but the southern shore of Iceland has warmer winters than New York City due to the influence of the Gulf Stream. That was probably as true during the Wurm–Wisconsin era as it is now. The fact is Ice Age travelers on the Atlantic ledge were not looking at a climate much more severe than today's in those same latitudes so long as they stuck to the coastal zones.

Fact is, the weather could have been more moderate in some sectors at some times than it is now. Nearly complete isolation of the Arctic Ocean, effected by emergence of the Atlantic ledge, would have prevented the cold Labrador current from flowing south between Iceland and Greenland in anything like the present volume. So the shores of Labrador and south Greenland, washed by moderate eddies of the Gulf Stream, could actually have been warmer than today during interstadial interludes.[1]

Thus, we are looking at a route to the New World that was fundamentally more moderate than the Bering Strait approach, weatherwise. Migrating groups would not have been required to shoot a frigid gap between continental glaciers. They would have needed only to hug the coastal strip washed by relatively warm seas, and make occasional short hops by raft or boat.

Beyond all this, the Ice Age climate of the North Atlantic, as we now know from the Greenland ice cores, was notably erratic. It was punctuated by frequent

---

1 It is known that the south coast of Labrador was never glaciated, even during the Wisconsin maximum, and that it was occupied by a wide variety of mammals even then.

marked moderations that pushed back the glacial fronts — from the Labrador coast for instance — making for easier travel. The pronounced interstadial episode known as the Denekamp, circa 37,000–38,000 BP would have provided optimum conditions for transit.

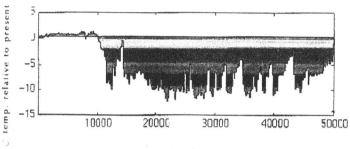

Years before the present

Fig. 8. The graph illustrates the eccentric nature of the Ice Age climate in the North Atlantic as revealed in the Greenland ice cores. The glaciers backed off enough for passage by Upper Paleolithic peoples several times 37 and 27,000 years ago. North American and European interstadials tracked those of the North Atlantic, chronologically, but were relatively less pronounced.

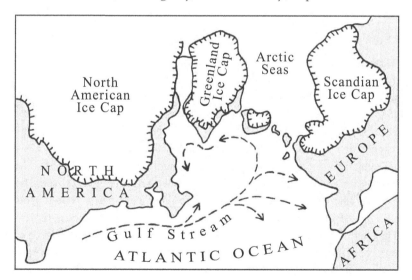

Fig. 9: The geography of the North Atlantic at the time of the initial European transit to the New World, ca. 35,000 years ago. Ice caps were not quite fully developed. Sea level was almost -400 meters below today's level relative to the Atlantic ledge. Note that with the substantial isolation of the polar seas, the entire southern shore of the migratory route was washed by the drift of the Gulf Stream. The south of Greenland and the coast of Labrador may have had a more

moderate climate than today. (Modern winter temperatures at the south tip of Greenland are not particularly severe, similar to those of coastal Maine.)

A trans-Atlantic migration in that distant era really faces no very serious problems, certainly none that the burgeoning mentality of the new sapiens breed could not overcome. Since the evidence says that humans were in the New World during the mid-Wisconsin, and since there is no good reason they could not have been, the conclusion seems obvious.

Bear in mind that unlike their Asian contemporaries, the Upper Paleolithic Europeans, with their stitched fur clothing and easy command of fire, would have been quite at home in arctic conditions. These were not "cavemen" but the people who pioneered the lifestyle of present-day arctic folk such as the Eskimos, Lapps, and Aleuts. They were an accomplished maritime-oriented breed, as well as formidable trekkers.

Our inherent predisposition is to assume that people living forty thousand years before our own enlightened era could not have been as adept and clever as ourselves. Habitually, we picture such folk as dull-witted, slow and inept. But all that is comic book anthropology. Not only was the native ingenuity of these early sapiens quite the equal of our own, their ability to cope with primitive environments was, in some ways, superior. It is a safe bet that their exploits and achievements exceeded our modern-day assumptions by a wide margin.

THE SOLUTREAN TREK

As seen earlier, some of the clearest evidence for transatlantic Pleistocene migrations involves the Solutreans' evident transit to the Americas where they spawned the Sandia/Clovis culture. The putative passage had to occur sometime between 24,000 and 16,000 years ago, the approximate duration of the Solutrean complexes in western Europe. Glaciation was quite heavy for most of this period, but there was a moderating interstadial about 17,000–18,000 calendar years ago, during which the ice would have retreated enough to ease the way to the New World (see fig. 8). This date of passage fits well with the material recovered from Virginia's Cactus Hill — unfluted Solutrean-type spear points, dated around 18,000 years BP that are plainly the precursors of the Clovis lithic culture.[1]

The confluence of data supporting the Solutrean passage is very close to compelling: the striking similarity in the Sandia–Clovis tool tradition, plus the occurrence of a North Atlantic climatic moderation at the very time archeology points to a trans-migration. It was simply a case of opportunity meeting capability. Perhaps the most advanced people of their era, the Solutreans were fully adapted to the glacial times in which they lived, quite comparable in nearly all respects to

---

1 Rose, Mark, *Cactus Hill Update*, www.archaeology.org/online/news/cactus.html, April 2000.

the pre-Columbian Eskimos — who reportedly made sporadic voyages to Iceland, and maybe even the Orkney Islands of Scotland.[1]

It was the Solutreans, about 20,000 years ago, who invented the sophisticated pressure flaking technique (later widely used in America) that makes their stone work the best of the Upper Paleolithic era. Pressure flaking involves the removal of the very thin flint flakes, not by striking, but by pressing them off with a hand-held punch. Some of the finer implements turned out by the Solutrean tool makers can only be described as technological works of art.

The most significant Solutrean innovations, though, may have been maritime. Although asthenospheric lag would have kept the Atlantic ledge near peak elevation for several thousand years past peak planetary rotation, sea level was less depressed ca. 37,000 years ago than it had been. Thus, the transit across the Faeroes-Iceland water gap must have involved a hop of a hundred miles or so. This means the Solutreans were sailing out of sight of land: They had developed a real seagoing culture by 18,000 years BP, and would seem to be the obvious progenitors of the North Atlantic Maritime Archaic culture which blossomed a few thousand years later — and which will have our attention shortly.

Since all, or nearly all, of the path followed by our Upper Paleolithic wanderers is now beneath the Atlantic seas, the odds are long against finding direct physical evidence of the ancient migrations over the Atlantic archipelago. The migrants must have clung to the warm southern coastal strip of the ledge, now submerged. What remains subaerial — the isle of Iceland, for example — was covered with glacial ice at the time of the migrations.

There is an outside chance that some cranny of land in southern Greenland or Iceland might harbor an arrow head or a piece of bone that would confirm our case beyond doubt. Hopefully, this book might motivate an eccentric or two to start looking for that cranny.

THE STRANGE CASE OF THE WELSH INDIANS

The Solutrean transit to the New World is easy enough to account for: All the geological and archeological data dovetail neatly. A somewhat more perplexing problem is presented by suggestions of a later transit, one occurring after the evolution of the nascent Indo-European speech but long before recorded times.

Vague but persistent traditions from the colonial era of American history tell us that some Amerindian tribes seem to have been speakers of some Celtic or proto-Celtic tongue, or at least a language to which Celtic had made some contribution.

These yarns are given small credence by established historians for they can perceive no way any Celtic element could have reached primitive North America.

---

1 Babcock, William H., "Eskimo Long-distance Voyages," *American Anthropologist*, 15 (1913) pp.138-41.

Still, there are many reports of so-called "Welsh" speaking Amerindians encountered by white settlers along the coast and in the Ohio and Missouri valleys. For the most part, these accounts originated with perfectly respectable citizens who were familiar with Celtic speech. So frequent were these reports that the existence of Welsh Indians in America was commonly accepted as a fact on the 18th century frontier. Even so, present day experts, long after the people in question and their tongues have disappeared, blithely dismiss the whole proposition. It does not fit with the prevailing concepts of an exclusively Asian origin for the Native Americans.

The credentials of the "Welsh" Indians, though, are not easily discounted — particularly in the case of the Mandans of the lower Missouri. The first explorer to reach the Mandans, Sieur de la Verendrye, known as a scrupulous observer, concluded that these light-skinned, sometimes blue-eyed natives who lived in villages laid out in streets and squares were at least partly European in ancestry.

Fortuitously, Verendrye left behind a couple of his more academically-inclined cohorts to study the language of this curious tribe.[1] They reported that the Mandan tongue had evident affinities to the language of Brittany, a Celtic dialect.[2]

Far the most famous character witness for the singular nature of the Mandans was the noted frontier artist George Catlin, who, while actually living with the tribe for an extended time, came to essentially the same conclusion as Verendrye's group: that there was indeed a European strain in the Mandans, specifically a Celtic one, more specifically, Welsh. Catlin could be accused of being prematurely precise here since the evidence was not quite adequate to determine which Celtic dialect had influenced the Mandans, but the fact that both he and the earlier explorers heard Celtic echoes is persuasive.

Catlin lists in his classic study of the American natives words which bear a close resemblance to Welsh (fig. 10). Significantly, these words are mostly quite basic ones, such as personal pronouns, in which true linguistic relationships are most likely to show. These language similarities, coupled with the European physical traits of the Mandans, were enough to convince a man of Catlin's keen perceptiveness who was an eyewitness to the facts. We are in a poor position at this date and distance to dispute him since the Mandan tribe was essentially wiped out by a smallpox epidemic in 1837 with the few survivors absorbed by neighboring tribes.

---

1 The history of the Mandans is, of course, imperfectly known. However, it is believed that the tribe had lived in the Ohio River Valley before migrating to the Dakota Territory.
2 *Mysteries of the Ancient Americas*, Joseph L. Gardner, Ed., Readers Digest Assoc., Pleasantville NY, 1986, p.35.

To judge from Catlin's word list[1] and other evidence, the Celtic element in the Mandans was subtle, somewhat remote. But among some other tribes farther east, it appears stronger. One of the signers of the Declaration of Independence, Francis Lewis, attests to the case of James Girty, a renegade who learned to speak something close to Welsh while living with an Indian tribe in the Ohio basin. Girty compiled a lexicon of Welsh-like terms and phrases that he claimed to have learned from the tribe, showing some 350 similarities between the Indian tongue and the Celtic.

Other encounters with Welsh Indians were reported by a minister and an Army officer. Even allowing for some embellishment, it is hard to account for the origin of these stories unless a real resemblance to Celtic was actually noticed by some pioneers. There is no arguing the fact that certain Native American languages of eastern North America did utilize typically Celtic sounds that are quite uncommon in other languages.

Fig. 10: An excerpt from Catlin's classic work on the North American Indians in which the author invites the reader to compare for himself the similarities, especially in personal pronouns, between Welsh and Mandan:

The Mandan canoes, which are altogether different from those of all other tribes, are exactly the Welsh coracle, made of raw-hides, the skins of buffaloes, stretched underneath a frame made of willow or other boughs, and shaped nearly round, like a tub; which the woman carries on her head from her wigwam to the water's edge, and having stepped into it, stands in front, and propels it by dipping her paddle forward, and drawing it to her, instead of paddling by the side. In referring to Plate 240, the reader will see several drawings of these seemingly awkward craft, which, nevertheless, the Mandan woman will pull through the water at a rapid rate...

How far these extraordinary facts may go in the estimation of the reader, with numerous others I have mentioned in Volume I, whilst speaking of the Mandans, of their various complexions, colours of hair, and blue and gray eyes, towards establishing any opinion as sound theory, I cannot say; but this much I can safely aver, that at the moment that I first saw these people, I was so struck by the peculiarity of their appearance that I was under the instant conviction that they were an amalgam of a native, with some civilized race; and from what I have seen of them, and of the remains on the Missouri and Ohio river, I feel fully convinced that these people have migrated from the latter stream.....

In adducing the proof for the support of this theory, if I have failed to complete it, I have the satisfaction that I have not taken up much of the reader's time, and I can therefore claim his attention a few moments longer, whilst I refer him to a brief vocabulary of the Mandan language....

---

1 lxvi Catlin, George, *Letters and Notes on the Manners, Customs, and Condition of the North American Indians*, Ross and Haines, Inc., Minneapolis, 1965, Vol. II, p.261.

English	Mandan	Welsh	Pronounced
I	Me	Mi	Me
You	Ne	Chwi	Chwe
He	E	A	A
She	Ea	E	A
It	Ount	Hwynt	Hooynt
We	Noo	Ni	Ne
They	Eonah	Hwna (masc.)	Hoona
		Hona (fem.)	Hona
No (there is not)	Megoah	Nagoes	Nagosh
Head	Pan	Pen	Pan
Great Spirit, or sovereign	Maho penata	Mawr penaethir (act as sovereign)	Maoor Panaether

Some other remarkable resemblances between Welsh and Mandan:

ENGLISH	WELSH	MANDAN
Boat	Corwyg	Koorig
Paddle	Rhwyf (ree)	Ree
Blue	Glas	Glas
Bread	Barra	Bara
Partridge	Chugjar	Chuga

Within the past several years, the once solid wall of academic resistance regarding Celtic influence in America has begun to show some cracks. James Whittall, Director of Archaeology for the Early Sites Research Society, was impressed by the startling similarity of the Druid Hill site at Lowell, Massachusetts, to stone circles he had seen in Britain — particularly since the standing stones at Druid Hill have proved to be astronomically aligned, just like their European counterparts.[1] Whittall is also persuaded that the Algonquin language is heavily spiked with words of Celtic origin.

There are as many cultural as linguistic associations between the ancient Celts and the Amerindians. Already we have seen that such prehistoric Celtic trademarks as the swastika and scalping were widespread among Indians. The

---

1 Angel, Paul Tudor, *Mystery Hill — America's Stonehenge*, www.crystalinks.com/mysteryhill. html (excellent quality site.)

mysterious Mandans also mirrored the Celts in their enthusiastic devotion to the art of tattooing, while Catlin notes the use among the Mandans of a small boat just like the Welsh coracle.

This is harder, more traditional evidence, too.

Perhaps the strongest conventional proof of early intercourse across the Atlantic is the striking similarity of some pottery, notably the Vinette I ware of northeastern North America, ca. 1000 BC, of the same design and made by the same process as north European pottery of the same period.[1] In any other context but a trans-Atlantic one, this parallel would be regarded as entirely conclusive proof of contact.

THE MADOC FANCY

There have been efforts to account for the Welsh tinge in early America through the Prince Madoc legend but this option fails on a number of counts. The prince was a storied Welsh navigator of the 12th century who supposedly sailed to the new World. Such as voyage, perhaps, is not entirely out of the question, but it can hardly account for the full aura of Celtic diffusion in the New World — the Vinette ware, for example. The Celtic influence in America is too elemental and at the same time too widespread to be accounted for by one relatively recent sailing/colonizing venture. Prince Madoc's expedition is supposed to have landed at Mobile Bay, and there are in fact some curiously atypical pre-Columbian stone constructions along the Alabama River which lend some support to legend; yet these are many hundreds of miles from Mandan territory.

Neither is there any evidence at all that any American Indian tribe possessed the arts and crafts of 12th century Wales. All the Celtic associations found among the Amerindians hearken back to times far antedating the era of Prince Madoc, if such a prince actually existed — a matter of some dispute among scholars.

In dealing with the Celtic issue, we are restricted by the question of when the Indo–European speaking Celts first reached the British Isle. It has long been the fashion, though no proof is possible (because there was no writing), to place the arrival of the Celts in Britain in the Bronze Age, the 2nd millennium BC, at the earliest. Some authorities even prefer the notion that the advent of the Celts coincided with the dawn of the Iron Age. Recently, though, Colin Renfrew of Cambridge has advanced the more likely theory that the spread of the Indo–European tongues was associated with the advance of agriculture in Europe[2] — which would put the proto-Celts in Britain in the latter 5th millennium BC.

To be sure, Renfrew pushed some aspects of his theory too far, engendering a good deal of academic opposition, but there is nonetheless substantial merit to his argument. In particular, it seems that the Neolithic Linearband ceramic cul-

---

1 Kehoe, Alice B., in *Man Across the Sea*, C.W. Pennington & R.L. Rands, Eds., University of Texas Press, Austin TX, 1976, p.288.
2 Renfrew, Colin, *Archaeology and Language*, Cambridge University Press, New York, 1988.

---

ture of central Europe must have been Indo–European. This culture originated in the mid-Danube basin before 5000 BC and spread over much of Europe in a few centuries. (The mid-Danube environment provides a very good match for the primordial Indo–European vocabulary as deduced by etymologists.) Hence, the whole Neolithic period becomes a candidate for Celtic contact with America.

This era may seem a surprising time for trans-Atlantic connections since the distances between the Atlantic stepping stones were by then about the same as today, requiring voyages up to 250 miles. But the prospect is much less surprising when seen simply as a continuation of what had gone on before, in the preceding archeological epoch — the Mesolithic of ca. 10,000–6,000 years ago.

THE RED PAINT PEOPLE

We have seen that Graham Clark, almost a generation ago, remarked on the Mesolithic correlations between opposite sides of the Atlantic. Any suggestion of a cultural connection may have seemed highly speculative at that time, but not today. Relatively recent research has uncovered a hefty accumulation of data supporting the idea of Mesolithic mariners in the North Atlantic waters. The people involved have even acquired an archeological designation: The Red Paint People (from their habit of using red ochre to cover their dead.)

The sites of the Red Paint People are scattered along the coasts of Labrador, Newfoundland and New England in the Americas, and from France north to Scandinavia in Europe. Besides the similar burial practices, the technologies at these sites on opposite sides of the Atlantic are so similar that any effort to pass them off as independently developed is nearly preposterous. Not only the tools but the art patterns are virtually identical. Dolmens are found at the American sites that closely resemble those on the other side of the ocean. Archeologists have finally noticed that the American Native teepees have a nearly exact parallel in the teepees of the Laplanders.

Most striking of all is the unequivocal evidence that the Red Paint People were deep sea fisherman.[1] They caught swordfish, a deep-water species, so they must have routinely sailed out of sight of land. The plummets used to weight their fishing lines are precisely the same on both sides of the Atlantic. The sites of the Red Paint People can be traced back some 7,500 years in both Europe and North America so there perfect chronological synchronicity. (The western branch of culture, typified by a burial mound at L'Anse-Amour, Labrador, is formally known in America as the "Maritime Archaic.")

Even with the overwhelming mass of corroborative data, there are still many who refuse to believe that transoceanic connections were possible in such remote times; they cannot accept that reality of the ancient mariner. Yet it is widely

---

1 See: Red Paint Sites, Univ. of Southern Main website, www.usm.maine.edu/gany/webaa; also: Schuster, Angela M.H., "Homing in on the Red Paint People" Archaeology, May/June 2000.

acknowledged that the Mesolithic and Neolithic peoples of northwest Europe were accomplished sailors and fishermen. The 1992 discovery of the Dover Boat proves that the Brits were already far advanced in the art of ship-building by the Bronze Age. The boat is a sturdily constructed plank vessel that must have been at least 50 feet long, easily long enough to qualify as sea-going. The ancient Beothuck Indians of Newfoundland built deep-water vessels as well as river canoes. The oceanic types were made of animal skins stretched tight over a wooden framework — almost identical to the Celtic curraghs, even to a sort of cabin to protect against the elements. Curraghs, which can be big enough to hold a dozen people or more, actually have been sailed across the North Atlantic in modern times.

In 1963, Dr. E.G. Greenman, of Michigan, noted the similarities between the early post-glacial cultures of Europe and those of northeastern America, particularly pictographs of Beothuck-type boats on both sides of the Atlantic.[1] Greenman proffered the hypothesis that there must have been transoceanic contacts but, needless to say, got a cold reception. Still, every scrap of new evidence on the issue pushes us to the conclusion that Greenman had it right.

Without much question, North Atlantic voyages were commonly achieved in the Mesolithic, and well before and long after. In fact, a solid case can be made that such voyages have been attainable, and sporadically attained, during the bulk of the time since the invention of boats.

There is a progressive logic to these ancient voyages. During the late Pleistocene when the water gaps were narrow, early man managed to navigate between the Atlantican stepping stones. When the Ice Age ended and the gaps enlarged, knowledge of the existence of these distant North Atlantic territories persisted; they were not quickly forgotten. Voyages continued even as the distances slowly widened because maritime technology tended to keep pace. Presumably, in Neolithic times, such expeditions were attempted only rarely and only by the most adventurous. But the Bronze Age was one of humanity's great maritime eras, and may have seen numerous Atlantic passages — enough to account for the Celtic tinge in early North America.

What eventually discouraged maritime expeditions was not just the widening waters. Adverse climatic fluctuations eventually made the North Atlantic islands inhospitable to anyone disinclined to an Eskimo life style. One such weather epoch, known as the sub-Atlantic phase, developed after the Climatic Optimum, a stretch of unusually mild weather, circa five to seven thousand years ago. The nadir of climatic deterioration was reached in the first millennium BC when voyages to Iceland and Greenland must have become so rare that the isles were largely lost to European consciousness, not to reappear again until the his-

---

1 Greenman, E.F., "The Upper Paleolithic and the New World," *Current Anthropology*, February 1963, pp. 41-91.

toric probes of the Vikings. Even so, there were still a few Celtic speakers on Iceland at the time of its Viking "discovery." (Later on, some Viking settlements on Greenland fell victim to weather-induced oblivion when the Little Ice Age took hold in the late medieval times. These Norse footholds were virtually forgotten until rediscovered by modern archeologists.)

Data developed by Whittall and Barry Fell support the view that prehistoric contacts continued across the North Atlantic as late as ca. 1000 BC. Fell found what he believed to be specimens of an ancient Celtic script at various sites along the North American east coast.[1] The script is a peculiar writing system call *Ogham* which evolved out of a sort of finger language and was used by Atlantic coast Celts of Europe for several centuries, starting as early as the 12th century BC. (While some argue that the system was devised in the early Christian era, Ogham inscriptions on the Iberian coast have been dated to 500 BC, and there is circumstantial evidence for an origin in the Celtic Urnfield culture centuries before.) Fell and many others contend that certain megalithic sites in New England, most notably Mystery Hill, were built by ancient Celts, and in fact, Mystery Hill does have a number of undeniable Celtic affinities.

Though Fell had a tendency to overreach at times, even some experts who have been critical of certain aspects of his work concede that some of his evidence is almost surely valid. And it is not without literal historical support. The memory of these ancient ocean voyages must actually have persisted into classical times to judge from passages in Plutarch's *Morals*. The scribe mentions an island five days sail west of Britain, which could only have been Iceland, and also states that the Atlantic Ocean is surrounded by a vast continent. He speaks too of a sun that scarcely sets in the summertime and of seas that are solid (frozen).[2] Plainly, such references are not the product of imagination but have their base in real maritime traditions.

Though peaking in the Bronze Age, the Celtic impact on early America dates from Neolithic times, early or late. Whatever the exact timeframe, we are not dealing with illusion here; we are dealing with history.

ARRIVAL OF THE ASIANS

Although the Americas were first trod upon by archaic Caucasoids, there is clearly a substantial Asiatic streak in most Native Americans tribes — the present day predominance of straight black hair and the prevalence of shoveled incisors, for example. Though trailing well behind the steps of the first Americans, the Asians eventually permeated most of the western hemisphere. But the farther the distance from the Bering Straits, the more diffuse are their genes.

The varying impact of the Asian migrations can be seen by comparing the Eskimos and Aleuts of northernmost America with the tribes of Tierra Del Fuego

---

1 Fell, Barry, *America BC*, Quadrangle/New York Times Book Co., New York, NY, 1977.
2 Plutarch, *Morals*, Vol. 5, v.1-v.12.

at the southern tip of South America. The former are predominantly Mongoloid, the latter mostly Caucasoid. Asiatic infusion was also weak among the east coast Indians of North America.

When did the Asians first manage to reach the American heartland? The Greenland ice cones show the Bolling interstadial of 15,000–14,000 calendar years ago (13–12k carbon years) was longer and milder than previously thought. Hence, the odds are that the ice-free corridor or the coastal route, maybe both, were open by then and very likely traversed. (As noted in Chapter 2, there is practically zero chance that any traversable path existed from Beringia to the American interior for about 20,000 years before the Bolling, if then.)

It is wholly unnecessary to postulate any intrusion from Asia prior to the Bolling Interstadial to account for the physical morphology of the Native Americans. We have no skeletal material from America that certainly predates the Bolling, but what Paleo-Indian fossils we do have are less and less Mongoloid in direct ratio to their increasing antiquity. The implications are that the Asiatic genes arrived relatively later and did not become pervasive until near the end of the Paleo-Indian period, or even afterwards.

Once begun, the Asian influx may have continued for a long time. The common assumption that the Bering Strait was submerged about 11,000 calendar years ago (ca. 10,000 C^{14} yrs.) is based on a uniform world rise in sea level. But we have learned that latitude makes a difference. Under Geopulsation Theory, the Bering Strait would have been swamped several centuries later than thought, as slowing planetary rotation finally allowed the earth's ocean waters to pour unretarded into the Arctic.

Including the Bolling phase, there must have been at least a couple of millennia around the end of the Ice Age when Asians poured unimpeded across Beringia and deep into the sparsely inhabited Americas. Even after this period, after the flooding of the Bering Strait, immigrations continued by boat, though at a reduced volume.

The genetic make-up of the Americoids is about what Hooten suspected, i.e., an archaic Caucasoid strain washed over by Asian gene flow. This view serves to explain a great many things otherwise inexplicable: everything from the Indians' lack of almond eyes to ear wax correlations.

The hyper-Caucasian characteristics that do not show up in Native Americans are missing for a couple of reasons: The traits were submerged by Asiatic genes or else did not evolve until after the archaic Caucasoids split into their American and European branches, that is, these traits developed only in the late Ice Age Europe.

Both factors may have been at work in making blondism almost unknown among the native peoples of the New World. We know the early Caucasoids were not blondish — they are not in their cave paintings — and they were further pigmented in America by the genetic infusions from Asia.

One typically Caucasoid trait, a tendency to hairiness, may have faded as much as through sexual selection as Asian gene flow. While bearded Indians, as we've seen, are not all that rare, hairiness was not generally favored among them and the men of most tribes made a practice of plucking out their whiskers.

The reason?

The Mongoloids, reaching America much later than the Caucasians, had a more advanced culture and technology, so the plucking probably started simply as an effort to look more like the "more cultured" people. Over time, a deep in-grained bias against facial and body hair developed into a selective evolutionary factor.

A parallel situation can be found in less remote times. When the Japanese invaded what is now their homeland it was occupied by the hairy Ainu. In the course of the conquest, hairiness became a mark of inferiority, and remains so even today.

It may be, then, that whatever hairiness typified the Caucasoids who first occupied America was bred out by a strong selective process. But the scarcity of hirsute Amerindians could also mean that those archaic Caucasoids of 40,000 BP were *less* hirsute than modern day Europeans, simply because they spent less time in the glacial trap of Ice Age Europe.

A CHANGE OF CLASSIFICATION?

Anthropologists who have relegated the Americoids to the status of a Mongoloid sub-race might want to revisit, and perhaps redraw, their charts. The Native Americans have had their own racial history and evolutionary path for nearly 40,000 years, arguably long enough to qualify as one of the ranking human races. Not only do they occupy a sprawling geographic area, they remain the predominant race throughout most of Latin America. Since the Caucasian element is more substantial than has been realized and actually has chronological precedence, the present classification lacks logical justification. Our findings support those analysts who argue that the Americoids are too distinctive to be lumped with the East Asians and hence should be accorded discrete status on a par with Whites, Blacks, Australoids, Mongoloids, and the "Capoids" or African Bushmen. This was the view, incidentally, of Linnaeus himself, who classified the Native Americans as *H. sapiens americanus*.

FAUNAL INTERCHANGE

Even though most of America's animal species migrated from Asia, it seems that some European fauna — the Svalbard variety of reindeer, for instance — utilized the North Atlantic ledge to reach the New World. Not necessarily during the last emergence but during earlier exposures. The ledge must have emerged on several occasions during the Pleistocene and had to be more elevated in some earlier glaciations than during the Weichsel-Wisconsin. For one thing, the ledge must have been somewhat eroded with time by repeated submergences and elevation. For another, some earlier glaciations are known to have been more severe than the last one and necessarily would have entailed more drastic alterations of land and sea level relationships.

Certain varieties of northern foxes, ermines and hares could have utilized the early Atlantic bridges as easily as the reindeer.

Most other animals, though, entered the Americas by way of the Bering shelf. The Geopulsation Theory of the Ice Age greatly facilitates faunal migration by this route as well as via Atlantica.

Why so? Because the Ice Ages were caused by the reduction in sea level, instead of vice versa. This means that sea fall did not lag the growth of the glaciers, but actually led it. In other words, the sea dropped below the level of the Bering shelf before extensive glaciation took place, not afterwards. So, a clear passage from Asia to interior America would have been available at the start of each major glaciation.

During each of these transition phases, before true Ice age conditions set in, there would have been a period when passage from Siberia to the American heartland would have been relatively easy. Once glacial conditions locked onto the planet, of course, passage would have been extremely difficult or impossible, even in marked interstadial phases. (As already observed, there is an utter lack of evidence that humans were able to utilize the last transition phase — more than 100,000 years ago — to transit to the western hemisphere.)

It may help to try to visualize what happened during one of the transitions from interglacial to glacial weather. If we could time-travel back 220,000 years, we would find the earth bathed in interglacial warmth. Hippos frolic in the Thames; palm trees grow in Ireland. There are no northern hemisphere ice caps, save perhaps a small one in Greenland. The tundra belt of today hardly exists. Northeastern Siberia and Alaska are covered with trees and grasses.

But gradually the rotation of the earth begins to accelerate. Sea level in the arctic slowly begins to fall until finally the Bering shelf is exposed. Temperatures drop a few degrees in Beringia but the ice caps are still in a nascent stage and there is a wide unglaciated plain in western Canada. Animals pass freely between the Old Word and the New — even such animals as the red fox and the red deer which cannot survive in a tundra environment.

But this condition, like all conditions on this earth, is transitory. After a few thousand years, the climate hardens, the glaciers spread. The easy passage is gone, not to reappear for a 100,000 years.

Thus, our revised vision of prehistory opens up a much-increased potential for faunal migration to America, one that goes a long way toward resolving what has been an insoluble problem for zoologists. And the resolution of this puzzle adds still more weight to the Geopulsation Theory.

* * *

At this point in our travels, unconventional thoughts begin to intrude. Various facts brought forth by our investigations begin to echo against background memories of ancient myth and tradition: facts like the presence of an early maritime culture in a North Atlantic Ocean subject to spectacular swings in sea level, and our finding that extraordinary episodes of volcanism and compression occur at intervals along the earth's ridge–rift system, in particular the great ridge running down the middle of the Atlantic. Meanwhile, the recent discovery of the supervolcano phenomenon shows that volcanic eruptions can be hundreds of times more destructive than anything recorded in our history books. Do these new realizations harbor implications about the mysterious olden legends of Atlantis?

We are pushed to consider whether the famous story might be something more than folklore. The compressional volcanism on the ridge presents the prospect that some millennia ago more land protruded above the Atlantic waters than just the present day Azores. And the existence of a truly ancient sea-going society hints that mid-ocean lands may have been populated far earlier than has been thought.

We are told that history is one thing and mythic traditions are something else. But is it always so clear cut? The line between the two has been obscured by Schliemann's discovery of Troy and Evans' digs in Crete that confirmed the legend of the Minoan sea kings. Could it be that those who dismiss the mythic sources are wrong yet again?

CHAPTER 8. THE SHADOW OF ATLANTIS

For sheer persistence, few if any legends can compete with that of the Lost Atlantis. For two and a half millennia, the tradition of a large island west of the Gates of Hercules (Gibraltar) has haunted the memory of humankind. The story has survived the damnation of skeptical scientists and the fevered exaggerations of devotees who feel compelled to find in Atlantis the source of all human civilization. (Some of the more extreme Atlantis enthusiasts have gone so far as to claim that the lost land was the scene of a culture more advanced than that of our own era.) The tale seems to have struck some mystic chord in the far recesses of our subconscious minds that still faintly vibrates and never quite fades away.

The roots of the Atlantis legend go back in time to Solon (ca. 600 BC), who, according to Plato, picked up the story from Egyptian priests in the city of Sais in the Nile delta. Plato relates the yarn in his *Timaeus* and *Critias*.[1] Atlantis, it was said, was the center of a powerful and aggressive society that launched crippling attacks on both Europe and the north coast of Africa. At the peak of its power, Atlantis controlled most of the shores within the Gates of Hercules as far east as Libya and Tyrrhenia (the west coast of Italy). Atlantis was finally defeated, so the story goes, by the ancient Athenians, and then, in a sudden cataclysm, the great island sank into the sea. All this, according to the Egyptians, took place some 9,000 years before Solon's time. But a "shoal of mud" still marked the grave of the lost land.

The tale was on the verge of vanishing into the twilight of forgotten mythology when Columbus discovered America. Scholars of the day were struck by an

---

1 See appendixes.

astonishing aspect of Plato's tale. It contained, it seemed, an exact description of Atlantic geography and appeared to refer to America:

> In those days the Atlantic was navigable; and there was an island situated in front of the straits which are by you called the pillars of Heracles; the island was larger than Libya and Asia put together, and was the way to other islands, and from these you might pass to the whole of the opposite continent which surrounded the true ocean; for this sea which is within the Straits of Heracles is only a harbor, having a narrow entrance, but that other is a real sea, and the surrounding land may be most truly called a boundless continent.

How could such a paragraph have been written by an ancient Greek unless the tale of Atlantis was true? The question was argued pro and con, even by such intellects as Voltaire and Montaigne. In 1882, Ignatius Donnelly published "Atlantis, the Antediluvian World," and gave new fire to the debate. But most of Donnelly's arguments were soon eroded away by geologists and archeologists. Today, few scholars are inclined to give credence to the Platonic accounts of the lost Atlantic isle.

As was the case with the Atlantic bridge, it was the doctrine of isostacy which permanently buried Atlantis in the estimation of science. The isle could not have existed because it does not exist today: Nothing could submerge so large an island in so brief a time.

We have learned, however, that there are alterations in land-sea relationships of a more rapid and profound nature than previously thought. And the very concept of a pulsating planet leads up to conclude that we have not seen, in the short span of recorded history, the farthest extremes of natural cataclysm. In fact, there must have been seismic and volcanic catastrophes that were completely off the modern-day scale during the phases of more rapid change in Earth's spin velocity.

It happens that in our analysis of the Ice Ages we have stumbled across some clues to the true origins of the Atlantis tradition. These will be detailed, but first a brief review of some of the more curious aspects of this ancient "myth."

To begin with, we are struck by an odd dichotomy in the chronology. Plato puts his Atlantean episode at about 9600 BC. At that time humanity was still in the Mesolithic era, lacking agriculture, metallurgy, cities, warships and organized armies. Yet Plato depicts an evolved culture and describes a massive military–naval onslaught by the Atlanteans into the Mediterranean. The maritime capability for such an adventure did not exist before about 3000 BC, so two seeming contradictory timeframes are here opposed.

Even odder, there is a passing reference in *Critias* which itself seems to subvert the 9600 BC date. Critias says that the Egyptians in their narrative "mentioned most of the names which are recorded prior to the time of Theseus" — who can confidently be placed in the latter second millennium BC. The implication is that Atlantis episode, whenever it started, did not end until after 1500 BC.

Archeology leads us in the same direction. It has been well established that the ancestral Greeks did not move into Greece itself much before 2000 BC.[1] So, if the early Athenian Hellenes were protagonists in the Atlantean war — as Plato relates — the war could not have happened before the early 2nd millennium.

WHERE IN THE WORLD?

The uncertainty about Atlantean chronology is compounded by the confusion about its locale. There have been efforts to link the legendary island with Crete, Malta, Tunisia, Cyprus, and a number of other Mediterranean sites. But Plato is quite specific about Atlantis being in the Atlantic Ocean beyond the Gates of Hercules. Gibraltar is so obvious and unique a geographic feature that is hard to conceive that the philosopher means anything but what he says. Moreover, none of the other ancient commentators on the subject — and there were several — give any hint that the island empire was anywhere but in the Atlantic.

Yet those seeking Atlantis in the Atlantic face a broad expanse of waters and many possible sites. Some of the less fantastical notions include Saint Paul's Rocks between Africa and Brazil, the British Isles, the Canaries, and western Iberia. Scandinavia has been fingered as a possibility, as have some seamounts off the Iberian coast. Then, there is Madeira and, of course, the islands of the Azores.

Most of these candidates are not hard to depose. The Iberian seamounts suffer from the defect of diminutive area, even assuming a substantial fluctuation in the oceanic crust. Only an incredibly large elevation of the sea floor could make these submerged volcanic peaks large enough to support a major maritime power. The same point holds for Madeira which is only a larger seamount which happens to still protrude above the surface. From the present shoreline of the isle it is a precipitous drop to the deep ocean floor.

Scandinavia is so far north that it can scarcely be made to fit Plato's descriptive phrase "in front of the pillars of Heracles." Moreover, the recent geological history of Scandinavia is the exact opposite of what is required by the Atlantis legend. The area has been rising steadily since the melting of the great Scandian ice cap 9,000–10,000 years ago.

Conceivably, St. Paul's Rocks might do as an Atlantis site except for the extremity of their location. It would appear implausible that a locale so distant from any ancient maritime society, could have been reached — much less developed into a powerful nation — before the era of Theseus. Even if that were possible, the notion of launching an invasion of the Mediterranean basin from a base three thousand miles southwest of Gibraltar strikes a most improbable note.

---

1 Branigan, Keith & Vickers, Michael, Hellas, McGraw-Hill Co., U.K., 1980, p.64.

The Canary Islands offer some attraction as a site for the "lost continent." They were surely occupied by the time of Theseus, perhaps even a few centuries before. (The islanders are mentioned by Homer and believed to have traded with the Phoenicians.) Yet this takes us back only to the very late Atlantean era, dimming the prospect that the Canaries were the Atlantean homeland. Worse, no evidence of any high culture exists in the Canaries until relatively late. Some intriguing step pyramids, reminiscent of the far larger Mayan ones, have been found on Tenerife but these probably do not pre-date the first millennium BC. Notably, the earliest known Canary inhabitants, the Guanche, held a memory of escaping from a cataclysm that destroyed their homeland — a legend reinforced by the fact that the Guanches were oddly blondish for the latitude. Ergo, the Canaries were not very distant from the fabled island, but they were not Atlantis itself.

Another negating factor is to be found in the writings of antiquity's Marcellus. As quoted by Proclus, he related the tradition that all the extant islands of the Atlantic were once ruled over by a large but now lost island.[1] Since classical writers knew of the Canaries, the implication is these isles were only adjuncts of the Atlantean domain.

There is also difficulty in constructing any hypothetical "large island" from the Canary group. Each of the isles is but the top of a sizable volcanic mount, quite separate from the rest, unjoined by any submarine plateau. Neither are there any traditions that the Canaries were ever any larger or more prominent in human affairs than now.

The credentials of another pretender to the Atlantean title are a little harder to dismiss. The peninsular site of Spain and Portugal — Iberia — was the scene of civilization before any other part of mainland Europe. The techniques of massive stone construction developed there more than 6,000 years ago. The great Megalithic Culture, of which Stonehenge was a kind of culmination, spread along the European Atlantic coast as far north as Denmark and included France, the British Isles, and the west Mediterranean basin, as well as Iberia itself. This culture was characterized by hefty dolmens and menhirs such as we see at Stonehenge, and by rock-hewn passage graves. Metal-working was not characteristic of the earliest phase of the Megalithic Culture but was practiced in Iberia earlier than anywhere else in western Europe. The vast extent of the megalithic structures and their coastal distribution make it clear that the builders had a mastery of seamanship. (The geographical pattern, in fact, suggests that megalithic mariners routinely sailed well beyond sight of land on voyages from Portugal to Brittany, or Brittany to Ireland.) The passage graves and dolmen complexes indicate a powerful religious motif in the culture. Such Iberian sites as Los Millares and

---

1 Cory, Isaac P., *Ancient Fragments*, Wizards Bookshelf, Minneapolis, MN, 1975, p. 43

Zambujal,[1] dating from the 3ʳᵈ and 4ᵗʰ millennia BC, are clearly the work of a highly organized and focused people.

The very presence of the Megalithic Culture in such an early timeframe in the far west is, of course, something of a circumstantial reinforcement of the Atlantis tradition — especially since modern investigation has established that the megaliths are far more ancient than was assumed in pre-Carbon 14 days. Indeed, the culture is so ancient that it vaporizes the old platitude that "All light came from the East." Some of these stone constructions are far older than the more finely constructed tombs of similar design in the eastern Mediterranean long assumed to be their prototypes.

But there are hitches in the notion of an Iberian Atlantis. Obviously, Iberia is no island; it is a peninsula. And it has not sunk beneath the sea. Nor has any significant sector of its shoreline, judging from the bathometric maps. There is also a statement in *Critias* that seems to cancel out Iberia as a prospect for the Atlantean homeland. Plato says that one of the sons of Poseidon "obtained as his lot the extremity of the island towards the pillars of Hercules, facing the country which is now called the region of Gades [Cadiz]."[2] Since the region of Gades is actually a part of Iberia, Iberia itself could hardly be described as "facing" the region of Gades. The implication is plainly one of looking toward Gades from some distant and distinct land.

MORE REMOTE PROSPECTS

Plato's mention of elephants has led some to suppose that Atlantis might be found in northwest Africa; but the sage does not say the elephants were native to the country. Then too, northwest Africa is not an island, or even a peninsula. Worse, it was not the locale of any notable early metal age culture. It was, in fact, a stagnant and relatively primitive sector of the Mediterranean basin. This, in itself, is about enough to eliminate the region from the Atlantean sweepstakes.

The British Isles have held some attraction for Atlantis detectives for a few good reasons. Brito-Ireland is easily large enough to qualify for the honor,[3] and extensive areas of the shallow British shelf were inundated 7,000 to 10,000 years ago by the rising tide of the glacial melt era. Further, the islands house some of the most spectacular achievements of the megalithic era — Stonehenge, Avebury, Newgrange, etc.

A sufficiently ingenious advocate could probably construct a fair case for a Britannic Atlantis, but there are daunting problems.

---

1 See: Hawkes, Jacquetta, *Atlas of Ancient Archaeology*, McGraw-Hill, New York, NY, 1974, p.89

2 *Critias* 114

3 Prior to ca. 7,000 years ago, Britain and Ireland were both considerably larger than today and connected by land bridges. However, Britain was also connected to the continent and thus did not constitute a true island.

The submergence of the British shelf, so far as science can tell, was gradual, thus lacking the necessary catastrophic element. And nearly all the flooding occurred well before the flowering of the Megalithic Culture. Perhaps the most elemental problem is the British climate, which is — as those who have spent time there will attest — well short of Plato's idyllic description. Much as the Brits may love their islands, Mediterranean peoples like the Greeks have always regarded the North Atlantic region as relatively harsh and foreboding. Surely, too, ancient Mediterraneans would have described the islands as "north" of the Pillars of Hercules rather than simply beyond them. Unless and until these difficulties can be resolved, the British Isles have to be classed as a slender prospect in our search.

A few of the more desperate Atlantis hunters have driven to advocate various spots in the New World as the Atlantean homeland. But these arguments are easily collapsed. There is no trace in the Americas of any metal-casting culture old enough to qualify, and an Atlantean invasion of the Mediterranean from the Americas verges on the fantastical.

A highly-publicized solution to the Atlantis mystery relates it to the destruction of the Aegean island of Thera (Santorini) in a volcanic explosion. But Thera was and is a tiny isle — hardly an iota of what Plato describes — and could never have been any kind of substantial power. It does not lie anywhere near the Gates of Hercules or any geographic feature that could possibly be confused therewith.

Marinatos, Galanopulos, and a number of others, have argued that the Thera eruption destroyed the Minoan civilization on Crete, that this was the great power that was brought down by the cataclysm. The notion seemed almost credible when the blast was tentatively dated "around 1500 BC" since the archeological record shows great destruction in Crete just a few decades after that date. The absolute chronological date of Thera's eruption has been the subject of lively argument,[1] but it is now clear that it happened in the Late Minoan IA era, while the Cretan collapse occurred at the end of the subsequent Late Minoan IB period.[2]

This sequence blows the whole Thera theory as sky high as the ash from volcano itself. The chronology is completely out of whack. Plainly, the Minoans were flourishing on Crete for something like a century after the Thera eruption: The Late IB phase is usually considered the apex of the Minoan civilization. It is beyond serious argument that the Minoan destruction of ca. 1450 BC could only have been the work of the invading Achaean Greeks (Mycenaeans) from the mainland.

There is little real question about this; virtually none at all.

The whole hypothesis that the Thera explosion was fatal to the Minoan society is a flawed concept. Quite likely, the north coast of Crete was hit by tidal

---

1 The mid-16th century BC appears most likely. See discussion, Chapter 9.
2 Pomeroy, S.B., et al, *Ancient Greece*, Oxford University Press, 1999, p.18.

waves, but few significant Minoan towns or cites were on that shoreline. Of those that were, most were built well back from the sea or on high bluffs — perhaps to avoid the threat of tsunamis. The idea has been put forth that the volcanic ash spewed by the Santorini eruption had a devastating effect on Minoan crops and thereby led to the nation's demise. Doubtless, some quantity of ash reached Crete, but was it destructive?

The evidence is that most of the fallout was blown east and that the ash dumped on Crete was only a few centimeters deep — and only on the eastern end of the island.[1]

It takes a great deal of ash to seriously damage crops. The huge volume of volcanic debris dumped by Mount St. Helens over eastern Washington State was supposed, at the time of the eruption, to presage agricultural disaster. But, in fact, the next crop was bumper crop, well above average in yield. Far from being the crop killer predicted by the experts, the ash from St. Helens turned out to be marvelously productive fertilizer.

There is no evidence, then, that the Santorini event destroyed or crippled the Bronze Age society of Crete. There is no evidence of physical damage to the Minoan cities at the time of the eruption, and no reason to believe there was any substantial impact on agriculture. The episode had no more permanent effect on the Minoan island than St. Helens had on Washington State — that is, practically none.

Another sticking point for the Thera/Crete hypothesis lies in the fact that the whole episode would have taken place in the Aegean, obviously an area better known to the Greeks than to the Egyptians. The idea that the Greeks could entirely forget a catastrophic destruction in Crete strikes an implausible note; yet there is nothing in Hellenic tradition that tells such a story.

Thera, then, can safely be consigned to the well-populated graveyard of proposed Atlantis locales. But we have another and more formidable candidate to contemplate.

THE AZORES

There is an old but incisive adage among Atlanteologists that is certainly true: "Either Atlantis was in the Atlantic or it was not Atlantis." And right in the middle of the broad Atlantic waters is perhaps the most popular of all suggested Atlantis locations: the area of the Azores islands, actually the island peaks of a huge submarine massif. Without doubt, the site is tantalizing enough to merit a serious look.

These idyllic isles are a good distance from the Gates of Hercules, but not nearly so far as the Rocks of St. Paul. The Azores lie about 800 miles from the

---

1 "Akrotiri on Thera, the Santorini Volcano and the Middle and Late Cycladic Periods in the Central Aegean Islands" (Lesson 17), *The Prehistoric Archaeology of the Aegean*, http://projectsx.dartmouth.edu/classics/history/bronze_age/.

coast of Iberia, less than that that from Madeira. The locale, almost astride the Atlantic rift, is often shaken by violent earthquakes and eruptions. Villa Franca, the original capital of San Miguel, largest of the Azores, was utterly buried by a volcanic convulsion in AD 1522. In 1811, a good-sized volcanic island rose in Azorean waters, dubbed "Sambrina" during its short existence. Sizable chunks of the island of Corvo have been swallowed by the sea since its discovery. In short, the whole archipelago is a zone subject to powerful tectonic forces. No great leap of imagination is needed to visualize sizable parts of this unstable massif thrusting farther above the surface in times past. Our own investigations, in fact, have greatly enhanced the prospect that the western Azores, at least, were much more elevated in late glacial times. We have seen that the Atlantic ridge is subject to colossal compressional pressures during Earth's spin deceleration. This lateral compression must have forced a sharp elevation of the ridge in the late Wisconsin era. Over time, the ridge would subside in wracking jolts to normal levels because it roots would be pushed into a deeper, hotter zone, finally melting away. But for lengthy era, most notably ca. 25,000 to 10,000 BP, much of the ridge must have stood hundreds of meters higher than today.

There is, then, a geological mechanism that can easily account for the existence of a large mid-Atlantic isle in the vicinity of the westerly Azores that may not have sunk to its present level till after the dawn of the Age of Metals.

Ancient reports testify that even in post-Atlantean time, the Azores were more elevated than now. Aristotle says that the Carthaginians knew of an island big enough to have navigable rivers in far Atlantic waters. None of the present-day Azores meets that description, nor do the Canaries or Madeira, but it could apply to one of the Azorean group when they stood higher than today. Marcellus states in his *Aetheopiaka* that one of three large Atlantic islands, among seven smaller ones, was 1,000 stadia (125 miles) long. He almost has to be talking about the Azores. (A middling uplift there would produce three sizable isles.) None of these isles now approaches that size, and there are now only nine, not ten, suggesting later subsidence.

More direct supporting data is not lacking. Smooth rocks and seashore sand have been found in deep waters off the Azores. Some cores drilled into the ocean floor near the mid-Atlantic ridge show large amounts of volcanic ash. The ash layer, mainly just east of the ridge, is heaviest close the ridge axis.[1] There was then, *subaerial* volcanism along the ridge, maximized, the datings tell us, around 10,000–12,000 years BP.

Of course, this subaerial activity only proves some volcanic peaks were poking above the surface on the ridge axis — which does not necessarily confirm the existence of any great island. According to Plato, Atlantis was bigger than "Libya

---

1 Malaise, René, "Oceanic Bottom Investigations and their Bearing on Geology," *Geologiska Foreningens I Stockholm Forhandlinger*, Mars-Apr., 1957.

and Asia together" and contained a huge plain ca. 230 miles wide and half again that long. Both "Libya" and "Asia" were vague terms in ancient times. "Libya" originally meant Cyrenaica but was later applied to most of North Africa. When the Greeks spoke of Asia, they were basically referring to Asia Minor. The terms *Libya* and *Asia*, then, are not a lot of help in estimating the size of Atlantis. But when combined with the description of the great plain, Plato looks to be depicting an extensive landmass.[1]

We might suspect something to be askew with the Platonic portrayal of the island's size — or our comprehension of it — since Atlantis was supposedly destroyed "in a single day and night." It is not geologically feasible for a land of the size indicated to be obliterated so quickly. An obvious possibility is that centuries of verbal tradition confused the island of Atlantis with the extent of the Atlantean empire. (And as our search progresses, we will find considerable evidence that such was the case.) Even so, the fact that Atlantis controlled a large empire mandates that the central island itself must have been substantial, on the order of several thousand square miles, at least.

Could lateral compression along the Atlantic ridge create so large an island? Uplift of ca. 1000 meters would be indeed — a lot, but not off the scale of feasibility. Meanwhile though, there is difficulty with the great plain. The sea floor in the rift/massif area is quite rugged and the Azores easily provide the high mountains described by Critias, but there could not have been a plain approaching the size he specifies.

The insights provided by Geopulsation Theory leave the impression that a sizable mid-Atlantic isle could have been there in appropriate timeframe, though it would not have been so vast as Plato seems to say and its topography would not entirely jibe with his description.

What about the location, climate, flora, fauna, etc., of the Azores when compared to the words we find in *Timaeus* and *Critias*?

The geographic local of the islands, in the mid-Atlantic at about the latitude of Gibraltar, is more than acceptable: It is practically perfect. It is this factor, of course, more than any other, that has led so many investigators to conclude that the Azores must indeed be the remains of the legendary Lost Atlantis. Moreover, at the east end of the island group there are extensive shoals — the Formigas reefs — which would account for Plato's statement that "shoals still mark the place."

The enviable Azorean climate seems apropos enough — though it lacks the true dry season implied by Critias. The towering mountains portrayed by Plato are spectacularly evident (volcanic Mt. Pico is over 7700 feet high), and stood even higher when the Azorean plateau was more elevated than it is today.

---

1 Nowhere does Plato call Atlantis a "continent." The term is a modernism.

But Plato says Atlantis had a rich fauna: "There were a great number of elephants on the island; for as there was provision for all other sorts of animals, for those which live in the lakes and marshes and rivers, and for those of the mountains and plains, so there was for the animal which is the largest and most voracious of all."[1]

This statement presents a fairly serious difficulty. The impossibility of native elephants on the Azores is not the big problem. Since the sage does not say they were indigenous, they might have been work elephants imported from Africa. (African elephants are difficult but by no means impossible to train.) But the Azores, due to their extreme isolation, have always had an impoverished fauna. There are a few rats, weasels, ferrets, and rabbits on the islands, but that is about all in the way of wild land mammals. Even this limited fauna must have been introduced by man since there is no other way any land animal could have reached the islands since the Age of Reptiles.

It can be argued that these introduced animals were already on the islands when they were officially discovered by Cabral in 1432. He dubbed the islands the Azores because of the large number of hawks (acores) that he found there. Hawks are flesh-eating birds, which suggests that the small creatures we have mentioned must already have been there; otherwise, the diet for hawks would have been sparse. There is, in fact, a strong tradition that there were rabbits on some of the Azorean isles when they were first reached by the Portuguese. It is also a matter of record that one of the isles was originally dubbed Goat Island — the intimation being that goats were on it when it was found.

A chronological uncertainty remains, of course. We have no information on when these animals might have been brought to the Azores, except that it was before Cabral. On the other hand, there is nothing to say that the creatures were not transported to their mid-Atlantic locale by early Atlanteans.

While the fauna of the Azores scarcely fits the Platonic parameters, there is less trouble with the flora. Almost anything will grow in the lush subtropical climate of these isles and they are clothed in a remarkable variety of native grasses, heaths, shrubs, junipers, and mysterious Criptomeria trees, plus various plants introduced in historic times. Since the isles are but the mountain tops of a once more elevated archipelago, the vegetation must have been even more varied in remote antiquity. The Azores are copious producers of citrus, pomegranate and other fruits and vegetables, and in this regard match what we might expect of Atlantis.

CAN YOU GET THERE FROM HERE?

One of the puzzles attending the notion of an Azorean Atlantis is blithely ignored by almost all writers on the subject (which says something about the

---

1 *Critias*, 115.

level of analysis that has been applied to the Atlantis mystery). That is the question of original occupation.[1] If the islands were settled in pre-classic times, how did those first colonizers reach them? Skeptics can argue that the archipelago is, after all, a long distance out to sea, not connected by any island stepping stones to the Mediterranean region, and the prevailing winds and currents are not very propitious for accidental discovery. True enough; yet ships have been blown to the Azores from time to time. In fact, Cabral's voyage of discovery was prompted by a report from another mariner who was carried within sight of the isles by a gale. What happened a few centuries ago could have happened a few millennia ago as well.

Then too, time and geologic processes change the odds. There is evidence that the Horseshoe Seamounts off southwest Iberia were more elevated in antiquity, likely due to compressional forces. Even today, these mounts are only tens of meters below the surface, and one (Josephine) is barely 500 miles from the Azores — maybe five days sail. As late as Phoenician times, some of the Horseshoe peaks must still have poked above sea level. Aristotle relates that Phoenicians "sailing outside the Pillars of Herakles with an east wind for four days, came to some desert islands full of bushes and seaweed which were not submerged when the tide ebbed but were covered over when the tide was full." (On Marvelous Things Heard, 136). Modern research lends support. In 1974, Russian submarines photographed what looks to be the remnants of a stone block wall on the Ampere seamount. To early mariners, the existence of these seamounts islets would have suggested that the Atlantic had numerous islands, inciting marine exploration.

It is hard to doubt that the Azores were known to west European sailors of the pre-Christian era since the diligent Plutarch relates that Sertorius, while sailing beyond Gibraltar, landed at the mouth of the Quadalquivir and there met seamen "recently arrived from the Atlantic isles ... distant from the coast of Africa by 10,000 furlongs."[2] That is exactly the distance from Morocco's shores to the eastern Azores.

Under Geopulsation Theory, the elevation of the Atlantic Ridge during the Ice Age would have been more and more pronounced towards the equator. So parts of the Azorean massif could have been raised by up to 1,000 meters, enough to create one large island of roughly Corsica's size (ca. 3,400 sq. mi.), extending southwest of Pico-Faial. It must have diminished some by megalithic times but still remained substantial (the 125-mile island of Marcellus?). To the east of it were several enlarged isles based on today's eastern Azores. To the west were more islands, now lost (map, fig. 11a). Overall, this island group, while featuring

---

1 The issue can be side-stepped by making Atlantis so huge that it approaches the shores of Iberia, but since there is no trace of any granitic continental bloc in the mid-Atlantic, such a speculation is beyond the bounds of geological feasibility.

2 Plutarch, *Parallel Lives*, (Sertorious vii), Dryden translation.

no isle as large as the popular image of Atlantis, was easily extensive enough to develop into a major sea power, i.e., much larger than Crete's famed Thalassocracy.

Meanwhile, the whole Atlantic milieu alters via the prism of Geopulsation, opening up alternate possible avenues to the Azores. Along hundreds of miles of the Atlantic Ridge spine were once strewn a number of islands, since submerged, dotting the now sparsely-isled Atlantic. The more islands an ocean has the easier it is to explore. Discovery of any one of these isles by the early Celts or even the Red Paint mariners could have eventually led them to the Azores.

It is all but obvious that the lattice of mid-Atlantic islands of megalithic times — and maybe later — was the inspiration for many of the lost isles of legend, such as Avalon, Tir nan'Og, Antilla, Hy Brazil, and the Isles of St. Brendan. That these traditions persist among Atlantic people is itself proof of the validity of our new geographic view and further implies that some of these isles must have persisted to near the dawn of historic times — and must have been explored.

How much hard evidence is there that the Azores were settled in the pre-classical era? There is not a lot, but there is more than a little — about what might be expected from the remnant peaks of a largely submerged land. For one thing, a story is preserved that when the Portuguese discovered the archipelago they found on the isle of Corvo an equestrian statue, subsequently lost when it was broken while being dismantled for shipment to Portugal. There are credible reports the Carthaginian coins were found in the Azores by the earliest Portuguese settlers. Theopompus of Chios (agreeing with Aristotle) states that the Phoenicians and Carthaginians at Gades (Cadiz) had a long-held tradition of a large island in the Atlantic — probably Pico-Faial which would extend a good 70 miles to the south if elevated a few hundred meters.

It is well established that Arab geographers knew of the Azores centuries before there were found by Cabral. They knew the location, the number of the isles, and that they were home to large numbers of hawks. Since the Arabs were not themselves great navigators of the Atlantic, they must have obtained this information from either classic or Carthaginian sources.

Of course, the Carthaginians were abroad in the historic, post-Atlantean era so we are still short of the right timeframe. It could well be that the Carthaginians — or their Phoenician precursors — first learned of the Azores from the Tartessians. Tartessos was a great maritime city on the southwest coast of Iberia, going back to at least 1100 BC, or long before if it is true that it traded with the Minoans (1500+ BC). The fact that Hercules visited this fabled Silver City — pausing to erect the Pillars of Hercules — suggests that the Achaean Greeks knew of it before 1300 BC. Its location raises the prospect that Tartessos might have been an Atlantean colony. According to Stabo and Poseidonius, the city claimed a history of 6,000 years — presumably an exaggeration but still indicative of great antiquity. There is still a town named *Tharsis* in the Rio Tinto valley near Huelva which has been a mining center for 5,000 years.

A key piece of evidence comes not from the Azores themselves, but from West Virginia: the Grave Creek Stone, found in 1838 and bearing a form of Phoenician writing used in Iberia in the early first millennium BC. It cannot be a forgery because this form of writing was not known in 1838. The similarity of the scripts is well beyond coincidence according to David Kelly (University of Calgary), a recognized authority in the field.[1] Obviously, if Iberians reached America's coasts almost 3,000 years ago, they must have been in touch with the Azores long before.

The Greeks themselves, even before Plato, provide us with plenty of tradition about isles at the edge of the world in the Atlantic: the Hesperides or Fortunate Islands, the Isles of the Blest, which sound like the Azores. Though no one seems to have noticed, Homer's far west Elysian Plain, on the shores of Okeanos, echoes overtones of the great plain of Atlantis. All these were idyllic lands of endless summer and golden apples where heroes resided after death. Greek legend makes Atlas the ruler of the Hesperides, a point favoring their association with Atlantis. These Hellenic traditions go back to the Achaean days — the mid 2nd millennium BC.

Once again, some passages in Plutarch's *Morals* are of service. In his discussion of Atlantic *geography (see p. 80)*, the ancient historian relates that the coast of the opposite continent across the Atlantic was visited by a Greek sailing expedition in the era of Hercules (mid-second millennium BC). At about the latitude of the Caspian Sea, the Greek sailors are said to have encountered a large bay about the size of the Sea of Azov. This geographic description points strongly to Chesapeake Bay in Maryland, clearly implying a mid-latitude crossing of the Atlantic. (Some of the Greek sailors, we are told, took a fancy to the "barbarian women" there and elected to stay.)

If the Greeks traversed the Atlantic at that latitude, they were certainly in prior contact with the Azores — which would account for their legends of the "Fortunate Isles," etc., in the western seas. A likely enough scenario is that the Greek voyagers encountered Azorean settlers, perhaps some survivors of the Atlantis disaster still holding on somewhere in the archipelago, who passed on the lore of a vast continent to the west.

Adding all the bits and pieces together, there is still enough evidence to conclude that the Azores were known, and colonized to some degree, during the maritime explosion that marked the mid-second millennium BC.

A YELLOW LIGHT

Our serendipitous discovery of a geological mechanism that accounts for the rise and subsidence of the Azorean plateau presents an almost irresistible temp-

---

1 Stengel, Mark K., "The Diffusionists Have Landed," *The Atlantic Monthly*, August 2000, p.39.

tation to pronounce the riddle of Atlantis solved: to proclaim the Azores as the true locale of the fabled isle and dismiss the other pretenders. Certainly, of all the usual suspects, the Azores have the best credentials — as well as the most serious advocates, including Berlitz and Donnelly.

Even so, some nagging questions dissuade us from shouting "Eureka" just yet. While there are many aspects of the Azores that meet the parameters of Plato, there are a few that give us pause. One is the puzzle of the great plain with plenteous wildlife, a feature that does not fit easily into the Azorean milieu. And, though they were certainly explored much earlier than has been assumed, we lack any indicator that the Azores were reached prior to the 2nd millennium BC, the first great nautical era in human history. Such a timeframe provides an uncomfortable short span for the build-up of Atlantean power.

The Platonic statement that Atlantis ruled over "divers islands in the open sea" is also bothersome since this phrase sounds very much like Azores. If not Azores, what is referred to? Plato's "other islands" on the way to the "opposite continent" also aptly fits the Azores. And a fragment from Theophrastes, a friend of Aristotle, speaks of colonies of Atlantis in the midst of the great sea. Were the Azores, then, just adjuncts of the Atlantean empire rather than the site of the home island itself?

The most troublous aspect of the Atlantis tale, though, is certainly Plato's statement that the island was destroyed "in a single day and night of misfortune." Such a scenario does not really suit the Azores, which must have subsided by fits and starts over many centuries as their sub-crustal roots gradually dissolved into the asthenosphere. Some of these seismic adjustments may have been catastrophic in scope, but there must have been many of them over a protracted time — not just a single cataclysmic collapse. Fact is, the shockingly sudden finale outlined by Plato is not appropriate to any Atlantean title contender, save the otherwise unqualified islet of Santorini. It is the manner of the island's destruction, more than anything else, that has been the Achilles heel of nearly all Atlantis theories. The explications have been either counter-scientific or entirely speculative — impossibly large earthquakes, sliding crusts or planetary flips, asteroid impacts, etc.

In the end, the Azorean islands seem almost plausible as the Atlantean home — but we are left with the vague suspicion that they are not the whole story, that the truth is more complex than commonly thought and that the crucial aspect of the whole issue has to be the question of what exactly caused so abrupt a destruction. One thing for sure: It must have been a force more powerful than anything in the annals or memory of present-day humanity.

Chapter 9. The Day the World Ended

The brief tick of recorded history gives only a hint of the catastrophes sometimes visited upon our small azure planet. We now know that bolides from space have at times struck with such impact that many or most species on the earth have been obliterated. There is another threat, equally great but less widely known, which we have only lately begun to comprehend — what are termed "supervolcanoes." Occupying thousands of square miles, these dwarf anything in our history books. Disasters such as Krakatoa, Tambora, Pelee and Santorini are mere sneezes compared to some colossal eruptions of the more distant past.

About 74,000 years ago, for instance, a supervolcano called Toba on the Indonesian island of Sumatra exploded with such force that it imperiled the very existence of the human race. The eruption spewed nearly 3,000 cubic kilometers of ash and rock debris into the atmosphere — about a hundred times as much as Krakatoa or Santorini, and ten times more than the biggest explosion of our direct knowledge: the 1815 blast at Tambora, east Java. Pyroclastic flows from Toba covered some 20,000 square kilometers, and megatons of sulfuric acid were spewed into the air.[1] The ash fall was so heavy that it must have wiped out much of the vegetation in southeast Asia. Temperatures plunged up to 20 degrees (F.) over much of the world and did not recover for at least six years — the ultimate "nuclear winter." Some investigators believe the cataclysm may have reduced humanity to no more than several thousand souls, worldwide. Toba left a crater (caldera) 100 km. long and about 40 km. wide.

---

1 Volcano World — Toba, Sumatra, U. of N. Dakota website, http://volcano.und.nodak.edu

Such supervolcano eruptions are far more frequent than catastrophic comet and meteor impacts from space. So, if Atlantis was destroyed in "a single day and night," the odds are the smoking gun will turn out to be a supervolcano.

There are some lines in the Platonic account that have not been given enough attention. Critias (108) refers to an "impassable barrier of mud" facing voyagers sailing from the Mediterranean to any part of the (Atlantic) Ocean after the Atlantis disaster. This line has been commonly interpreted to mean that the remnants of Atlantis remained for a time just below the surface, but might mean something else. It could as easily refer to a sea surface clogged with volcanic debris, i.e., floating pumice. It is hard, after all, to see how the subsidence of the island could block passage to *any part* of the ocean. In other passages, the Atlantic is described no longer navigable in the wake of Atlantis' destruction.

After the eruption of Krakatoa, the surrounding seas were covered with floating rafts of pumice thick enough to support a man. Some of this material stayed afloat for nearly two years. If a supervolcano explosion rocked the eastern Atlantic near the Gates of Hercules at the dawn of history, navigational access to the ocean from the Mediterranean would have been seriously impeded for the small sailing vessels of the day. Such a degree of naval impairment mandates that the eruption could have been no more than a few hundred kilometers from Gibraltar.

WHAT LIES BENEATH

If we scan the seafloor between Iberia and the Azores, a striking bottom formation stands out clearly. Less than 200 miles due west of Lisbon lies the Tore Seamount. But it is no ordinary seamount. It is roughly donut shaped and about 75 miles across — very deeply depressed in the middle. In other words, it has every appearance of being a gigantic volcanic caldera, comparable in size to that of the Yellowstone supervolcano which is perceptible only from the air (and which has erupted about every 600,000 years with devastating consequences in North America.)

The great central depth of the Tore seamount caldera demonstrates that this supervolcano must have blown in relatively recent geological time, i.e., the last few thousand years. Unless they abruptly go extinct, volcanoes will slowly rebuild themselves upward after an eruption.

As earlier noted, we can be sure the demise of Atlantis happened after 2000 BC, the approximate date of the Hellenic occupation of Greece. And the catastrophe could not have occurred much after 1500 BC — otherwise, it would be a much stronger feature in the Greek chronicles than it is. Thus the basic timeframe is the first half of the second millennium BC.

It happens that there is solid evidence of a massive volcanic eruption in the mid-17th century BC, doubtless in the mid latitudes of the northern hemisphere. Supporting data come from tree ring studies in Sweden, Ireland, and Arizona, assorted carbon 14 evidence, and ice cores in Greenland.[1] This event has been taken to be the Thera (Santorini) blast, but there is a serious hitch: The eruption date is badly out of synch with the carefully worked out classic chronology of the eastern Mediterranean which shows that Thera blew in Late Minoan IA — about 1540 BC. Since it is highly unlikely that the established chronology is off by a full century, it is near certain that the catastrophe of ca. 1640 BC was *not* Thera. Further, the known vast expanse of the 1640 ash cloud implies an explosion of far greater magnitude than Thera's. Some carbonized materials from the Aegean isle have been C14 dated to ca. 1600–1625 BC but others are chronologically all over the place. An active volcano, Thera has blown with varying intensity numerous times in its history. The SCIEM 2000 project concluded that C14 dating, somewhat inexact, cannot distinguish between high and low chronology for the major Thera event.[2] Accordingly, most experts remain doubtful that it took place in the 17th century BC.

We see, then, that a mammoth eruption occurred in the northern hemisphere in the mid-1600s BC of which no record exists — except in the tomes of a certain noted Greek philosopher. In other words, the mega-explosion of ca. 1640 was Tore.

A supervolcano blast at that time exactly matches the Platonic parameter for the destruction of Atlantis.

Not only is the timeframe optimal, but the location is dead on — exactly where Plato puts Atlantis: not far beyond the gates of Hercules and barely a couple days' sail west of the Iberian coast. The locale is close to the sea lanes traveled by megalithic sailors — so close that this now sunken island must have been discovered and settled very early, probably before 3000 BC. (The isolated little isle of Malta was reached by ancient mariners well before 5000 BC.) So there would have been plenty of time for the build-up of a major sea power on a Torean Atlantis prior to the Achaean age of the Greeks

Before its volcanic destruction, the isle would have been extensive in area — ca. 4500 square miles — about half the size of the great island of Sardinia and much larger than Crete, home of the great Minoan sea power. The eruption of Tambora in historical times blew off the top 1200 meters of that volcano, so it easily feasible that the vastly larger Tore eruption pulverized the top 2500 meters of that island-mount: We are looking at volcanism on a scale almost incomprehensible to contemporary minds. Afterwards, the base of the shattered supervolcano must have subsided several hundred meters, leaving the remnant structure where it is today, some 2000 meters deep. The 850 meter volcanic mount of Krakatoa — tiny compared to Tore — collapsed 350 meters into the sea after its eruption.

---

1 Kuniholm, P.I, "Overview and Assessment of the Evidence for the date of the Eruption of Thera," www.arts.cornell.edu/dendra/thera.html.
2 www.science2000.info/ (Project 8).

The Tore cataclysm would have dumped millions of megatons of floating pumice onto the surrounding waters, making the Atlantic in that region as difficult to navigate as Plato says. Colossal tsunamis were sent crashing onto the shores of Iberia, the Atlantic isles, and other littorals. These waves must have been up to a hundred meters high in some instances, dwarfing the 15-meter waves that wreaked such shocking havoc in the Indian Ocean in 2004, or even the 40-meter tsunami produced by Krakatoa which killed over 30,000 people. The myriad flood legends among the Celts may be traced to these tsunamis: the tales of Y's, Lyonesse, Cantre'r Gwaylod, etc. All these disaster stories have underlying similarities and must represent localized interpolations over time of some ancient seismic cataclysm.

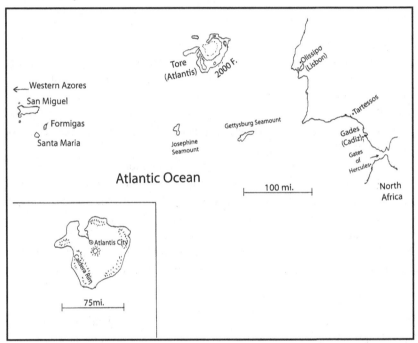

Fig.11: The base of the old Tore supervolcano off Iberia is plainly evident at the 2000 fathom line. The rim remnants project upward from there to within about 2000 meters from the surface. Two major seamounts and the eastern Azores are shown as the probably appeared in Atlantean times. The inset show the island Atlantis as it might have looked before being blown asunder by the eruption of the 17th century BC. *The Atlantean realm was not strictly insular. It apparently held outposts on the mainland at Olissipo and Tartessos.*

The case for the Torean Atlantis is further enhanced by another feature in Plato's description. He tells us that in the center of the island's plain was a flat-topped mountain — which sounds very much like a volcanic cone in the middle of the supervolcano's caldera. A perfect match is provided by the climate which would have been very similar to Lisbon's: warm and mild with adequate rain in the winter but dry enough in summer to benefit from irrigation. The rich volcanic earth would have yielded an agricultural bonanza and would also account for the red, white and black building stones mentioned by Plato. His noted hot springs would be abundant, and the high rim of the caldera accounts for the fact that Atlantis was "lofty and precipitous on the side of the sea."

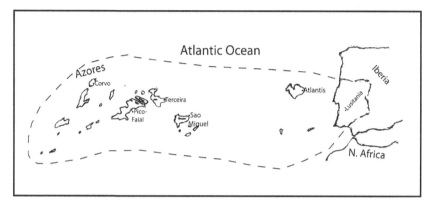

Fig. 11a: The map shows the extent of the Atlantean empire before its destruction by the Tore supervolcano, when the Azores *were far larger and more numerous than they are today.*

So there really was an eastern Atlantic island closely matching Plato's Atlantis, and its destruction "in a single day and night" occurred during the chronological window intimated by the archeological record — in fact, during the most feasible century. Without much question, then, the Tore seamount was the original Atlantis — at first just a minor island kingdom but soon to extend imperial tentacles to other isles as well as sectors of the mainland.

Obviously, the existence of a sizable island off the coast of Iberia greatly enhances the case for early colonization of the Azores, barely 500 miles to the west. Tore/Atlantis was a busy maritime center, with ships constantly coming and going up and down Europe's Atlantic coast. If the Azores were not discovered in some other fashion, it is near certain that some vessel was windblown within sight of them by the later third millennium B.C. The ensuing colonization would have developed Atlantis into the major maritime power of the west.

Any Atlantean colonies established in the Azores, of course, were destined to be shattered and/or submerged a few centuries later by the Tore sea waves and related aftershocks. (The explosion of Tore was likely tied to a major downthrust of the Azorean massif.) The settlements there must have been reduced to a few isolated villages populated by shocked survivors, most of whom soon would have abandoned the isles since they were still subject to jolting, periodic seismic down-thrusts.

Seeing the bulk of their islands steadily sinking, even the hardiest occupants must have eventually concluded it would be only a matter of time until all was swallowed by the sea. Thus, it is hardly surprising that the Azores were found uninhabited by the Portuguese. Though the early occupation of the Azores was not very prolonged, just a few centuries, it still bears directly on the intriguing issue of Atlantean influence in the New World. (See Chapter 12.)

THE CASUALTY COUNT

The total number of deaths inflicted by the Tore/Atlantis eruption is, of course, hard to estimate but must have been in the scores of thousands, even in that less populous era. Odds are that the great bulk of the Atlantean population did not make it off the island in time. Though volcanoes usually give advance notice of eruption through early tremors, people typically tend to ignore the signs of impending disaster until it is too late. In the case of Mount St. Helens, for example, volcanologists were warning for weeks ahead of time that an eruption was likely. Still, outdoorsmen continued to hike, fish, and camp in the vicinity of the volcano, and some old-time denizens of the area simply refused to leave. Many who did pay some casual heed to the warning had no concept of the damage-at-a-distance that an erupting volcano can do through roaring pyroclastic flows that incinerate people in seconds and fiery volcanic bombs that can be hurled for miles. Sudden torrents of mud and water slurry (lahars) can sweep people away and bury them, or they maybe asphyxiated by rolling clouds of sulfurous gasses. Some who mistakenly though St. Helens might be just a spectacular show belatedly found they were much too close. Nearly 60 of them died.

We can surmise that most of Atlantis' population, while expressing some concern about the frequent tremors, went on buying and selling their goods, loading and unloading their wooden ships, attending their parties, meetings and shows. By the time they realized that something cataclysmic was impending, the whole caldera was about to explode under their feet in one of the greatest supervolcanic blasts in all history. By then, there was small chance of escape. The Atlantean palaces, piers, and temples did not just collapse: They were utterly blown to bits; so it is next to impossible that any remnants can ever be found.

Deaths from the attendant tsunamis may have equaled the toll from the volcanic blast itself. These waves give little warning — outside of a brief, temporary tidal drop — before hurling themselves onto the shore. The west coast of Europe held a substantial population at the time of the disaster, and Olissipo (Lisbon) must have been virtually obliterated. Even some the fishing tribes of the Americas were doubtless hit. The coastal inhabitants of the Azores, perhaps thousands in number, must have been all but wiped out. Other more indirect deaths would have occurred as well. Though we do not know the then prevailing wind direction, the enormous quantity of dust and debris in the air most likely buried many mainland crops and may have caused something like a nuclear winter, and famine, over large areas. Even far to the East — in the only literate locale of the time — there seem to have been dramatic repercussions. The date of the Tore eruption coincides closely with the Hyksos invasion and conquest of Egypt (ca. 1640 BC), an event that many scholars believe was impelled by famine.

The evidence for a catastrophic supervolcano eruption in the exact timeframe most likely for the destruction of Atlantis is not coincidence — not when we also see the remnants of a supervolcano just where Plato locates the lost island. The time factor also meshes well with Geopulsation Theory. Other things being equal, we would expect the most horrific volcanic eruptions to occur in the latter part of a compression phase of the geopulsation cycle, or else at the time of the maximum rotational change rate. The Tore explosion happened late in the last compression phase as a gigantic underground magma chamber, building for 45,000 years, finally went ballistic. Notably, the preceding supervolcano eruption at Toba happened at the exact time of the planet's maximum rotational acceleration, 74,000 years ago.[1]

PLAIN CONFUSION

Resolving the crux of the Atlantis problem — its locale and manner of destruction — does not leave our path ribbon smooth. A wrinkle remains in the disparate descriptions in *Critias* of the Atlantean plain (or plains.) One depiction paints a plain of huge dimensions, about twice the size of Portugal. Yet, when describing the plain around the capital city, Plato says the city was near "the center of the island" and only 50 stadia (six miles) from the sea (to which it was connected by a canal.) This description is not appropriate to a vast, sprawling island though it does fit the Tore Seamount if the city was at the head of an inlet about 25 miles long (see map fig.11). Here again, an odd geographical dichotomy is to be found in the Platonic narrative.

This and other descriptive aspects give the impression that Plato's tale may mix features of two distinct but related territories. What begins to emerge is the prospect that some other land than the island itself is somehow integral to the Atlantis story. One area, as we've seen, was a sizable volcanic island off the coast of Iberia with Azorean satellites; the other a larger region dominated by a sprawling plain with continental fauna — almost surely located on the west European coast. If we remember that Atlantis is said to have controlled large areas of the

---

1 This pattern provides some degree of comfort regarding the risk of another supervolcanic eruption at Yellowstone, even now slightly overdue. Geopulsation Theory suggests that the next era of maximum risk is likely to be some 20,000–25,000 years away — though there are other factors involved and we cannot be sure we have that long. We only know that beneath America's favorite national park there is a magma chamber as big as Rhode Island and many miles deep that will someday become uncontainable.

mainland, this disparate geographic portrayal is easy enough to understand. Some of this mainland territory must have been dominated very early, and thoroughly integrated into the Atlantean society; so there was more to Atlantis than just the capital island and the Azores.

That a somewhat skewed description of Atlantis should have emerged in the ancient eastern Mediterranean is not at all surprising; in fact, it might be expected, given the vague comprehension of Atlantic geography among the Greeks and especially the Egyptians. Add to that the many centuries that elapsed between the Atlantean era and that of Solon, plus the disrupted and semi-literate nature of those intervening times.

Elements of both space and time need to be factored into the descriptive synthesis that finally filtered down to the classical Greeks, and ourselves. First, travelers passed along varying depictions of Atlantis on their arrival in (or return to) the east, depending on whether they came from the island Atlantis or from its continental adjunct. Sometimes they were talking about one, sometimes the other, but using the term "Atlantis" in both cases — just as a traveler might say, "I'm just back from New York" (the state or the city?). Those coming from the mainland portion would have emphasized the features of the great plain and the lofty northern mountain ranges. But visitors from the island talked of its capital city and bustling harbor, and its idyllic ocean environment. Over time, the continental sector expanded in size and importance and even after the destruction of the island, most of the mainland portion would have bounced back in a generation or so. Thus, the earlier tales about Atlantis would have centered on the insular locale, whereas later ones had more continental trappings. Eventually, over centuries, these varied oral traditions melded together into the diffracted composite picture that was at last written down by Plato.

Plato's slightly meshed up geography, then, helps to account for the fact that the Atlantis mystery has been so hard to solve. His description cannot be made to fit any single locale, simply because both parts of the Atlantean nation, the islands and the mainland territory, are merged in that description. This explication also handles the vast size of Atlantis as reported by the philosopher. Including both the insular and continental sectors, the nation must have approached Britain in land area and sprawled much farther in extent. It is about a thousand miles from old Castile to the western Azores.

If our analysis is correct, there should be some not-very-distant coastal region in the European mainland closely approximating the description of the Great Plain of Atlantis. It should not be hard to discern.

Some Less Famous Places

Everything points to Iberia as the site of the prime Atlantean continental colony. Not only is it the closest mainland mass to the island Atlantis, this warm-temperature peninsula also has the requisite broad plains and high mountain ranges, most running east-west and providing shelter from the north wind (*Critias* 118). Iberia has very great cultural antiquity and is the preeminent land of chestnuts, cited as an Atlantean crop. Plato also mentions a fruit with a hard rind that some have taken to be the coconut but is more likely the pomegranate, which thrives in the Iberian climate. In short, the whole Iberian milieu — climatology, topography, crops and archeology — easily fits into the Atlantis narrative. All that remains, really, is to find the exact sector of Iberia that matches the depiction of the great plain.

The clearest aspect of Atlantis is its location in Atlantic waters. Not only does Plato place the legendary nation beyond the Gates of Hercules, he also says the Atlantic Ocean itself was named after Atlantis' first king, Atlas. Hence, the great Atlantean plain should be found on the littoral of the Atlantic, rather than, say, inside the Mediterranean. Fortuitously, the dimensions of our sought-for plain are provided by Plato: about 2,000 stadia wide and 3,000 stadia long (ca. 225 by 340 miles). While well shielded from the north by mountains, part of the plain was said to be open toward the south.

This description is really quite specific. If there is credibility to Plato's story, we should see some closely matching geography in western Iberia.

Only two large plains in Iberia border the Atlantic. The famous Andalusian plain in the far south is almost large enough (150 by 250 miles) but lacks the "rectangular and oblong" form Plato specifies. It is distinctly wedge-shaped or triangular.

A little to the northwest of Andalusia lies the Portuguese coastal plain which merges with the Estremadura plain of western Spain. This locale, very nearly the old Roman province of Lusitania, lays out in the proper shape and exact size delineated by Plato (map fig. 12).

The plain here only deviates from its basically rectangular form — as per *Critias* — where it follows the great "circular ditch" winding around the plain — obviously the Tagus and Guadiana Rivers. Critias reports the ditch to be a canal but with ill-concealed skepticism: "The depth, width and length of this ditch was incredible, and gives the impression that a work of such extent, in addition to so many others, could never have been artificial. Nevertheless, I must say what I was told."[1] The two rivers cut deeply, ditch-like, into the surrounding landscape. Their combined length, about 1,070 miles, is strikingly close to the 10,000 stadia (1,135 miles) given for the great ditch. The shielding mountains to the north, the Sierra de Gato and Sierra de Credos, soar up to 8,500 feet high. Somewhat lower ranges define the eastern and southeast boundaries of this plain of Lusitania — an idyllic land that may have inspired not only the far western Elysian Fields of the Greeks but also the Egyptian "Fields of Peace." These fields are portrayed in the Egyptian Book of the Dead as a fertile plain with the proper 3:2 length-width

---

1 *Critias*, 118.

ratio, cut by waterways. In some cases the western boundary is shown to be the ocean.

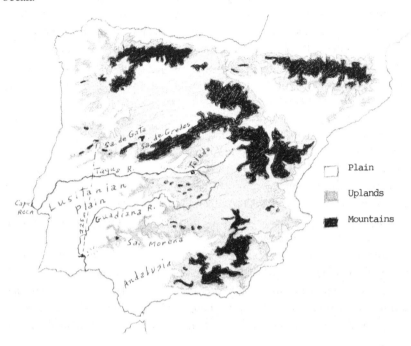

Fig.12: The map shows how closely the Lusitanian Plain of Iberia corresponds to the geography of the great plain of Atlantis. Plato describes the plain as roughly rectangular, largely surrounded by mountains but with part of it open to the south; specifically, mountains shield it from the north winds. "Across the center inland" the plain measures ca. 225 miles wide, exactly the distance from the Sierra de Gata range to the foothills of the Sierra Moreno. Lengthwise, according to Critias, the plain extends about 340 miles, the distance from Cape Roca up the Tagus valley to the vicinity of Toledo. Going around the plain was a great canal or "ditch," actually the rivers Tagus and Guadiana which cut deeply into the landscape and together measure very nearly the length prescribed by Plato, ca. 1100 miles.

Geographically, this Lusitanian plain fits so precisely with Plato's prose that the case cannot be mere happenstance. This landscape is doubtless part and parcel of *Critias*.

The correlations go on and on. In antiquity, Iberia was rich with silver, gold, copper, zinc, and tin (very rare in Europe), fulfilling the description of Atlantis as a land abundant in metallic ores. Though now somewhat denuded, Iberia was once heavily forested with pine, oak, beech, and chestnut, easily meeting this Atlantean parameter.

The storied faunal diversity of Atlantis is mirrored by that of Iberia, which harbors most of the usual European species plus a few African ones. Of particular note is Plato's mention of elephants. Elephants inhabited Iberia in prehistoric times; just when they died out is not known. It is possible they could have survived on the peninsula into the third millennium BC. Or they might have been imported for heavy lifting from neighboring North Africa.

Lusitania's weather is as close to the Atlantean as can be: adequate rains in the winter but sunny and dry enough in the summer to require irrigation of some crops. Doubtless many of the supposed canals in Atlantis were really tributaries of the Tagus and Guadiana, but some artificial waterways would have been dug out for irrigation.

Atlantean features that are not part of Lusitanian environment are all characteristic of the Tore/Atlantis island site, i.e., an insular location, geological instability, hot springs, a precipitous coast, red and black volcanic rocks. Some key markers are shared since the flora — chestnuts and pomegranates, for example — would have been much the same in both places. Thus, if the classic depiction of Atlantis is seen to cover both the insular and Iberian parts of the Atlantean nation, all the requisite parameters are readily met.

The problem with the Atlantean analyses heretofore is that the focus has simply been too narrow. Atlantis was not just an island; it was an empire.

The physical congruence between "Atlantis" and the Tore-Lusitania-Azores region, however striking, is not only consideration that matters. Plato paints the Atlantean nation as the seat of a very early and accomplished culture, so this aspect has to be seen as well. Nothing at all survived from the insular sector, of course, but archeology provides plentiful evidence that Lusitania, particularly the lower Tagus River area, was the site of a remarkably ancient and dynamic society. The sites of Zambujal, Palmela, and Villa de Sao Pedro establish that the people of this region were constructing rock monuments and communal tombs before 4000 BC. They were well into the Copper Age and building elaborate hill forts with massive walls ca. 3000 BC — before the first pyramids in Egypt. The rest of continental Europe lagged far behind this Atlantic culture. It was as impressive as Plato implies.

But one chapter in the Atlantis story remains somewhat indistinct, and seemingly incongruous — the chronological scheme.

THE TIME WARP

It is commonly overlooked that *Critias* is only the opening chapter of what was to be an epic historical tale, one never finished, perhaps because of the death of the author. There is a little additional information in *Timaeus*, but what we have from Plato is the barest outline of an Atlantean history that had to span centuries, during which the society's fortunes must have shifted, ebbed and flowed, over a wide geographic era.

Time really is a fourth dimension, and without a grasp of it most historic story lines are likely to seem incoherent. Future archeologists, finding English language inscriptions in North America, Britain, southern and eastern Africa, India, Australia and New Zealand, might see that this geographical distribution as baffling, near incomprehensible, if they did not know the sequence of events during the colonial era.

The narrative information in *Critias* isolates the timeframe of the Atlantis chronicles between the dawn of metallurgy in the west (ca. 3000 BC) and a time just "before Theseus," which works out to be about 1300 BC according to Parian Marbles.[1] Yet the specific chronology provided by Plato is much different. At first glance, it appears inexplicable, abounding with aspects both implausible and contradictory at the same time. It will be our thesis here though that the Atlantean timeframe is much less bizarre than it seems once a couple of points are grasped.

One fault is partly our own: the tendency to assume, perhaps because the story in *Critias* is short and its end abrupt, that the Atlantean War was a brief episode of history, rather like World War II. In fact, it was more on the order of the struggle between Islam and the West which raged for well over a thousand years and has not entirely subsided to this day. In other words, we have grossly foreshortened the tale, in effect condensing a novel into a news item. Once this is understood, the Atlantis tradition takes on a new dimension entirely, one that makes it much less a puzzle.

The second fault is less ours than the Ancients'. They were more than a little slipshod about recording historical time, especially when dealing with extended periods involving centuries or millennia. In fact, there was a well-established tendency to err on the side of chronological exaggeration — to the point where it was not unusual for an error factor of three or four to creep into their records.

It would be amazing if the Atlantis legend had survived to Plato's time in undistorted form. In the mostly illiterate centuries between the Atlantean era and classical Greece discrepancies had to develop. Even so, we are struck by the outright implausibility of 9600 BC as the reputed date for the Atlantean adventure. There was, as previously noted, nothing that could be classed as civilization at that time — not around Lusitania, not around the Aegean, not in Egypt, not anywhere.

There is no question the date is wrong. But why so far wrong?

One obvious prospect is that the Egyptian priests who told the tale simply inflated the time line for effect. It is clear in *Timaeus* that the Egyptians were trying to impress Solon with the great antiquity of their historical tradition. One of the priests sniffs that the Greeks have "no ancient tradition, nor any science which is hoary with age."

---

1 Forsdyke, John, *Greece Before Homer*, WW Norton Co., NY, NY, 1964, p.55.

Some commentators have suggested another explanation: that the Atlantis episode occurred 9,000 months before Solon instead of 9,000 years. They propose that the original version of the story was framed in terms of "moons ago" which somehow got twisted into "years ago."

Nine thousand moons before Solon, ca. 1300 BC, takes us back to Theseus, but that is hardly far enough. Other names cited by the Egyptian priests predate Theseus by several generations. Cecrops and Erechthesus, for example, among the earliest remembered kings of Athens and, thanks to the Parian marbles, can be dated with some accuracy. The marbles place Cecrops in the early 16th century and Erechthesus in the late 15th century BC. So the "moons" hypothesis is unsatisfactory.

Another suggestion offered to account for the chronological distortion: the unlikely possibility that an extra zero was added to the actual number of years through mistranslation or mistranscription. Then the Atlantis era would be 900 rather than 9,000 years before Solon, around the mid-second millennium.

But none of these conjectures is really very convincing or necessary. The fact is that the great historian, Herodotus, indirectly supplies us with a reasonably close date for the Atlantean episode. Herodotus visited Egypt about 140 years after Solon and gives an account in his famous *History* of the Egyptians' chronological methods.[1] He says they had a list of 341 kings who had ruled Egypt since the first king — who can be placed about 3500 BC.

Actually, the first Egyptian king known to us was Narmer, who dates from about 3150 BC and was probably the father of Menes, traditionally the first king of unified Egypt.[2] But it is known that Upper and Lower Egypt were ruled by separate kings for a good four or five centuries before unification. Most likely, these were included on the Egyptians' list of royalty.

Each name on the list was assumed to represent a generation, three generations to a century, so the sum of the years since the first king was calculated at 11,340 years before Herodotus' visit. In reality, of course, the average reign of these kings was much less than 33 years, what with wars, plagues, palace coups and other hazards of kingly reign. Also, in times when Egypt was not united but ruled by rival monarchs, the names of these various rulers would be included on the list even though they were contemporaneous. There were other errors as well, but the point is that if the classic Egyptians placed their first king at 11,000 years before Herodotus, then the Atlantean era ("9000 years" before Solon) was obviously after that king's reign. Using a proportionate time scale puts the Atlanteans on the historical stage about 3000 BC.

1 Herodotus, *History*, Book II (142).
2 Some think that Menes and Narmer were the same person. More likely, Narmer was the southern king who first subjugated Lower (northern) Egypt while Menes (the Egyptian "Aha") was the first to be enthroned as the acknowledged Pharaoh of both Upper and Lower Egypt.

This date agrees with an important chronological marker contained in *Critias* where Plato specifies that copper, tin and brass were utilized by the Atlanteans. The mention of brass but not bronze is significant because it places Atlantis in the Copper Age, roughly the third millennium BC in southwest of Europe. (While Bronze making did not reach Atlantic shores until after 2000 BC, natural copper-zinc compounds will produce brass.)

But if Plato's "nine thousand years" actually translates in real time to about 3000 BC, what exactly is the significance of that date? It is commonly taken to mark the drowning of Atlantis but, strictly speaking, that is not what Critias says. What he is talking about when he uses this date is the war "said to have taken place between those who dwelt outside the Pillars of Hercules and all who dwelt within them."

Both the statement itself and simple logic compel the conclusion that a confrontation so vast must have involved numerous powers besides Athens over a span of many years. Did the struggle perhaps last for decades, or even centuries? One could speak of the "war between the Turks and the Europeans" which persisted almost without surcease for more than 800 years.

There is no way to tell from the texts of *Timaeus* or *Critias* whether the specified time marks the beginning or the end of this great conflict, or some phase in between. Critias himself would not have known the answer since he is only repeating a tale he heard as a youth. Fortunately, the question is answered by archeology. It happens that the time around 3000 BC signals the onset of a conspicuous clash between Atlantic and Mediterranean Europe that is clearly marked in the archeological record. It was a confrontation that occupied several centuries, one we will shortly detail.

Meanwhile, it is worth noting how well the onset of the third millennium BC fits into the putative Atlantean era. This was the very dawn of written history when myth, tradition, and the still sparse records were most likely to be fused. It was also the dawn of the Age of Metals and of sea-going warships, both integral to the Atlantis tale. It was prime time, too, for the western Megalithic Culture, the one most likely to be tied to Atlantis.

Our interpretation of the Egyptian chronology also comports with another date given in *Timaeus*. The priests of Sais told Solon that their city's constitution went back some 8,000 years — again an obviously rough and inflated figure. But using what we have gleaned from Herodotus, we could calculate the city constitution of Sais to circa the 28th century BC, a date in good accord with what we know about the development of writing in Egypt and the history of Sais.

The Egyptians, by the way, conceded to Solon that Athens, though its citizens had forgotten their own past, was actually older than Sais.[1] To those nurtured on

---

1 Timaeas 23.

notions that Egypt was the cradle of world civilization, the statement may seem surprising, perhaps even dubious. But it is neither.

Even though the Egyptian can be fairly classed as the most spectacular of the very ancient civilizations, it was not the first. The early Mesopotamian culture rose before Egypt. And long before even these, sizable Neolithic towns based on agriculture had sprung up in various parts of the near eastern region, including Greece. It is credible enough, then, that Athens was established as a Neolithic (pre-Hellenic) town before Sais.

Block by block, the Atlantis timeframe begins to fill in. The Atlanteans were on the world stage not long after the 30th century BC. Since they could not have attacked the Greeks before 2000 BC (because the Greeks were not in Greece till then), the implication is that the Atlantean advance through the broad Mediterranean basin took the better part of a millennium to penetrate the Grecian waters at the far east end. Such a scenario is hardly surprising. Great powers do not have short histories.

But even though the broad chronological perspective has started to materialize, there are still a few blank spots in the time line yet to be addressed.

CHAPTER 10. THE SCEPTERED ISLE

If there is any prehistoric culture that provides the bedrock for Atlantis is has to be the great monument-building society of ancient western Europe, the Megalithic. Not only does the timeframe fit (4500 to 1500 BC) but so does the geography. The sprawl of the Megalithic culture is quite close to Plato's delineation of the Atlantean — along the coasts of Atlantic Europe and around the western Mediterranean.

The Atlantean empire, if more than mere legend, was surely some Copper Age manifestation of this societal complex. But is there proof that the megalithic people were once under unified rule? Could one group of preliterate ancients ensconce itself as dominant over so vast an assemblage of tribes?

Literacy is not necessary to the art of empire building. The Incas ruled an expansive realm in South America, hundreds of thousands of square miles, even though they never learned to write. All that is really needed is a will to conquer and the ability to do so, which usually means some sort of organizational or technical superiority. Of course, in the absence of scribes, edicts and bureaucrats, some other unifying ethos is helpful to empire builders. Among the Incas, it was a religious belief in a divine emperor. An even more dramatic illustration of the power of religion in history is the case of the early Moslems, whose zealotry spawned a compelling military force that transformed much of the Old World.

We know religion was a strong motif in megalithic society: The chamber tombs and lithic monuments like Stonehenge offer proof enough. The melding of civil and religious authority was more common than not in ancient times, and the closing paragraphs of *Critias* indicate just such a fusion in the government of Atlantis. It is widely known that the primitive Celts were dominated by a powerful network of Druids who combined religious and civil authority as priest-judges. If a similar structure existed among the Atlanteans, it would have been easily capable of controlling an extensive empire. Though the origins of Druidism are unknown to us, they must to very deep into prehistory — some think even back to Stonehenge.[1] Druids figure prominently in Ireland's *Book of Invasions*, a folkloric account of the island's earliest history with roots many centuries deep into the pre-literate era. As we will soon see, the shadow of Atlantis can be discerned hanging over the British Isles of the Copper Age, and most investigators believe Druidism spread through the Celtic social structure from Britain. A close chronological correlation exists between the construction at Stonehenge and the Atlantean era; so if the Druids did in fact build the monument, we might suspect that Druidism itself may have had Atlantean roots.

Religion, then, may have been the glue of the Atlantean empire. And religious fervor could have been a factor in its expansion even if it was not the primary motivation. In the end, simple old-fashioned greed may be the most likely driver, especially considering Plato's comments about Atlantis' ethical decline.

This much is known for sure, though: At about the time construction began on the first phase of Stonehenge (Henge 1), dramatic changes overtook the whole megalithic world. It was utterly transformed by a powerful new force.

Proofs abound that a massive intrusion along the coast of west Europe and into the Mediterranean began ca. the 29th century BC, continuing for hundreds of years. It came from the western fringes of the known world: It was a thrust from the Atlantic — and Atlantis.

Archeologists call this "the Beaker explosion," because it was first traced through the distribution of a particular shape of pottery known as a bell beaker. This ware had the shape of an inverted bell and carried incised hatching marks on the sides. The Beaker Folk, as they have come to be known, produced a characteristic type of copper dagger. They were expert bowmen who fired tanged and barbed arrowheads of copper or flint while wearing stone wrist guards. There can be no question that the Beaker People were accomplished sailors and more warlike than they properly should have been.

They swept over most of the Megalithic society including Iberia and France, Britain, parts of central Europe, and much of the west Mediterranean basin. By 2000 BC, the Beaker Folk dominated the equivalent of the Western Roman Empire, two millennia before the Caesars. More to the point, the Bell Breaker sway tallies neatly with Plato's description of the Atlantean empire just prior to its at-

---

1   Historians generally date the Druids from the first writings about them by classical authors in the 2nd century BC. There is little real logic to this view, obviously. In fact, it was said by Polyhistor that the 6th century BC mathematician/philosopher, Pythagoras, was taught the Druidic doctrine of reincarnation by a Celt. Conventional views notwithstanding, the prospect remains that the brilliant, if eccentric, antiquarian William Stukeley was right after all, in his claim that Stonehenge was built by the Druids.

tack on the Greeks: "The men of Atlantis had subdued the parts of Libya within the columns of Hercules as far as Egypt, and of Europe as far as Tyrrhenia."

BACKTRACKING THE BEAKERS

The origins of the Beaker Folk have been an ongoing academic squabble for decades with no real consensus achieved. The rapidity of their initial expansion makes it less than obvious, archeologically, just where it all began. The Portuguese say Lusitania, and they have something of a case. Traces of the culture are actually most pervasive in the British Isles, but evidently it did not start there. A disproportionate number of brachycephalic (broad-headed) skulls are found in Beaker tombs, pushing prehistorians to the quite logical conclusion that round-headed people must have carried the culture to (long-headed) Britain.[1] Some think these people came from the lower Rhine valley but they could as easily have come from Brittany on the northerly French coast. Some of the oldest Bell Beaker pottery, the so-called Maritime variety, is found very early (ca. 2800 BC) in the Lisbon area and not long after in Brittany. In due time, this new copper culture dominates the whole megalithic west European littoral and intrudes deep into the western Mediterranean. Since Lusitania was part of the Atlantean empire, it is not much of a stretch to see the Bell Beaker genesis in Atlantis.

A long-running argument rages about whether the Beaker culture was spread by migration or cultural diffusion. The most probably answer is "both." The initial wave of expansion, along the Atlantic Coast and up its river valleys, and into the western Mediterranean, was almost certainly accomplished via aggressive migration. From that point, much of the spread into the interior of central Europe could easily have been by way of cultural diffusion.

Significantly, the onslaught of the Beaker Folk is tied to a key date in the Atlantean annals. Their explosive expansion along the western European coastline manifests itself not very long after 3000 BC. It was about that date that they mastered copper smelting, a transforming event in their history. They seem to have been the first people — at least in the west — to grasp the potential of copper metallurgy for the production of weaponry. Copper arrowheads and daggers could be produced at unheard of rates compared to the tedious process of working stone. Armies of unprecedented size could be equipped with these new weapons. Here was the answer to Atlantis' expansionist dreams.

Armed with their new technology, the Atlantean Beaker Folk soon swooped north to England and the Netherlands, then pushed up the Rhine valley. Meanwhile, after overrunning much of Iberia, another wing of Atlantean warriors drove into the Mediterranean. These soon overwhelmed the south of France, the Balearics, Sardinia, and Sicily, as well as parts of Italy and North Africa.

---

1 Laing, Lloyd & Jennifer, *The Origins of Britain*, Granada Publishing, London, 1980, p.183.

Always they were looking for more copper, a metal they used for more than more utilitarian purposes; it was also a prestige metal valued for ornament and adornment. Copper, it seems, had something like the fascination of gold for the Atlantean mind. Before 2000 BC, the Beaker Folk were in control of all the big copper producing regions of Western Europe.

In order to see the Beaker culture as the Atlantean it is necessary to dispose of one of the goofier notions in archeology — that the Beaker Folk were just "maritime traders." If so, why the prominence of weapons in their tool kit? Could mere traders have left so dominant a stamp on the lands they visited? No, these people had to be more than transient peddlers. Many were buried in the great tombs of the lands they overwhelmed. They were a new ruling warrior class in the megalithic territories during the Chalcolithic and early Bronze Ages.

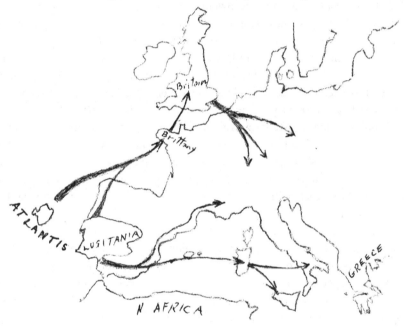

Fig.13: The map shows the main attack routes of the Beaker Atlanteans in western Europe during the third millennium BC.

A recent breakthrough in bone analysis, using strontium isotope ratios, strongly argues that the maritime trader school got it all wrong, that the Beaker Folk were in fact a real migratory influx that altered the genetic base in the lands they intruded upon. The data show that in the early phases of the Bell Beaker expansion, a third to a half of the hundreds of people found in Beaker graves were born very far from their burial sites.[1]

---

1 Price, T. Douglas, "Tracing the Migrants Trail," *Discovering Archaeology*, Oct. 2000.

It may seem a spectacular feat for a single people at so remote a time to establish themselves over so vast a domain. But technical superiority, which the Beaker warriors clearly possessed, can have startling results. Consider that a relatively small number of Europeans, with the advantage of firearms (and abetted by disease germs), overwhelmed all the sprawling terrain of the Americas in little more than three centuries.

The fogs of antiquity have settled over some aspects of the Beaker explosion. But prehistory clearly tells us this: that well-armed maritime folk from the far west had swept over a huge expanse of territory by 1900 BC — the very same territory said to have been subjugated by Atlantean warriors. This imperial power was one of the most formidable in the ancient world; and it was distantly remembered as such by the ancient Greeks and Egyptians. The center of this empire was a now lost isle off the coast of Iberia — the island of Atlantis.

But even as their reign expanded, a colossal subterranean pressure was building, unsuspected, beneath the foundations of the Atlanteans' home island. The day of destruction dawned benignly, like most days. But soon violent tremors began to shake the ground, worse than any previously know. Even citizens who had been through many a quake in their time began to take fright. Some must have headed for the numerous ships anchored in the harbor to buy hasty passage out, destination no longer an issue — the Canaries, Iberia, the Azores — anywhere at all. But most would have found they had waited too long: There were nowhere near enough ships. Then, as the rumbling shock waves grew exponentially, all the man-made constructions of Atlantis must have disintegrated like sand castles. Reaching a safe distance, the last few evacuees may have looked back to see towering columns of black smoke and ash reaching into the high stratosphere. They would have heard apocalyptic explosions reverberating across the north Atlantic seas as the entire island was blasted to bits in a supervolcanic Gotterdammerung. A great chalcolithic center on the far western edge of the know world was obliterated and engulfed by the worst cataclysm in 70,000 years — one that spawns undying tales of a monumental lost civilization. Today, about the only reminders of this once thriving isle are rolling waves of the Atlantic and a few paragraphs in the writings of an ancient Greek philosopher.

FACT OR FICTION?

By now, we can safely jettison the official explanation of the Atlantis story: that Plato simply made the whole thing up. The idea that he would purposely deceive his readers hardly squares with the philosopher's obsession for truth. In the conversations of Timaeus and Critias, it is plain that Plato is not playing games. Rather, he is passing along a fascinating story of historic significance that had come into his purview. His motivation was simply to preserve the record, and, we may suspect, to find some moral in the tale.

Beyond this, we have the word of Proclus that Crantor found the Atlantis story still extant in the Egyptian annals at Sais three centuries after Solon's time.[1] The Roman historian Ammianus Marcellinus tells us the Egyptian intelligentsia considered Atlantis a historical fact. The loss of the ancient Egyptian records is in no way surprising. As waves of conquest poured over ancient Egypt, most of the historical literature was lost. Hundreds of thousands of volumes of irreplaceable manuscripts and scrolls were incinerated in the burning of the great library of Alexandria. Among those, we can only imagine what references to Atlantis were sent up in smoke.

Yet we have not lost everything. A fragmentary work by the 4th century BC Greek writer, Theophrastus of Lesbos, talks about islands in the sea — most like- ly the Azores — that were colonies of Atlantis. Timagenes of Alexandria (first century BC) relates that one of the tribes of Gaul held a memory of coming from a distant island in the Atlantic. The oft-stated argument that the Atlantis Legend rests only on the testimony of Plato doesn't quite wash, after all.

Whatever the explanation of the Atlantis Legend, the least likely is that it was pure invention. In his discourses on Atlantis, Plato repeatedly states the nar- rative is not fiction but "actual fact." As usual, he meant what he said. An ancient Athenian festival, called the Panathenaea, was held to thank the goddess Athena for the victory over the nation of Poseidon (the god most associated with At- lantis). According to tradition, this event, which included a solemn procession, dated from the time of Theseus. Since this observance antedated Plato by centu- ries, he could not have concocted the Atlantis legend.

No flippant dismissal of the Platonic chronicle is credible in light of the myr- iad Atlantean cross-coordinates to be found in the Tore seamount and Lusitania — and in the Beaker explosion which so closely parallels the sage's account of At- lantean aggression. With stout ships and strong bows, a militant seafaring breed did thrust themselves into the grey dawn of Mediterranean history, advancing along the coasts and river valleys, invincible — if Plato has it right — until they encountered the Athenians.

What then, are the historical prospects for an Atlanto–Athenian clash?

The Beaker Folk reached Sicily and south Italy around 2000 BC, about when the archaic Hellenic tribes overwhelmed mainland Greece. Two aggressive soci- eties, both more inclined to warfare than diplomacy, then faced each other across the not-very-broad Ionian Sea. No crystal ball was required to foresee the course of coming events.

---

1 Proclus, Lysios, *Commentaries on Plato's Timaeus,* (cited by L. Sprague de Camp, *Lost Continents,* Dover Publications, 1970, appendix A.)

Archeology indicates that the Atlantean empire did not persist as a monolithic structure very far into the 2nd millennium BC. After settling in Tyrrhenian lands, the intruding Beaker Folk came into contact with more developed cultures. Gradually, the old Beaker ways yielded to alien influences and geographic sprawl. The distinctive Beaker pottery that makes their early wanderings so easy to trace slowly passes out of fashion in the early 2nd millennium almost everywhere except in parts of Iberia and Britain.

This circumstance, of course, does not at all imply the evaporation of the people who made the pottery. Styles changed then, even as now, if much more deliberately. But the vast expanse of a single culture was evolving into a number of more regionalized societies, still related and coordinated, but individualized in various ways. The great unity, exemplified by the classic Bell Beaker Culture, was giving way to something resembling a confederation.

The fact that the Beaker-Atlantean empire was diversifying not long after its initial thrust into the eastern Mediterranean does not mean its assaults were curtailed. The loot was still there for the taking, and the similar heritage of the associated tribal states makes it all but certain they would have continued to push on in concert. Plato himself implies the invaders from the west were, in fact, a kind of a confederacy when he speaks of "this great power gathered into one."[1] He also uses the plural "*kings* of Atlantis" referring to the leaders of the invasion.

The situation is somewhat analogous to the breakup of the British Empire. The empire is gone: yet it is not gone. It persists in the customs and associations of its former constituent parts. In matters of foreign policy, economics, and in many other ways, the Commonwealth nations habitually act in a coordinated fashion.

The analogy may reasonably be carried further. Great Britain remains, to this day, something of a "first among equals" in the Commonwealth. Several member states, though essentially independent, still recognize the wearer of the British Crown as their official head of state. That a similar status was enjoyed by Atlantis proper in the early 2nd millennium BC can hardly be doubted. Until its obliteration, the capital island of Atlantis held sway as the preeminent member of a sprawling confederacy that completely dominated the western Mediterranean. The several affiliated Mediterranean tribes, and their territories, were surely know as "Atlantean" at least until the capital's destruction, and even for some time afterwards. When we probe their intrusion into the Aegean area, we will find that many of these tribes have a traceable history.

Perspectives in Stone

The historical canard about enlightenment coming out of "The East" is so imbedded in western minds that a note on civilization's true course might be

---

1 *Timaeas* 25.

worthwhile before moving on to the late Atlantean wars. Typically in human history, sporadic and varied rays of light come not from a single source, but from here and there — east, west, north, south. It was no different in prehistory.

Though given short shrift in the classroom, the megalithic era was one of the most remarkable manifestations in the human chronicle. The stunning assemblage at Stonehenge was only the culmination of an awesome dawn-age culture that erected thousands of huge stone monuments and chamber tombs along Europe's Atlantic littoral, structures now known to have predated and influenced those of the Near East. The oldest monumental constructions in our world are not in Egypt or the Fertile Crescent but on the shores of western Europe. So, the persistent tradition that the Atlantean culture was humanity's oldest is not so bizarre as some people might think.

The stone monuments and tombs begin to show up almost simultaneously in widely separated locales in Brittany and coastal Iberia about the middle of the fifth millennium BC. The exact point of genesis is beyond certain knowledge, but it was somewhere in the far west European coastal zone. The odd initial distribution points to something significant — a very early command of the sea. Routine long-distance ocean transport and communication were unquestionably commonplace along the megalithic Atlantic shores more than a thousand years before the first Egyptian pharaoh was enthroned.

The finest of the chamber tombs are in the Boyne River Valley of Ireland — namely, Newgrange, Knowth, and Dowth. All three date from the third millennium BC, and all are sophisticated in both design and workmanship, extraordinary achievements for their time. They incorporate ornamental stone art and appear to be astronomically oriented like Stonehenge. The Boyne Valley tombs demonstrate contacts with Iberia; they contain decorated stone basins and a particular type of bone pin typically found in the Iberian Peninsula.

There was contact, too, with northern Scotland: The Boyne tombs plainly served as an inspiration to the builders of Maes Howe. There is no question that the whole Megalithic Culture was a unitary society, each part in close contact with most of the rest. We have here a civilized complex stretching from northernmost Britain to Gibraltar,[1] and from there into the west Mediterranean Sea, a world that evolved on a separate track from that of the Near East.

In addition to the tombs, standing stones called menhirs began popping up along the Atlantic coast of Europe in megalithic days. The purpose and meaning of these is unknown. Most likely, they had some kind of religious or ceremonial significance. Most are undecorated, but some are carved with anthropomorphic or occulus motifs.

1   Laing, Lloyd & Jennifer, *The Origins of Britain*, Granada Publishing, United Kingdom, 1982, p.167.

The engineering feats of the megalithic workmen are so mind-bending that some commentators have been swept into the realm of fantasy. But the ability of ancients to transport and erect huge stone blocks does not mean they were aided by space aliens. It merely means our ancestors were a good deal more clever and better organized than most might suppose.

The largest stone in the assemblage at Stonehenge is barely less than 30 feet long. Near Saumur, in central France, four capstones weighing up to 86 tons each, were used to roof one of the great megalithic tombs. Sometimes, these ponderous stones, through some astonishing technique, were hauled scores of miles from their quarries. Obviously, the architects of megalithic times had mastered the principles of leverage, and maybe the power-multiplying force of pulleys as well.

Metalworking appears so early in the megalithic society that it may have developed there independently, though diffusion from the Near East is equally plausible. Shortly before the dawn of the 3rd millennium, metal-smelting settlements evolved in southern Spain (Los Millares) as well as along the lower Tagus River in Portugal. Not long after, the Megalithic culture began to press into the Mediterranean basin, the Balearics and Sardinia, Malta and parts of Italy. On Sardinia and Minorca, the megalithic manifestations took on new forms. Boat-shaped rock tombs called navetas were built along with taulas — T-shaped stone constructions of unknown significance.

The navetas serve to emphasize the nautical orientation of the megalithic people. The fact that the Mediterranean leaders of this culture were entombed in such a fashion can only mean that ships played a prominent role in their lives — all of which jibes with the coastal, insular and river valley distribution of the whole megalithic regime.

In short, a great monument-building society, highly organized and with notable maritime capabilities, arose surprisingly early on the far west frontier of Western Civilization. It was the island of Atlantis that was the hub, the Rome, of this society during its Chalcolithic stage.

THE SARDINIAN MANIFESTATION

One of the lands overwhelmed by the Beaker expansion was Sardinia, the second largest Mediterranean isle, a place of sunshine, olives and grapes, mostly mountainous but with some fruitful plains. The island has seen its greatest days and now lies outside the mainstream of events — archaic, a bit detached.

But it was not always so. At times, Sardinia has teamed with vitality and progress; at times, it has impacted world affairs.

One such time was four millennia ago. It was on the island of Sardinia that the Atlantean society reached something of an apex. And an impressive one it was, worth examining because it demonstrates that while the Atlanteans may have lagged the Near East in some respects, they were far from bumpkins. Since Sardinia is much closer to Greece and Egypt than Atlantis itself, there is every likelihood that Sardinia colored the East Mediterranean perception of Atlantean society.

Fig. 14a: Nuraghi Ruins. An idea of the scale of these great Bronze Age structures can be gained from the human figures visible at the left of picture below. (From "Sardinia" by Margaret Guido).

Fig. 14b: Some examples of the sculpture of the Nuraghian (Atlantean) civilization. (From "Sardinia" by M. Guido).

Circa 2000 BC, a culture complex now called the *Nuraghian* appeared on Sardinia. This notable, if little known, civilization is distinct form anything to the east but has close similarities to the Atlantean as described by Plato. What we find in Sardinia provides insights into what the drowned city of Atlantis may have been like.

Plato tells us the Atlanteans were elaborately organized, the land being divided into military districts, each with its own chief in charge of maintaining a quota of armed men. The Bronze Age of Sardinia, as revealed by archeology, shows a population living in villages dominated and defended by massive circular stone towers called nuraghi and surrounded by circular walls. The capital of Atlantis, 'tis said, was completely enclosed by a circular wall.

The nuraghi, which usually included storerooms, work rooms, and a religious center, were almost surely the castles of district chieftains. These structures were built of a variety of stone, including basaltic, confirming Plato's observation of multi-colored stones utilized by the Atlantean builders. There are literally hundreds of nuraghi in Sardinia, some of them huge structures that must have been garrisoned by up to 300 men. Some of the central turrets are three stories high, rising 50 feet or more above ground level.[1]

Notably, round towers similar to the nuraghi were built in Scotland and Ireland during the early Iron Age. Whether these had any direct connection with Sardinia is unknown, but they could well have been late constructions of now lost building types used in the drowned Atlantis.

Critias describes large temples and statues in Atlantis' capital city. The remnants of Bronze Age Sardinia include some fairly imposing temple ruins as well as huge monoliths carved to represent figures. These works, of course, are not made in a classic style. But Plato specifically says that the structures of Atlantis presented a somewhat "strange and barbarous appearance."[2]

The philosopher makes reference, too, to the fact that the Atlanteans constructed fountains and cisterns with buildings around them. Sardinia is fairly teaming with the ruins of sacred wells with elaborate enclosing structures built in the early Bronze Age.

This Nuraghian culture, developed out of the Beaker/Atlantean, was almost exactly contemporaneous with the Achaean of the Aegean a few hundred miles to the east. There was commerce between the two. Aegean wares have been found in Sardinia, dating from around the 16th century BC.

While contacts with the eastern civilizations may have affected the Sardinians' society and technology, the interchange did nothing to modify their marauding instincts. From the Tyrrhenian lands of Sardinia and Sicily, it is only a

---

1 See *Nuraghi: Charm in Sardinia* web site, www.sarnow.com/sardinia/nuragl.htm for both photographs and text.
2 *Critias* 116

short voyage to the Aegean and the riches of its antique civilizations. In history, warships are seldom far behind the wakes of trading ships.

FROM OUT OF THE WEST...

Both tradition and archeology point to the Sardinians with some of their neighboring Atlantean tribes as leading protagonists in Plato's Graeco–Atlantean War. There is no "history" here, of course, since neither the Greeks nor the Atlanteans had attained the art of writing in the early 2nd millennium BC. Even the Minoans of Crete were just beginning to develop the art. Our sources are thus limited to stone and bones, folklore and legends. But there are enough of these to outline the picture.

The Sardinians had intruded into south Italy in their Copper Age. This is apparent from ruins in the "heel" of Italy's boot that correspond closely to the Sardinian nuraghi, chamber tombs and menhirs. Though little known, there are more than just a few of these; they are all about the place. The militaristic Sardinians, then, were ensconced just across the Strait of Otranto from the equally militaristic Achaean Greeks — about 60 miles away — with predictable results.

The mainland Greeks, though, were not the initial Atlantean target. The legends of Crete relate that Sardinians invaded the island during the reign of King Minos (the name of at least two Cretan kings) but were driven off by Talos, the island's great bronze, bull-headed defender.[1]

The imagery is clear enough: The victory over the invaders was attributed to the Minoans' highly developed bronze armor and weaponry, markedly more advanced than that of the Sardinians. (Notably, Talos was also the name of a marvelously gifted bronze-smith of Hellenic legend.)

The date of this Sardo–Atlantean thrust into the Aegean can easily be fixed in the chronological cross-hairs: circa 1700 BC. The palaces at Knossos and Mallia are badly damaged at this time and Phaistos is leveled by fire.[2] Most archeologists are inclined to attribute this destruction to an earthquake on the grounds that Crete is "quake prone." Maybe, but it is not a land of mega-quakes. Since it is over 40 miles from Phaistos to Mallia, only a shock of huge amplitude and extent could account for the damage of 1700 BC. There is nothing comparable in all of Crete's known history. (The devastation once called "the quake destruction of 1450 BC" was almost certainly the work of invading Achaean Greeks from the mainland.) The Phaistos fire has every mark of an intentional burn. There is evidence of fire at Knossos, and a palace at inland Monastriaki was clearly torched at the same time.

The famed Phaistos disc which dates from the 17th century BC likely commemorates the assault on Crete by Atlantean tribes. The disc has never been de-

---

1 Robert Graves, *The Greek Myths*, George Braziller Inc., N.Y. 1957, 92.m

2 Hawkes, Jacquetta, *Atlas of Ancient Archaeology*, McGraw-Hill, New York, NY, 1974, pp. 113-128.

ciphered but its glyphic message is plain. It shows pictograms of shields, plumed warriors, ships, ocean waves and grieving women — patently the story of a sea-borne invasion.

Plate II: The famous Phaistos disc, found on the island of Crete, dates from the time of the Atlantean intrusion into the Aegean and appears to tell the story of a seaborne attack on the isle by warriors with plumed helmets, the typical Atlantean gear. The obverse side of the disc bears similar glyphs.

It also shows the Sardinians were not working alone. They had allies.

A key clue on the Phaistos disc is the "feathered" headdress of the warriors etched upon it, plumage that was an emblem of terror in the Mediterranean for centuries and seems to have been standard equipment for most Atlantean affiliated warrior bands.[1] The gear is known to have been worn by at least four warlike

---

1 It is not certain whether the headdresses really were made of feathers or just look like it in the surviving art of the era. See: Sanders, N.K., *The Sea Peoples*, Thames & Hudson, London, 1987, p. 134.

tribes that anciently assailed the shores of the eastern Mediterranean: the Pele-sets, the Sicels, the Denyens and the Lycians. These tribes regularly joined with the Shardana (Sardinians), who wore horned helmets, in depredations through-out much of the second millennium BC. The logical inference here is that bands of plumed warriors, coordinating with the Shardana, were the burners of Phaistos in 1700 BC, while their Sardinian allies simultaneously assaulted Knossos on the isle's northern side.

The Sicels plainly came from Sicily, and the Denyens and Lycians, as we shall see, betray western roots as well. Representations of the plumed headdress have been found as far west as Iberia. (The Picts of old Britain were commonly por-trayed with feathered headgear although the source of this convention is not known.)

The most intriguing of these feather-crowned warriors, the Pelesets — the Philistines of Biblical fame — had a vagabond history. When encountered by the Egyptians in the 13th century BC, the Pelesets' culture had already acquired a marked Aegean veneer, indicating they had spent a protracted time along those shores. According to the Bible, they came to Palestine from Captor (Keftui), i.e., Crete. Despite the repulse of their initial thrust, then, at some point Peleset–Philistines must have sojourned awhile in Crete. But they were not Minoans, or Mycenean Greeks either.

It is not just a matter of the trademark feathered headdresses. The Philistines' political organization, a confederated system, was nothing like the Hellenic model, or the Minoan. It was, though, very like the Atlantean system as described in *Critias*.[1] Their language, though little known, was assuredly not Greek.

A number of investigators believe the Pelesets must have some relationship to the Pelasgians, the pre-Hellenic natives of Greece. Both names are derived from the same root: Pelaskoi. In the era of classical Greece there was a tribe known as the Brutti in the far southeast of Italy whose customs had marked affinity to those of the Pelasgians. Tradition has it that the Brutti were once called "Pelaskoi."

It looks very much, then, as though the Pelasgians were not quite obliterated by the Achaean invasion of Greece, circa 2000 BC. Some must have fled south to Italy — Atlantean territory — where, as the Pelesets, they became part of the piratical confederacy of Sardinian and other Atlantean tribes. (We know the Shardana had a reputation as warriors and sea raiders at least as early as the mid-second millennium.) Southern Italy, then, is the likely forward base for the Shardana–Peleset assault on Crete in 1700 BC — and a later and stronger on-slaught as well.

---

1 *Critias*, 119

THE EXPLOITS OF ATHENS

Archeology confirms the mythic testimony that the first foray of the Atlantean tribes into Crete was beaten back. The destroyed palaces were soon rebuilt, grander than before, and there is no sign of any significant change in Minoan society in the wake of the assaults of ca. 1700 BC. The Bronze Age defenders of Crete did their job.

The familiar story of the fire-breathing Cretan Bull wreaking destruction around the island is easily seen as a mythic reflection of the Atlantean attacks. The bull was reported to be a creature of Poseidon — appropriate to a seaborne intrusion and also to Atlantis which Critias says was founded by Poseidon[1]. Later, we are told, this same bull swam to the Argolid on the mainland where it spread similar havoc as the Bull of Marathon. The malevolent bovine is supposed to have killed hundreds of men on its way from the Argolid to Marathon where it was finally overcome by the Athenian hero, Theseus.

This phase of the yarn can only reflect an attack on the mainland by Sardinian warriors and their plumed allies following their raids on Crete, and supports Plato's statement that the Athenians were the ones who finally repelled the Atlanteans. Theseus is just a figure of Athens here, since he could hardly have been alive yet. The Greek myth-makers tended to roll up the glorious events and exploits of earlier generations into the lives of a few superheroes. (It is very likely true, though, that Theseus was a leader in a subsequent struggle against a later manifestation of Atlantean aggression.)

Backing up this interpretation of events are the ruins of Lerna, a sea-coast settlement in the Argolid, destroyed and abandoned approximately 1700 BC.[2] Either Lerna was brought low by the invading Atlanteans or by the Achaean Greek effort to re-capture it. The latter may be the case in light of the legendary slaying of the Lernaean Hydra by Hercules. This hydra, they say, had a hundred heads — which clearly ties it with the tradition of the *centuriae* who raided the Argolid from Lerna. Hercules' harrowing struggle to dispatch the monster implies that the Atlanteans were expelled from the town only after an extended time and with greatest difficulty.

Since the timeframe in question is pre-literate we have as much evidence as can be reasonably expected confirming the Platonic account of an attempted Atlantean conquest of the Aegean area. Athens played a leading role in turning the tide — just as the philosopher says.

Plato explains that the Greeks lacked a record of the Atlantean episode because of a natural cataclysm which afflicted Greece soon afterwards. In fact, the primary reason is simply that the Greeks had not yet learned to write. The cataclysm — even though it did occur — is just an excuse. We do not have to look far

---

1 *Critias*, 113
2 *Lerna*, Hellenic Ministry of Culture — Archaeological sites website, www.culture.gr

for evidence of this disaster: Obviously, it was the eruption of Thera in the mid 16th century BC, not long after the battles at Marathon and Lerna.

Tsunamis emanating from the Thera eruption must have done a good deal of damage along some coastal littorals in the Aegean. Just such a watery onslaught is reflected in the myth that a peevish Poseidon flooded Attica's Thriasian plain with great waves after losing his contention with Athena for possession of Athens.[1] This legendary enmity between Poseidon and Athena — though no one seems to have noticed — is an obvious mythological reflection of the Athenian conflict with Atlantis. (Poseidon was not only the reputed founder of Atlantis but also its primary god.) The sea god also contended, so the story goes, with other gods for control of various localities in the Peloponnesus, a region directly on the Atlantean invasion path. There is, then, substantial mythic backing for Plato's historical thesis.

Fragmentary memories of the Thera tidal waves seem to have survived among ancient historians. Diodorus relates that the coast of Asia Minor, directly east of Thera, suffered "pressing and grievous calamities" in the flood of Deucalion. The Parian chronicle places this event at 1529 BC, maybe a tad late but remarkably close considering the pre-literate state of the Greeks at the time. The legend of great flooding on Samothrace during Dardanus' visit to the isle might also be a reflection of the Thera event.

While Plato's narrative is but a bare bones account of a long, complex epic, he implies that the destruction of the Atlantean capital happened during the same overall historical era as the natural disaster in the Aegean — which comports with our dating of the Tore super-eruption in the mid 17th century, circa 1640 BC.

The destruction of their insular capital had to be a body blow to the whole Atlantean psyche, their religious outlook in particular, and must have left the affiliated continental tribes in something of a state of shock. But since Lusitania must have recovered within a few decades, the disaster did not mark the absolute end of the Atlantean nation. A new capital city eventually emerged in Lusitania — presumably ancient Olissipo (modern Lisbon) at the mouth of the Tagus. We know that Olissipo goes back at least to Phoenician times, almost certainly well before. Greek legend has it that the city was founded by Ulysses which would put it in the Achaean era (13th century BC). Archeology, in fact, suggests that the Tagus estuary was already a major center before 2000 BC since the concentration of Bell Beakers there is extremely heavy. Though Olissipo must have been severely damaged by the Tore eruption, it ultimately rose again. The city appears to have crept into Plato's description of Atlantis since, at one point, the sage locates a major city where the great canal, i.e., the Tagus River, "let off into the sea." At

---

1 Graves, Robert, *The Greek Myths*, George Braziller Inc., New York NY, 1957, 16c

least part of Plato's picture, then, may have been painted from descriptions post-dating the volcanic disintegration of the original Atlantean capital.

It is safe to assume that the nations of the eastern Mediterranean shed few tears over the catastrophic demise of the island Atlantis. But if people of those nations thought they were safe, they were badly mistaken.

CHAPTER 11. BLOOD AND FEATHERS

Those prone to assume the permanence of civilization are likely unacquaint-
ed with the latter 2nd millennium BC, an era of cascading catastrophe at least
as traumatic as the collapse of the Roman Empire. Before this age of chaos was
ended, virtually every society in the Mediterranean area had been shattered or
badly disrupted. Egypt alone, though battered, managed to maintain some cultural continuity.

The Atlanteans apparently had long memories, and a thirst for revenge. Following their 17th century set-backs in the Aegean area, the Atlantean tribes re-
grouped and updated their military and naval forces while mastering bronze
technology. By ca. 1400 BC they were ready to launch more successful and far
more damaging attacks on the great cities of the eastern Mediterranean. What
resulted was an almost unparalleled time of troubles.

The insignia of this Bronze Age apocalypse was a familiar one: the feathered
headdress worn by most of the Atlantean tribes — the Denyens, Pelesets, Lycians and Sicels. These and the horn-helmeted Shardana were joined at various
times and places by other tribes in a long series of depredations that brought a
Dark Age to the East Mediterranean, collapsing the Minoan, Hittite, Syrian and
Mycenaean societies.

Though a good deal is known about some of these tribes, such as the Shardana
and the Pelesets, we have only enough data on others to allow rough sketches.

Of special interest are the Lycians or Luka, infamous sea raiders in the mid-
second millennium BC who may have come from the Lusitanian Atlantis. Aside
from the similarity between "Lycian" and "Lusitani," Greek mythology holds that
Lykos, son of Poseidon and one of the Atlantides, was settled in the western Isles
of the Blest — a likely reference to Atlantis. At the beginning of the historical

record, the Lycians are identified with an area on the southern coast of Anatolia (Asia Minor) but Herodotus says they came there from Crete. Since that isle could hardly have been their original home, the statement points to the likelihood that the Lycians were involved in the dimly understood 14th century destruction of Cretan Knossos, afterwards opting for the Anatolian coast where they overwhelmed a Luvain tribe, the Termilae, and modified but did not fundamentally alter its language. There, the Lycians set up a governmental system based on the Atlantean model, i.e., a confederation of city states. Archeological support for a far western Lycian homeland can be found in the fact that the earliest alphabet used in southern Anatolia bears a striking resemblance to engravings on the Turditan Stone of southern Portugal.

Another intriguing tribe of these "Sea Peoples" (as they came to be known) was evidently Celtic and must therefore have originated in Gallic west Europe — an indicator of the wide sweep of the Atlantean confederation. The feathercrowned Denyens or Danuana (the vowels are uncertain) have a name with a distinctively Celtic ring to it. D-n is very common in Celtic names — people or places — and not usual elsewhere. A name starting or ending with such a syllable is apt to be of Celtic origin (Donegal, Dundee, Denbigh, Danube, London, e.g.). Tradition says the first Celtic invaders of the Emerald Isle were the Tuatha de (tribe of) Danaan.

Though they were no doubt around earlier, the Denyens enter history in the 14th century BC, apparently from a forward attack base in south Italy where they were in cahoots with the Shardana and the Pelesets. A tribe of "Daunians" was recorded still living in Iron Age times in the province of Apulia[1] — the same province where we find those nuraghian stone constructions. Since there are strong archeological infusions into Apulia from the south of France in the mid-second millennium BC, it appears the Denyens came to Italy from Celtic Provence, probably arriving with their Shardana allies.

BY THE BOOK

The Denyens hold a certain historic fascination since they show up in the Bible: Some of them evidently became the Israelite tribe of Dan after settling on Palestine coast circa 1200 BC.[2] Several anomalous attributes typified this tribe, including the fact they were the only seafaring Hebrews. Curiously, a number of Hebrew words appear to have been adopted from the Celtic — in particular words that would have to do with the sea or Druidic ceremonies. Some of these, which could only have been borrowed from the Denyens, are:

---

1 Pallottino, Massimo, *The Etruscans*, Indiana Univ. Press, 1975, p.47.
2 See: Sanders, N.K., *The Sea Peoples*, Thames & Hudson, NY, 1987, pp.163-64.

English	Hebrew	Irish
To divine	kasam	geasam
sorcerer	ounan	oinin
enchanter	nahhash	neas
charmer	cheber	geabhar
knowing one	iadanani	deadanan
oracle	iod	iodh
ship	gnabhara	cnabbra
bark	barichim	barc
mariner	melach	meilachoir
covenant	berit	berit
meridian sun	darom	daram

We might suspect also a connection between the Semitic god *Baal* and *Bel*, the Celtic sun god. From a distance of 3 ½ millennia, it is hard to say whether the god was borrowed by the Celts from the Semites, or vice versa — though the former looks more likely. Either way, the Denyens provide the intercultural link.

The fabled feats of the biblical Samson become comprehensible if we remember that Samson was a member of the tribe of Dan. The smaller Mediterranean folk, awed by the size and strength of some of the Celts, often referred to them as "giants." Samson, then, was something like a big brawny Irishman possessed of what seemed to the locals to be super-human strength.

The Celtic strain also helps account for the tradition that there were giants among the Philistines, of whom Goliath was only the most famous. The Philistines were affiliated with the Denyens long before both settled in Palestine, and intermarriage between these allied tribes must have been common.

THE FINAL FLAMEOUT

The shattering paroxysm that left the island Atlantis beneath the seas, ca. 1640 BC, did little to dampen the marauding instincts of the Atlantean tribes in the Mediterranean. They actually did their worst damage during a kind of Atlantean Epilogue in the 14ᵗʰ and 13ᵗʰ centuries.

The era that would ultimately end the Greek Heroic Age begins about 1375 BC with the sudden destruction of Knossos, chief city of Crete. This disaster was long assumed to be the work of Achaean Greeks from the mainland but it now established that the Achaeans took over Knossos ca. 1450 BC at the same time they overwhelmed the rest of the island. Who then, were the invaders of 1375?

The Minoan veneer of the Philistine society dictates that the tribe must have spent at least a few generations in Crete. It is all but obvious, then, that it was the Pelesets — probably assisted by the Lycians and the Shardana — who in 1375 ravaged Knossos, avenging their discomfiture of 1700 BC. Not coinciden-tally, very soon after the sack of Knossos, the earliest references to the Shardana and the Lycians begin to appear in the inscriptions of the ancient Middle East. While the Lycians and most of the Shardana soon moved on to other targets, the Pelesets chose to settle down in Crete to enjoy the fruits of conquest and soak up some Minoan culture.

The Homeric epics tell us that Crete had been ethnically factionalized by the close of the Heroic Age and that the Pelesets were among the factions. The Odys-sey contains this description of Crete's population:

> Some are Achaeans; some are Eteocretans, a proud people who claim to be the true Cretan stock. Some are Kydonians, and there are the Dorians with long, flowing hair, and the splendid Pelasgians.[1]

As noted earlier, the Pelesets were Pelasgians who settled in Atlantean south Italy to escape the Achaean conquest of Greece. After 1375, Kydonia in the far west of Crete seems to be under the control of Sardinian forces. Recent excava-tions at Kydonia (modern Khania) have uncovered strong affiliations between western Crete and Sardinia/south Italy in late Minoan times — not just trade connections but actually colonization from the west. And Kydonia replaces Knossos as Crete's premier city.

Herodotus remarks that Crete was once populated by "barbarians," which can only mean people who were neither Greeks nor Minoans. After 1375, the isle's culture, though still more Aegean than anything else, betrays marked alien influence — not Minoan, not Hellenic.

Even the archeology of the Greek mainland supports the idea of an invasion of Crete from the west. In the 14th century BC, the mainland cities, which had been unfortified, begin to construct thick protective walls, a policy change that could only mean a dangerous new aggressive force had entered the geopolitics of the Aegean.

The apprehensions of the Achaean mainlanders were justified soon enough. In the late 13th century BC, the militant multi-tribal coalition known collectively as the Sea Peoples, rampaged full force onto the Mediterranean stage. With fire and sword they dispensed unrelieved havoc along the coasts of the Aegean, Asia Minor, Cyprus, the Levant and Egypt itself. The attacks were so vehement, wide-spread and destructive that the ensuing Dark Age lasted up to four hundred years in some sectors.

This martial *volkwanderung* involved up to ten tribes acting in concert. Thanks to Egyptian chroniclers, their names have been preserved. Among them were sev-

---

1 Homer, *The Odyssey*, Book XIX, St. 171-175.

eral old Atlantean tribes. By the mid-14th century, the Denyens were working out of a base in southern Anatolia around Adana. The Lycians, to their west on the same coast, were already occupying themselves with piratical raids on Cyprus and the Levant. The Pelesets and Shandana, as already mentioned, had taken control of parts of southern Italy and most of Crete. The Sicels evidently still retained Sicily as their main base of operations.

Aside from these familiar tribal names, there are some additions.

The Egyptians' "Tursha" can be identified with the Tursonoi (Etruscans) of west-central Italy,[1] a conclusion bolstered by the know presence in historical times of Etruscan pirates on the Aegean isle of Lemnos. Most obviously, these pirates must have been the remnants of Etruscan marauders running with the Sea Peoples in the late second millennium.

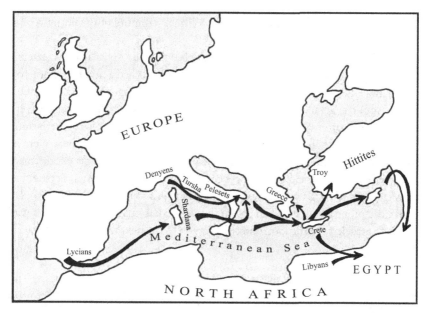

Fig.15. The map illustrates the depredations of the Sea Peoples, most of which were old Atlantean Empire tribes, in the 14th and 13th centuries BC. Their opening thrust into the eastern Mediterranean was directed at Knossos, ca. 1375. After establishing a base in Crete, the Sea Peoples launched assaults against Cyprus, Egypt (ca. 1220) and the Hittites (who were attacked by northern enemies at the same time). The Sea Peoples ravaged almost all of Greece except Athens around 1200 BC, then swept through the Levant to mount another strike on Egypt (ca. 1186) but were again defeated there. In time, the remnants of the Sea Peoples were slowly absorbed into surrounding cultures.

---

1 Some think the Tursha were the ancestors of the Etruscans, but they have probably got it backwards. See section on Etruscan origins.

The Libyans (perhaps composed of more than one tribe) were among the Mediterranean marauders. The "Ekwesh" may have been war-like Achaean Greeks (from eastern Crete?) who joined in the melee for fun and profit.

EGYPT STANDS ALONE

Of all the east Mediterranean states, only Egypt was able to hold back the torrent of the Sea Peoples. The Pharaoh Mereptah repulsed their attack from Libya ca. 1220 BC but they were not finally defeated until about 1186 by Rameses III. Rameses crushed the invaders on both land and sea and thoughtfully provided historians with a detailed record of his successes — including vivid battle depictions on the Medinet Habu reliefs.

In between these two defeats though, the swords of the Sea People swept through the Mediterranean littoral like scythes through a wheat field. Nearly every coastal city was sacked. The socio-political structure of the entire region was virtually demolished.

Most historians have been loath to assign the fall of the Achaean (Mycenaean) civilization to the raids of the Sea Peoples and have hatched a number of not-too-convincing alternative scenarios: civil strife, earthquakes, etc. The fact is, though, that most of the great Achaean citadels — Pylos, Mycenae, Gla, Tiryns — were destroyed soon after 1200 BC, at the exact apex of the Sea Peoples depredations. The linear B tablets from the last days of Pylos show that officials there were in dread of a sea-borne attack.[1] Since the Sea Peoples were then *the* extant maritime threat, they are the obvious suspects in this historic mayhem. It is true that Greece shows few signs of foreign occupation ca. 1200 BC, but the Sea Peoples were more prone to raiding than colonizing. Their habitual modus operandi was simply to attack, take the loot, and then run on to the next target.

THE TALE OF TROY

Not all the tribes that ravaged the Aegean were of Atlantean heritage. The most famous historic enemies of the Achaean Greeks were, of course, the Trojans, who would have been prone to join any assault on the Greek lands. The context of the legendary Trojan War has long been argued but there is one scenario that makes a good deal of sense.

About 1225 BC, some Achaean cities, including Athens and Mycenae, were attacked though their citadels did not fall. Most of the Sea Peoples were then occupied with an assault on Egypt, but, with the help of Troy, those still in the Aegean would have been able to mount attacks and raids on the Greek mainland. Some Hellenic women must have been among the valuables carried off in these forays. Ergo, the tale of the abduction of Helen. The Achaeans countered with the assault on Troy, capturing and burning the city after a long siege.

---

1 *Wonderous Realms of the Aegean*, Dale Brown, Ed., Time-Life Books, Alexandria VA, 1993, p.142.

This scenario puts the fall of Troy VIIa — obviously the victim of an invading army — around 1215 BC, very close to the date (1209) given by the Parian marbles. The most popular traditional date, 1184 BC, cannot be right since the Achaeans could not possibly have mounted the siege against Troy after the destructions of 1200 BC. (Archeology cannot settle the dispute over the year of the fall since it lacks the needed degree of chronological exactitude.)

Indicators of a coalition between the Atlantean Sea People and the tribes of the Troad are several. Homer relates that contingents of Lycians and Pelasgians (Lukka and Pelesets) fought beside the defenders in the Trojan War.[1] One of the more obscure tribes in the Sea Peoples' assault on Egypt, ca. 1186 BC, was the Tjerker, who can be identified with the Teurci of the Troad. Moreover, the Trojans who survived the flames of dying Troy are reported to have fled to Tuscany, the land of the Tursonoi, one of the original Sea Peoples.

But the Greek victory at Troy was as ephemeral as Hannibal's triumphs over the Romans. About 1200 BC, the Sea People, with their accumulated allies, returned to strike Greece again — this time with fatal effect. The weakened Mycenaean society folded under this renewed assault. Of the Achaean cities, only Athens survived — a lone last haven for refugees, overlooking the wreckage of a once great Bronze Age civilization. The Hellenic genius would not stir again for nearly four centuries.

The ultimate denouement of the Sea Peoples' intrusion into the eastern Mediterranean was, then, barely short of apocalyptic: Oblivion enveloped almost everything. The Aegean, Hittite, and Levant societies all went up in flames. At the last, the old Atlantean tribes were beaten down and eventually absorbed by their neighbors. About the only memento of it all at the end of the second millennium was a name on the map, "Palestine" — given to the land where the Pelesets settled after their defeat by Egypt's Rameses III. The Pelesets (as the Philistines) managed to survive as an ethnic entity for a few centuries more before being overrun by greater Middle Eastern powers.

Academic Follies

The prevailing, though not unanimous, view in academe holds that the Shardana, Sicels and Tursonoi were native east Mediterranean tribes that moved into the west after their defeat at the mouth of the Nile and gave their names to the lands that they settled (Sardinia, Sicily, and Etruria.)

The theory is hard to take seriously.

First off, there is no trace of these peoples in the eastern Mediterranean, nor any feasible homelands for them, prior to the middle of the second millennium BC. Neither is there any evidence that Sardinia or Etruria was invaded or subjugated in the wake of the Sea Peoples' easterly assaults. Sicily had been overwhelmed by

---

1 *Iliad*, Book 2, 840 & 875.

the Sikels, but centuries prior to Egypt's battles with the Sea Peoples, and assuredly not from the east. The tradition is strong that the Sikels intruded into Sicily from south Italy. Thucydides says so[1] and so does archeology.

Statue menhirs in southern Corsica, just across the strait from Sardinia, depict warriors fitted out like the Shardana who invaded Egypt, and these menhirs pre-date the wanderings of the Sea Peoples. Moreover, the notion that the Shardana, after being crushed by Pharaoh Rameses III, could have achieved a conquest of the great island of Sardinia borders on silliness.

As for the Etruscans (Tursonoi), the view is steadily growing that they were in Italy centuries before their first recorded encounter with the Egyptians (13th century BC), and therefore could hardly have been refugees from Lydia or the fall of Troy as some have hypothesized. (More on these intriguing folk shortly.)

The only solution to the mystery of the Sea Peoples that makes sense is the obvious one: They were a conglomerate of western Mediterranean folk, mostly of Atlantean heritage or affiliation, who were joined in their escapades by a few opportunistic east Mediterranean tribes.

By the end of the Dark Age, only fragments of this ancient story lingered in the Mediterranean memory: There had been a mighty struggle with a coalition headed by an Atlantic Island power; this isle had been lost in a cataclysm and there had been a corresponding disaster in the Aegean (Thera); the dauntless Athenians had once repelled the invaders (ca. 1700 BC) and alone had held against the later attacks of ca. 1200 BC, providing a haven for refugees of the wars.

Actually, the Athenian Theseus appears to have delivered one other blow against the Atlantean enemy. The common notion that the Minotaur tale reflects the Achaean seizure of Crete in 1450 BC suffers from real problems. First off, the Minoan society was not an aggressive one, making it hard to believe that the Minoans extorted Athenian youths for sacrifice. Much more likely, the Atlantean conquerors of Knossos (1375 BC) levied the infamous tribute. Secondly, the Parian chronology firmly places Theseus in the early 13th century BC, not the 15th.[2] The final destruction of Knossos as a populated center did not occur until about 1300 BC. This is a much more feasible date for Theseus' famous retaliatory raid. The expedition against the Minotaur was just a late episode in Athens' lengthy struggle against the Atlantean tribes.

ECHOES IN TIME

Undeniably, the chief legacy of the Atlantean intrusion into the Mediterranean was one of chaos and destruction. But few historical events are unrelentingly negative.

The tradition that Atlantis possessed a relatively advanced technology is not entirely fabulous. The Atlanteans did not have airships or laser weapons, but they

---

1 Thucydides, *History of the Peloponnesian War*, Book Six, 2.
2 Forsdyke, John, *Greece Before Homer*, W.W. Norton Co., NY, 1964, p.55.

did possess some prodigious engineering capabilities. Long before any others, they were moving massive blocks of stone over extended distances. The Egyptians did not start building their pyramids until well after the Atlanteans had penetrated the Mediterranean basin in the early 3rd millennium BC. The chronology, then, suggests that the Egyptians picked up the fundamentals of megalithic engineering from the western intruders — though the Nile dwellers eventually carries the art to a higher level.

Beyond question, the Atlanteans were the master mariners of their time. Is it just coincidence that the greatest sea-faring nation of its age, Phoenicia, arose adjacent to the locale settled by the tribe of Dan, the Denyens? More likely, the Phoenicians learned their maritime expertise and navigational lore about the far Atlantic west from the Denyens. How else to explain the Phoenician fascination with such remote and distant shores?

The astronomical orientation of Stonehenge and many other sites demonstrates that the Atlanteans were expert astronomers, on a par perhaps with the star-obsessed Babylonians. The metalwork in copper, gold and bronze of such Atlantean locales as Sardinia and Wessex (in southern Britain) is remarkably proficient for its time and some the artistry is truly extraordinary.

But the most important impact of the Atlanteans on western civilization was probably quite indirect, coming by way of those enigmatic Etruscans.

The origins of these unique people remain a mystery despite intensive study by prehistorians. The Etruscan language is but dimly known, but it is not Indo–European and so must have been intrusive to Italy which was surely overwhelmed by the Indo–Europeans well before 2000 BC. The Etruscans culture was an amalgam of eastern and western influences, further confusing the question of origins. While some archeologists favor an east Mediterranean genesis, there is no language in that region related to the Etruscans' tongue. More likely, they came from the west as one of the Atlanto–Lusitanian tribes. The Rinaldone copper culture of Tuscany flowered just after the Bell Beaker folk intruded there, and the Rinaldones had very close trade and cultural contacts with Iberia. No break is found in the continuity of Tuscan Italy's archeology from then to historic times. A strongly maritime people, the Etruscans (Tursonoi) can be seen as true offshoots of the Atlantean root. We know that their basic political structure was Atlantean, that is, a federation of city-states — just like the Philistines. As one of the Sea Peoples intruding into the eastern Mediterranean, the Etruscans, of course, came increasingly under "orientalizing" cultural feedback from that area.

Except for the obscure Lusitanian Turditani, who were finally crushed by Rome in the 2nd century BC, the Etruscans survived as an ethnic entity longer than any other Atlantean tribe — well into the 4th century BC. They were the last Atlanteans of which we have much knowledge. What is most significant, the bulk of Roman culture, which one day would dominate the Western world, was derived from the Etruscans — social and political organization, religion, arts, engineering, and architecture. The fact that they viewed the Etruscans as a little decadent, too fond of luxury and ease, did not deter the Romans from wholesale imitation of Etrurian ways.[1] Indirectly, by way of Rome, the whole of Western civilization owes much of its character to the Etruscan Atlanteans. We are in many ways, as many have long suspected, heirs of Lost Atlantis.

Whatever light the Atlanteans may have bestowed on the East, the most enduring was a chapter of west European history: the Atlantis legend itself. If it was not carried to Egypt prior to 1200 BC, the Sea People surely told the tale on the Nile. In their final battle with the Atlantean tribes, the Egyptians took thousands of prisoners — portrayed on the Medinet reliefs — most of whom were made slaves. Given the language differences, what the Egyptians got from their captives may not have been highly accurate but the Nile scribes got the essence of it down on papyrus.

The wonder is not that the details of the story became obscure. The wonder is that the tale survived at all in the maelstrom of the second millennium BC. The priests of Sais were right when they told Solon that they alone had the key to antiquity, because only the Egyptian chronicles survived the long plague of warfare.

---

1 Plato says in *Critias* that the Gods destroyed the Atlanteans because they lost their pristine character and became "debased."

CHAPTER 12. THE ATLANTIC CONNECTION

Devotees of Atlantis have always cited as one of their supporting arguments the curious similarities between the low latitude Amerindian civilization and those of the Mediterranean. Actually, many Atlantis enthusiasts take the view that these New World societies were merely reflections of the Atlantean, or even Atlantean colonies.

At the opposite end of the debate is a large body orthodox archeologists and historians who insist there was no connection at all between the early American cultural centers and those of the Old World. There is though, a growing cluster of moderates who allow for sporadic contacts between the eastern and western hemispheres which may have been responsible for some features of the Native American high cultures.

We have found that despite some mild distortions, the Atlantis story is substantially true. There was a real Atlantis, marine oriented, that dominated the bulk of the great megalithic culture complex before and into the Bronze Age. As noted in Chapter 6, persuasive proofs exist that the northern wing of the Atlantean empire, the Celtic wing, did make contact with the northeastern North America. The clear Celtic influence found in certain Native American languages thereabouts and some of Barry Fell's Ogham inscriptions are difficult to discount.

There are also a significant number of megalithic constructions on the eastern coast of North America that are almost certainly related to their counterparts on the western coast of Europe. The most famous of these is the Mystery Hill site in New Hampshire, a complex of stone chambers and henge stones with an evident astronomical orientation, strikingly similar to some megalithic structures in Europe. Carbon dates from the site indicate that it cannot be of colonial vintage, as some have argued. Fell maintained that inscriptions found at Mystery Hill are Celtic Ogham and Celtiberian.[1]

Other Megalithic constructions have been found on the American east coast, including dolmens and tholoi, and even stone circles, all too similar to their trans-Atlantic counterparts to be results of chance. Copper and Bronze artifacts, virtually identical with Celtiberian types, have also been uncovered in New England.

All in all, the case for Celtic contacts with America verges on the overwhelming. Indeed, "contacts" is too weak a word. The evidence is sufficient to support the notion that Atlantean Celts actually planted small colonies on the eastern shores of what is now the United States of America. These colonies, though transient in nature, probably were able to maintain contacts with — and loyalties to — their trans-Atlantic homelands for at least a few generations before communications broke down and fatal isolation settled in. So Plato looks to be correct when he states that the Atlanteans ruled over parts of "the opposite continent" (*Timaeus* 25).

But this penetration of North America via the high latitudes does not settle the question of whether the low latitude civilizations of the New World were entirely indigenous or were nurtured by megalithic influences from Europe. And if these cultures were not altogether home-grown, did the alien navigators make direct contact with Meso-America? Or were the American high cultures merely influenced in an indirect way, via the gradual transmission of certain arts and techniques from the northeast United States to warmer climates where they blossomed more brilliantly?

The latter possibility may not be outlandish, but one is hard-pressed to find much evidence to support it. The famous Mound Cultures of the Ohio and Mississippi valleys, for instance, are much too late in time to provide any such transmission link.

If the Old World affected the flowering of civilization in the New, the odds are that direct maritime contacts with Meso-America were involved. Such voyages can no longer be dismissed with a sniff and a wave of the hand. Not in light of the wide-ranging, maritime Bronze Age civilization we have found in the North Atlantic. And especially if we consider Atlantean colonization of the widely extended Azores in the 2nd millennium BC. This occupation, even though temporary, put daring sailors with seaworthy ships within marginal sailing distance of the West Indies.

The initial east-to-west transit, or transits, could have been either purposeful or accidental. A ship disabled in Azorean waters would nearly always be carried by the Canary Current directly to the region that gave rise to the New World civilization.

---

1 Barry Fell, *America B.C.*, New York, Quadrangle Book Co., 1976, pp.81-92.

Or, if megalithic navigators reached New England, what is the say that some of them did not continue to explore down the American east coast until they reached the Caribbean? It seems that discovery of Meso-America by the sailors of pre-classic times was not all that unlikely.

But did it happen? It's a complex question, this argument about early contacts between the hemispheres, so an overview of the parameters would not be out of order.

DIFFUSIONISM 101

The New World and the Old did not sprout civilizations at just the same time. Still, the timing is a little too close to be coincidental if no contact between the two is allowed. It was less than a couple millennia after the Egyptian and Sumerian societies began to flower that very similar things began to happen in Mexico and the Andes. If the Americas had always been isolated from the rising cultures of the Old World would this have happened?

True, there were basic differences between the ancient civilizations of the two hemispheres. In particular, the food crops, with a few possible exceptions, were divergent. Yet both worlds grew and wove cotton. There is no provable relationship between the Meso-American writing systems and those of the Old World. Still, the function of the Mexic hieroglyphics, part pictorial and part phonic, is the same as the ancient Mediterranean glyphs, and even a few of the signs are similar.

The architectural parallels are striking. The step pyramids of the Americas are markedly like the ziggurats of the Near East; and a particularly intriguing link between the two can be found in northwest Sardinia at Monte d' Accoddi. A truncated step pyramid there features a ramp leading up one side to a ceremonial platform at the top,[1] a design so similar to the Mexic pyramids that chance coincidence can be ruled out. Monte d' Accoddi, which dates from the latter 3rd millennium BC, seems to have been a ceremonial center for much of the western Mediterranean, if not the entire Atlantean society.

Then, too, the Native Americans developed astronomy and even a kind of astrology quite reminiscent of the Near East. They built paved roads even though they had no draft animals to pull wagons or chariots. Both the Americans and the Mediterranean's made pottery and practiced irrigation. Both also mastered the art of smelting and casting gold, silver, and copper. All these techniques (and some others to be noted later) were undiscovered or undeveloped at the time of the Pleistocene migrations into America. It follows, then, that such arts must have been introduced after the submergence of the Bering and Atlantican land bridges or else were evolved independently.

---

1 See: Service, Alastair, & Bradbury, Jean, *Megaliths and their Mysteries*, MacMillan Publishing, NY, 1979, pp.109-113; Also note: *Monte d' Accoddi*, Italian Institute for Experimental Archaeology website, cc-486.lettere.unige.it/iias/mtaccodi.htm.

Evidence exists that the Amerindians were, in a few locales, practicing agriculture of a primitive type long before the megalithic Atlanteans took to the sea lanes. Tentative indicators of agricultural activity — the cultivation of squash, chili peppers and avocados — have been uncovered in the Tehuacan Valley of central Mexico and carbon dated to ca. 5000 BC.[1] Recent discoveries in the Andes suggest incipient agriculture was developing there even earlier. It seems, then, that the concept of farming was not a gift to the New World from the Atlanteans — not if we define the Atlantean era as essentially the second and third millennia BC. We have seen, though, that there were sporadic earlier contacts, in particular by the Red Paint people who were roving widely in the era when primitive agriculture was developing. Thus there is some chance that the Red Paint mariners could have introduced the notion of crop growing to the Americas even though they were not primarily agricultural folks.

On balance, indigenous innovation looks to be more likely, but even if farming was devised by the American natives on their own, it does not follow that all aspects of the Amerindian civilizations can be explained in the same way. Agriculture does not necessarily lead inevitably to such arts as astronomy and metallurgy. There are still cultures on this planet that raise crops but do not cast metals or build monumental stone structures. It is easily credible to postulate that some post-agricultural advances were the result of trans-oceanic influences.

Fact is, there is an almost inexplicable cultural breakthrough to the west of the Yucatan peninsula about the time of the peak Atlantean activity. The whole Olmec civilization, the earliest in North America, and (depending on the definition of civilization) maybe the earliest in the New World, appears abruptly in the 15th century BC and soon develops to its zenith about 1200 BC.

THE ENIGMATIC OLMECS

The Olmec culture is conceded by many archaeologists to be intrusive in character. This conclusion, as Michael Coe noted in *America's First Civilization*, has shaken the notion of gradual self-evolution of the Native American societies.[2] The appearance of the highly organized, artistic, monument-building Olmecs on the east coast of Mexico dovetails with the native Mexic legends recorded by Father Sahagan. These tell of immigrant people arriving from across the waters in ancient times, landing at Vera Cruz and working their way south. The interlopers included "wise men" who carried with them "all the writings, the books, the paintings" of their culture.[3] They were bearers of the arts and sciences of civilization.

---

1 Coe, Michael D., *Mexico* (3rd Edition), Thames & Hudson, New York NY, 1984, pp.38-39.

2 Coe, Michael D., *America's First Civilization*, American Heritage Publishing, NY, 1968, p.37.

3 Ibid., pp. 117-18.

The legend of this landing is consistent with the archeology of the Olmecs whose culture was first manifested in the vicinity of Vera Cruz. The tradition is plainly akin to the tale of the bearded white god Quetzalcoatl, the deity of learning and knowledge whose promised return from across the seas so facilitated Cortez's conquest of Mexico. Though the tale of Quetzalcoatl cannot be exactly dated, it is clearly of ancient vintage, certainly extending deep into Mayan times and very plausibly back to the Olmec era.

The Quetzalcoatl legend aside, the traditions reported by Father Sahagan are easily seen as referring to an expedition by Atlantean refugees or explorers in Olmec times. Such an early Atlantean contact could have been the means by which metal-working, stone construction, astronomy, and certain religious concepts were introduced into the Mexic world. And the source of writing as well. (There is a certain kinship between some of the Mayan and some of the early Cretan glyphs.) The oldest known example of writing in the New World, dating to the tenth century BC, was uncovered recently (2006) in the San Lorenzo area of Olmec territory.

The similarity of some techniques utilized by Americans and early Mediterranean people is almost impossible to lay at the door of parallel development. Cyrus Gordon made some incisive observations on this score in his book *Before Columbus*. He pointed to two quite sophisticated technologies practiced on both sides of the ancient Atlantic: the *cire perdue* method of casting metals and the weaving of cotton fabrics.

In the cire perdue, or "lost wax" process, a model of the figure is made in wax and coated with clay. The mold is heated so that the wax melts and runs out. Molten metal is then poured into the empty cavity and the clay is chipped away after the metal has cooled. The process is complex enough to constitute an almost irrefutable proof of trans-Atlantic diffusion.

On the point of cotton weaving, Gordon has this to say:

> For the weaving of cotton, the plant not only must be cultivated, but someone has to spin the thread from the boll. The Old and New World looms are remarkably similar in design and the methods of weaving were strikingly alike in the Eastern and Western Hemispheres.[1]

Systematic cotton growing developed in Meso-America around the 3500 BC, a few hundred years later than in the Middle East — though utilization of wild cotton doubtless goes back centuries earlier in both hemispheres. Strange to say, the cultivated cotton of the Americas has thirteen large chromosomes and thirteen small chromosomes, and therefore looks to be a hybrid of wild cottons of the New World and the Old. Cotton is a pretty fair natural traveler but cannot cross whole oceans unless it is somehow carried or rafted. Yet the evidence is that the hybridization of American cotton occurred long before there was any possibility

---

1 Cyrus H. Gordon, *Before Columbus*, Crown Publishers Inc., New York, NY, 1971, p.145.

of trans-oceanic crossings by humans in the tropic or sub-tropic zones. The only proffered explanation of the mystery, however unlikely, hypothesizes that there might have one been a variety of Old World cotton in the Americas that subsequently went extinct.)

The hybrid nature of American cotton has been a known conundrum for decades but has long since been quietly consigned to the "Insoluble Enigmas" category. The context of Geopulsation Theory, though, offers a possible solution to the puzzle via the periodic alterations of the mid-Atlantic Ridge.

The seeds of wild cotton have enough buoyancy and resistance to salt water to be carried by ocean currents for five hundred to perhaps a thousand miles without loss of viability.[1] But it is a good 1,600 miles across the Atlantic from west Africa to the eastern hump of Brazil. The transfer of wild cotton seeds between these locales would be implausible except for one factor: the sharp rise of the Atlantic Ridge in the latter half of the glacial stages. The lateral compression of the ridge system (due to planetary spin deceleration) would have raised Saint Paul's and Saint Peter's Rocks by well over 1,000 meters. Now little more that shoals, they would then have comprised several large islands, some over twenty miles long and several hundred square miles in area. With these fertile way stations, the trans-oceanic migration of wild cotton becomes easily feasible via the ocean currents. Transfer by birds seems unlikely since birds will not touch cotton bolls.[2]

But what is most significant here is not that cotton was grown for fabric in both the Americas and the Old World; rather it is the striking coincidence of the weaving technologies. The loom is, after all, a complex machine, and it strains credibility to presume that virtually identical models were independently developed almost simultaneously oceans apart. Particularly, the vertical frame loom with two warp beams used by the Incas was a nearly perfect match for the looms used in Egypt in the second millennium BC.

Since cotton is a subtropical plant, the parallels strongly support, even if they do not absolutely prove, direct connections between the Mediterranean zone and Meso-America. There are, though, additional bits of data that become very nearly conclusive on the question. Consider this: The Quiche Maya, in their sacred book, the Popul Vuh, refer to their homeland as a paradise where Black and White people lived in peace until the god Hurakan (Hurricane) became angry and flooded the earth. The reference to Blacks is startling since there were none native to the Americas.

In addition to the many bearded images found in ancient Mexic Indian art, there are some that are emphatically Afroid. The only ready explanation of these representations seems to be that Mediterranean or Atlantean ships with Black

---

1 S.C. Stephens, in *Man Across the Sea*, University of Texas Press, 1976, p.406.
2 Gordon, Syrups H., *Before Columbus*, Crown Publishers Inc., New York, NY, 1971, p.145.

crew members reached the New World long before Columbus. There is more likelihood, obviously, that Mediterranean vessels would carry such crewmen than ships from the more northerly latitudes.

There are two cultural practices that are persuasive on the question of low latitude trans-Atlantic contacts: mummification and trephination.

Mummification, of course, is popularly associated with the Egyptians, but it was also widely practiced by the Canary Islanders (off northwest Africa) and among the Incas. Since all these practitioners were in the lower latitudes and since mummification was not practiced in more northerly climes, the implication favors lower latitude Atlantic contacts.

Equally illumining is the fact that trephination was practiced on both sides of the Atlantic. Trephination involves cutting a small disk from the skull of a living person, perhaps as a method of allowing evil spirits an escape route from the mind of the tormented. The real trouble, of course, was usually psychiatric in nature, or headaches or epilepsy. (Oddly, most of the patients survived the operation, and sometimes it even seems to have worked.) This early surgical procedure is known from Neolithic times in west Europe but was especially popular in the Chalcolithic era (roughly the millennium before 1800 BC). Trephination shows up in the Andean cultures about the mid-second millennium BC, the same time as several other signs of early trans-Atlantic contacts. Conjectures that all this is just "coincidental" are scarcely convincing — especially since the technique was so widespread among the maritime Beaker Folk. Inasmuch as trephination was unknown north of the Rio Grande, the southern route again provides the obvious connection.

A similar point can be made about the construction of reed boats which were built in North Africa and Meso-America but not in more northerly climates. Here is another complex technical development that could not have been transmitted via Atlantica but must have traveled through warmer latitudes.

Lately, the isolationists' position has been rocked further by discovery of tobacco and cocaine residues in some of the mummies of ancient Egypt.[1] (The find has been largely ignored by scholastics on the grounds it just can't be so.) These commodities are derived from American plants that did not occur in the Old World. Further, they are tropical/subtropical in nature and thus were surely transported via the low latitudes.

ON THE BANKS OF THE CHATTAHOOCHEE

There are two intriguing archeological finds from the southeastern United States that are persuasive on the broad issue of early low latitude trans-Atlantic contacts. Both sites probably date from the first millennium BC, so they do not bear directly on whether some features of the American high cultures were

---

1 F. Parsche, S. Balabanove & W. Pirsig, "Drugs in Ancient Populations," *The Lancet*, Feb 20, 1993, p.503.

spawned by European influences. The Olmecs were on the road to civilization well before they could have been impacted from either site. Even so, the Metcalf Stone and Bat Creek finds testify to surprisingly early navigational prowess.

Both of these antiquities were uncovered, barely 200 miles apart, near the Chattahoochee River in Georgia. The Metcalf Stone has signs in common with both Phoenician and Cretan scripts, and seems to be older than the Bat Creek tablet. The latter, from an ancient Amerindian grave, betrays what Gordon saw as an early Hebrew (or Canaanite) script, similar to Phoenician.[1] A possible source of both inscriptions might well be Gades, the Phoenician colony in southwest Iberia that dates back to ca. 1100 BC.

The now scattered (almost extinct) tribe that once occupied the area where the Metcalf Stone was found were the Yuchis who practiced an eight-day festival starting on the full moon of the harvest month, during which they lived in booths and nurtured a sacred fire. A similar ceremony is described in the Bible (Leviticus 23), and is still practiced in modified form by the Jews. Among the earliest known inhabitants of the Bat Creek area were a vague conglomerate known as Melungeons, whose origin is now beyond any certain diagnosis but is clearly disparate and atypical.

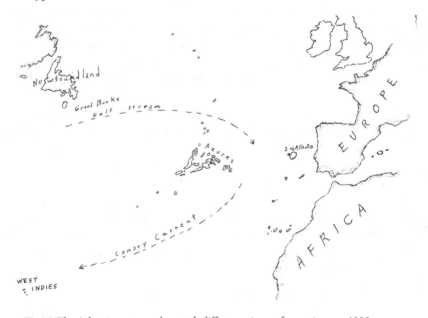

Fig.16: The Atlantic presented a much different picture for navigators 4000 years ago. Instead of nine small dots on the map, the Azores *were sprawling archipelago in mid-ocean that greatly facilitated the exploration of Meso-America.*

---

1 Gordon, Cyrus., *Before Columbus*, Crown Publishers, New York, NY, 1974, p.182.

The Chattahoochee finds lend further credibility to the even older Grave Creek Stone from West Virginia as well as the several other indicators of Euro-American contacts in the first and second millennia BC.

But there are more antiquated and more mysterious archeological surprises to ponder.

An ancient pottery style called *Chassey*, popular in west Europe in the 4th millennium BC (and a few centuries before and after), is closely duplicated in low-latitude America. These burnished, round-based pots were sometimes decorated with triangular and diamond-shaped hatching. In Ecuador, these same motifs have been found on similarly shaped pottery, in horizontal zones, with defining lines incised on the clay before firing, exactly as in western Europe.[1]

Pottery convergences like these are commonly seen by archeologists as solid proof of cultural contact. It may not be coincidental that the earliest known New World village, Caral (2600 BC), is found just to the south of Equator. Since ships and navigation in the 4th millennium were still in a developmental phase, these curious parallels may not indicate premeditated voyages. At the least, though, some ships carrying Chassey pots — seen as worthy of emulation by American potters — must have been storm-swept across the Atlantic to American shores.

Any vessels inadvertently carried by east winds and currents to the New World, of course, would have found it next to impossible to make their way back to their distant homelands. Nevertheless, the fact that this kind of thing evidently happened indicates that trading ships were plying deep Atlantic waters well before 3000 BC. These happenstance voyages help to establish the reality of a busy Atlantic maritime culture very early — even before the Bell Beaker era.

Sail On!

To professional archeologists — nearly all of whom fall into the category of "landlubbers" — the weighty evidence for ancient transoceanic voyages is more than a little flummoxing. But to a maritime mind, the geographic position of the Azores in the mid-Atlantic represents an obvious jumping off place to the Americas — so obvious that any seafaring man would think it implausible that Bronze Age navigators from the archipelago did not reach the Americas in due course. The enigma of what lay beyond the western horizon would have been nearly impossible to ignore. And once the Azores were occupied, fortune favored voyages to America since mariners were then astride the Canary Current, an oceanic conveyor belt to the West Indies. Those isles lie less than 1,000 miles from some then-emergent seamounts southwest of the Azores. A venture too far, a chance gale, a lost sail — and a landfall in the New World would have been realized.

Prior to 2000 BC, any landings on American shores must have been chance one-way trips rather than true exploratory ventures; so historically, they would

---

1 *Man Across the Sea*, Carroll J. Riley, et al., eds., University of Texas Press, Austin, TX, 1976, p. 269-270.

have been largely meaningless. Eventually, though, one such errant voyager could have managed a return trip home, carrying with him word of lands to the west.

And another prospect exists.

Atlantic navigators had sailed Newfoundland's waters and harvested the swarming fisheries of the Grand Banks very early — beginning actually with the Red Paint mariners. By the 2nd millennium BC, they must have worked their way down to Cape Cod, where the strong flow of the Gulf Stream becomes adverse to further southward probes — the same factor that stalled the small-sailed Viking ships 3,000 years later. The dauntless maritime spirit of the Atlantean age assures that this navigational challenge would not have gone unanswered for long.

But the situation called for a touch of genius.

Let us put ourselves in the place of a Bronze Age sea captain mulling the problem in the Azores. He has heard of a westward flowing current (the Canary) south of the Azores. A bizarre notion strikes his mind. Might it be feasible to follow this current west, then pick up the northward current that flows along the North American east coast? Could it be, indeed, that it is all the same current, that the westward flow turns north along the coast? If so, the whole North American shoreline could be readily explored. After restocking in Newfoundland, the trip home would be a breeze.

It is a startling conception, this, one that his nervous crewman suggest is tantamount to spitting in the face of fate. But the old sea dog is insistent. It is summer; the skies are clear with the North Star plainly visible almost every night. Further, the captain argues, if they do not make landfall after three or four weeks, they can simply swing north into the returning Gulf Stream flow. He mentions, too, that they can net a handy profit trading craft goods for the timber and smoked fish of the Newfoundlanders.

Reluctantly, the crew acquiesces. After all, the Old Man has survived many years on the high seas; he probably knows what he's doing. Besides, it would be quite a feat at that, one sure to leave the homefolks with mouths agape.

The ship heads southwest, then west. The naked horizon is daunting, but the sun and the stars say our paleo-mariners are on course. Day after day, they ply the endless expanse until, many days out, they espy a palm-topped hill some miles to the portside. They have drifted slightly south of their intended course and what they see is one of the Bahama islands. Like Columbus, millennia later, they have run smack into the West Indies.

If some such voyage took place ca. the 17th century BC, a feat well within the range of feasibility, exploration of the whole West Indian archipelago would have followed in a matter of decades — and evidently did.

In the shallows of the Bahamas, a number of curiously regular subsurface rock formations have been discovered by divers or spotted from the air. The best know is on the isle of Bimini — a stone causeway laid out in a fashion that looks suspiciously unlike a work of nature. The pro forma explanation, that these are just "beach rocks," is less than convincing because of their strikingly symmetrical arrangement. The "Bimini Road," as it is sometimes called, is perfectly straight for about a thousand meters, then curves into a neat 90 degree bend. It is not at all probable that the layout actually represents any kind of "road." Much more likely, it served as a harbor breakwater at a time when the sea was a few meters lower than today. Could this be a structure built by late megalithic colonists from the east, thousands of years ago?

The ongoing geological breakdown of the Azores must have caused sporadic evacuations from those islands around the mid-second millennium BC. Presumably, most of the quake-weary refugees opted for Lusitania or the Canaries, or various domains of the Sea Peoples around the Mediterranean. But not all necessarily fled eastward. Aware of the idyllic isles in the Caribbean, some headed for the western horizon. There is a real prospect that Bimini was an outpost of the late Atlantean society.

If so, it would explain a great many things, including the Quetzalcoatl legend. Bimini would have been an ideal base for exploratory expeditions to the shores of Mexico, making contact with the Olmecs and transmitting some of the Atlanteans' technical facility to the ancient Americas — including their remarkable techniques for moving heavy stone blocks. As the Azores are within easy sailing distance of North Africa, some Atlantean ships may easily have had Black crewmen, accounting for the otherwise baffling depictions of Blacks in pre-Columbian art. African contacts would also explain the reed boat technology of the New World.

A Mayan epic, the Chillam Balam, tells how the primal homeland of the Mayas was swallowed by the sea amid earthquakes and fiery eruptions.[1] A frieze from the temple at Tikal shows a boatman fleeing a sinking land, with a drowning man and an erupting volcano in the background. Evidently, refugees from the foundering Azores, perhaps Atlantis itself, reached Yucatan.

The proliferate legends of lost mid-Atlantic isles are mainly echoes of the more widely extended Azores of Atlantean times. These, along with the surviving Azores and Atlantis itself, contributed to the Greek notion of the Isles of Blest and the Fortunate Islands, while the great plain of Lusitania became the Elysian Fields. These traditions were carried throughout the Mediterranean by the Beaker folk and the Sea Peoples, surviving the centuries as vague but persistent folk memories.

The ocean is a barrier to some but a highway to the adventurous. To sailors with worthy ships and a yen for the horizon, the sea offers an irresistible challenge — one that was met and overcome many times by the mariners of prehistory.

---

1 Berlitz, Charles, *Atlantis, the Eighth Continent*, Fawcett Crest, NY, NY, 1985, p. 199.

THE INEVITABILITY OF REGRESS

These early Atlantic voyages represent something of a Bronze Age tour de force, a stretch to the outer limits of ability. They were achieved, but not easily and not often, and were not to go on indefinitely.

In the present age, most fall easily into the habit of picturing progress as a continuous forward motion, but of course it is not. The arts and sciences of yesteryear are sometimes lost, or decline, as in the Dark Ages of Europe and Dorian Greece. No craftsman today can duplicate a Stradivarius. And will anyone ever again achieve the musical heights of Mozart or the architectural purity of the ancient Greeks, or the grandeur of the Gothic cathedrals? Can anything as monumental as the pyramids ever be built again? Hardly likely.

The inhabitants of Easter Island forgot how, or even why, their ancestors erected the island's colossal stone heads. In navigational annals, too, there is precedent for the backslide phenomenon. The Polynesians achieved an incredible *tour de force* in their settlement of the Pacific isles, but many of these islands and island groups subsequently became totally isolated with no outside contact for centuries. Over time, the Polynesians largely lost their command of the open seas.

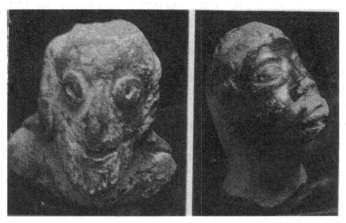

Fig. 17. The Tlapacoyan head (left) has blatantly Caucasoid characteristics; the Mixtec head is clearly Negroid. (Was there a Pre-Columbian Melting Pot?, Life, Oct. 16, 1970)

Even in our own era there are hints of parallels. It has been well over a generation since the US placed a man on the moon, a quantum leap requiring prodigious effort and technical innovation, plus a goodly measure of luck. It may be decades before anyone does it again — maybe many decades. If some sort of breakdown in worldwide technological development should occur before that happens, the story that men once walked on the moon could soon become a legendary tale, no longer believed by sensible people.

The notion that everything necessarily becomes more primitive as we go back in time is pervasive but baseless, as baseless as the notion that Bronze Age navigators could not have matched the feats of the Vikings and Columbus.

Where, really, are the grounds for skepticism about trans-Atlantic trips in BC times? Ships as seaworthy as the Santa Maria were available; astronomical reckoning was well developed. Some voyages are known to have spanned thousands of miles. Hanno reached West Africa's Cape Palmas, three thousand miles from Carthage, ca. 500 BC. The Greek Pytheas, sailing from Massilia (Marseilles) reached the Faeroes, and maybe beyond. Most remarkable, a Phoenician ship sailing for the Pharaoh Necho in the 7th century BC completely circumnavigated the vast African continent, a feat not duplicated again for more than two thousand years.

In his book *Four Thousand Years Ago*, Geoffrey Bibby has this observation on pre-Columbian contacts:

> If there is one theme that runs through this book, it is that during the Second Millennium, people were traveling more widely than ever before, trade goods were traveling even farther than people, and ideas farther than trade goods. And that if ever there was a period in the millennia before our own era when America might have been reached from Europe or Africa, that period was in the centuries between 1650 and 1300 BC.[1]

The topic of ancient mariners is subject to an incredible amount of scholastic fidgeting that is hard to justify. The oceanic probes we posit are pale achievements beside the settlement of the Hawaiian Islands by Neolithic sailors, a development requiring repeated trips over thousands of miles of open sea in outrigger canoes. And these were journeys to mere pinpoints of land in the vast Pacific, not continental masses.

The failure to recognize the maritime capabilities of ancient people has surely been one of the most egregious blind spots in the study of prehistory. Archeologists were boggled by the proofs that primitive man had reached island Australia at least 50,000 years ago. Yet even after accepting that fact they have been unable to apply its implications elsewhere — a consequence, perhaps, of the fact that archeologists are not sailors and so have little real grasp of the lure and lore of the sea. Whatever the basis of this odd opacity, archeology needs a total reassessment of ancient migration patterns and a far greater appreciation of early maritime cultures. It is long past time to abolish what Hooten called the "Archaeological Monroe Doctrine," the notion that no European set foot in the Americas before the modern age of discovery.

But the time has come to end our exploratory excursion of Atlantis and travel on to some deeper implications of Earth's rotational variations. So far, the concept has served well. Besides unlocking the Atlantis mystery, it has provided the

---

1 Knopf, NY, 1973, p. 280

key to the Ice Ages and revealed the avenues leading to the first settlement of America.

These are not the limits of the implications of Rotational Pulsation Theory. Its most fundamental impact may be in the province of basic geology. For it seems that the notion of earth pulsations provides the long sought mechanism behind the enigma of "continental drift" or "plate tectonics."

CHAPTER 13. CREEPING CONTINENTS

The evidence is everywhere that some cryptic power is at work, and has been for hundreds of millions of years, constantly warping and reshaping the crust of the earth. Some of the effects of this force are obvious — mountain ranges, for instance — even if the manner of its function is not.

According to present geophysical theory, the very continents themselves are being shoved about the surface of the globe in some improbable but evident process dubbed "plate tectonics" by science. In our investigation of the Ice Ages we uncovered a pulsation pattern which affects the shape of the earth itself. An obvious question presents itself: Could these pulsations have something to do with the long-sought mechanism underlying continental drift?

The notion of a migrating continent is so mind-bending that some readers may be disposed to think geologists spend too much time talking only to each other. (An occasional geologist might be inclined to agree since there are still a few that retain reservations about the theory.) Before going further then, we should devote a few lines to the protracted and often fevered debate about continental drift.

Long rejected, this once controversial notion has now attained something close to the status of engraved truth in the halls of academe. But it remains an enigma even to its advocates. They are in the awkward position of insisting that it must be happening even though they cannot explain *how* it could happen.

Despite this unhappy flaw as to causality, the proponents of drift can point to massive evidence favoring the concept. The initial clue — the remarkable fit between the west coast of Africa and the east coast of South America — was followed by actual matching of ancient rock formations on the two opposite coasts. A great breakthrough came with the discovery that Earth's magnetic poles have periodically reversed at irregular intervals. It was soon realized that these field reversals might provide a check on the validity of plate tectonics. Freshly ex-truded magma polarizes on the surface in accordance with the planet's magnetic field. The rifted submarine mountain ridge running down the center of the At-lantic was long suspected of involvement in the drift phenomenon. If the tectonic plates were separating, then magma must have been welling up through this rift to fill in the gaps in the ocean floor as the plates moved apart. This polarized rock would constantly be pushed to the east and west of the rift as new material was extruded. Investigation then, should reveal a "zebra stripe" pattern of alternate rock polarity on the ocean floor with the stripes running parallel to the mid-oceanic rift.

Investigation revealed exactly that.

The Atlantic Ocean floor, including the North Atlantic ledge, has been con-tinuously created out of subcrustal material seeping through the central ridge over the past hundred million years or so.

Another re-enforcement of the theory of tectonic plate migration is provided by the massive glaciation which took place in the Southern Hemisphere hundreds of millions of years ago in the Permian and Carboniferous Ages. These glaciations covered South Africa, part of southern South America, southern Australia, and even southern India with enormous continental ice sheets. Since these areas are now tropical or at least temperate in their climate, it seems that the continents themselves must have moved since the time of the glaciations. Furthermore, the direction and extent of the glaciations strongly suggest South America, Africa, India, and Australia were all joined together at the time of the Permian–Carbon-iferous Ice Age.

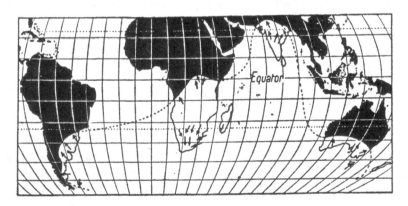

Fig. 18: Sketch-map of the southern latitudes showing the directions of the moving ice-sheets during the Permo–Carboniferous glaciation. (After A. du Toit in R. v. Klebelsberg 1949.)

THE MYSTERY MECHANISM

Even though tectonic plate migration is now seen by most as established fact, the motive force behind the phenomenon remains a subject of protracted controversy. It is fair to say that we are little closer to understanding this mechanism than was the German meteorologist Alfred Wegener on the day when he proposed the theory of continental drift in 1920 — to almost universal hoots of derision, incidentally, from the mainstream geologists of his day. (Sadly, Wegener did not live to see his "wild hypothesis" become the bedrock of modern geological science.)

Ironically, the interior of this Earth presents one of the most impenetrable mysteries in the physical universe. What comprehension we enjoy is due mainly to the study of seismic (earthquake) waves, the velocity and direction of which can be analyzed with the help of the many seismographs now stationed about the planet's surface.

Seismic studies show the earth above the core to be composed of a number of detectable layers, but basically the planet is solid down to a depth of about 1,800 miles except for a narrow zone at a depth of 100 to 250 kilometers that is characterized by lower-than-normal seismic velocities and must be somewhat plastic. This plastic zone, the top layer of the earth's mantle, is called the asthenosphere. The solid layer above the asthenosphere is termed the lithosphere, the top few miles of which make up the earth's "crust."

A significant feature of the Earth's lithosphere has been confirmed in recent decades. It is cracked. Exploring geophysicists, modern day Magellans, have mapped in detail a huge worldwide rift in the planetary crust, of which the great Atlantic rift is just one segment.

Magnetic and thermal anomalies characterize this planetary rift system almost everywhere, and on each side of the rift throughout most of its length are parallel submarine mountain ranges. In the Atlantic and Indian Oceans, the rift is located about equidistant from the continental blocs around the oceanic basins. This set of circumstances led geologists to suspect the crustal macro-crack must figure in the process of tectonic plate migration in some fashion. It was argued that the rifts must mark the boundaries of separate tectonic plates moving away from the rift axes and being subducted or folded in their consequent collisions with each other.

This is what geologists now believe is happening.

But do not ask them why or how.

IMMOVABLE OBJECTS, INCONCEIVABLE FORCES

Most geologists decided decades ago that something in the nature of mantle disturbances must be responsible for the disruptions and displacements of the earth's crust. The immediate assumption was that convection cells, created by the planet's internal heat, must exist in the mantle. It was theorized that hot mantle material must be upwelling in the regions of the crustal rifts, moving laterally beneath the surface, then descending in the vicinity of the submarine trenches (e.g., off the coast of South America). As the mantle material flowed under the continents, it was presumed to move them in the direction of mantle flow by viscous drag.

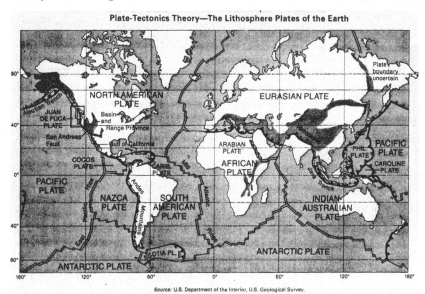

Fig. 19: The map depicts the ridge–rift system that divides the world surface into tectonic plates. It is the curious jostling of these plates against each other that causes earthquakes and builds mountains and produces continental drift.

At first the theory looked attractive. And it attracted wide support before coming apart under closer analysis. The difficulties with the convection cell theory are several and deadly. First, the study of earthquake waves shows beyond serious question that the mantle is not plastic enough to permit the formation of convection cells, except possibly in a zone a few miles deep just below the lithosphere. To explain the lateral movement of the continents, it would be necessary to postulate that the convection cells are continuous for very long distances — thousands of miles in some cases. It is inconceivable that these hypothetical cells could be so lengthy and yet so shallow. They would surely break up into a series of much shorter cells. Our knowledge of the upper mantle is not as voluminous as we would like, but almost everything we do know looks to run counter to the idea of convection cells.

Another of the hitches with the convection concept is the requirement that the upwelling mantle must necessarily be rising in a kind of curtain form along the rift lines, an extremely unlikely proposition. Upwelling in the form of a column is infinitely more likely since that format would meet the least resistance to upward flow.[1] All the clear manifestations of mantle upwelling that we know, such as those at Hawaii, Iceland, and Kerguelan, are in the form of plumes. While such plumes probably do figure in the break-up of the planetary crust, they cannot explain the whole phenomenon of continental drift.

Still another complication lies in the curious fact that most of the oceanic rifts tend to be centered almost exactly between the drifting continental blocs. The mid-Atlantic ridge is a striking example. This self-centering tendency is often hard to explain in convection cell terms. Unless the continental blocs were moving with uniform motivation against equal resistances, they would not be transported at the same rate.

Is it likely, for instance, that the supercontinent of Eurasia would move east as easily and rapidly as the much smaller North American continent moves west? Clearly not. Especially since it is incredible that a uniform subcrustal mantle current is flowing all the way from Scotland to Singapore. In fact, it is very hard to visualize the vast Eurasian continental land mass "drifting" at all. Yet the Atlantic ridge is just halfway between Europe and North America.

The relationship between Africa and South America presents an even more obvious difficulty. Under the convection cell theory, Africa would be sandwiched between two opposing convection currents, therefore should be more or less stationary. South America would have to do all the migrating involved in the creation of the Atlantic Ocean. Yet the Atlantic ridge between the two continents is precisely centered.

The discovery in recent decades that the solid lithosphere is really about 100 kilometers thick further undermines the convection cell concept since the viscous drag of convection flow is supposed to account for mountain-building. It might be barely credible to postulate crustal deformation through so tenuous a force if the lithosphere were only 5 to 30 miles thick, as once believed. But the prospect of this flimsy pressure folding and compressing solid rock over 60 miles thick borders on fantasy. Plainly, a far more powerful and direct crushing force is needed to explain lithospheric deformation.

The final epitaph for the convection cell theory is written in a well-known geological phenomenon called the "Hawaiian hotspot" — a point on the Pacific floor where hot mantle material punches up through the earth's crust. The hotspot is thousands of miles from the ridge–rift system which supposedly marks convection cell upflows. As the crustal plate slides over the Hawaiian hot spot, mantle material sporadically thrusts upward to create new islands, the latest being the big island of Hawaii itself. After the islands are carried away from the hotspot by

---

1 Rowan, Egon, "The Origin of the Oceanic Ridges," *Scientific American*, November 1969, p. 112.

the moving crustal plate, they tend to subside. (Beyond Midway, they are mere submarine remnants.)

All evidence is that the hotspot is essentially stationary over great stretches of geological time — tens of millions of years. But if the mantle is a mass of moving convection cells, how can this be? The problem is starkly obvious and beyond rational explanation: If the mantle is flowing laterally beneath the crust, the Hawaiian hotspot could hardly be stationary.

Since the convection cell model fails on this as well as several other counts, it can only be classed as untenable.

THE SEARCH FOR ALTERNATIVES

The difficulties with convection cell theory provoked a great scurrying among geologists to come up with an alternative hypothesis to account for continental drift and sea-floor spreading. A number of ingenious efforts have produced nothing persuasive so far. Perhaps the most imaginative was the "expanding earth theory." It was suggested that if the earth's interior were heating up due to radioactivity, then the entire planet should be expanding. The thought was that mere expansion of the interior of the earth could split the crust and produce the effects of continental drift entirely through the process of sea-floor creation — the new floor filling in the growing gasps between continents.

This admirably inventive tack failed to hold up under scrutiny. Most obviously, the amount of earth expansion required is much too great to be explained by heat expansion. To account for the present distribution of the continents, we would have to assume that the surface area of the earth has more than doubled since the crust solidified.

Another drawback in the theory lies in its inability to explain mountain ranges, i.e., crustal folding. An expanding earth provides no mechanism at all for lateral pressure — there would be no lateral movement of the continents, merely an ongoing creation of the ocean floor.

Another ingenious — but equally unsatisfactory — hypothesis has been proffered which argues that the tectonic plates are being pulled apart by the force of gravity. The notion is that the plates are simply sliding slightly downhill into the submarine trenches, supposedly pulled by the weight of the plate's sinking edge. Some such pull may actually exist since the descending segment is, after all, sinking. But the force involved is nowhere near enough to do the job. The sliding plate concept is pitifully weak in dealing with the build-up of the great folded mountain chains which must involve massive lateral compressions.

Aside from the convection cell, expanding earth, and gravity hypotheses, a number of other proposals have been put forth to rationalize plate tectonic theory. Suffice it to say that none of these comes any nearer to explaining the phenomenon.

The fact that no explanation of continental drift really works, or even comes close to working, leads us to suspect that there is some force at work here that has thus far gone undetected. Is it, perhaps, something related to the variations in the planet's rotation?

CHAPTER 14. THE PULSATION SOLUTION

Continental drift is essentially a reconfiguration of Earth's crust. In our probe of prehistory, we uncovered a previously unperceived phenomenon that produces rhythmic distortions of the earth's surface: geopulsation. We may begin to suspect, then, that this is the engine of the enigma.

The changing planetary geoid effectively expands and contracts the planet's crustal area over and over again. The surface is significantly larger when Earth is most distorted from the form of a sphere, i.e., during periods of more rapid rotation. The process then reverses as spin slows.

The chance that we are onto something is enhanced by the fact that the surface changes are of two kinds. There is sea-floor spreading which implies expansion of the crust. But there is also compression of the crust (mountain-building) which implies crustal contraction. The geopulsation concept provides for both of these effects, at different times, through distortion of the geoid and its return to "normal."

When geologists first faced the question of what caused the great mountain chains to form, their immediate conclusion was the crust was folding due to cooling/contraction of the earth's interior. That notion, clearly, cannot handle sea-floor spreading at all. And the cooling itself is suspect on a number of counts, including the constant volcanism of the lithosphere which is more consistent with heating than cooling of the earth. Moreover, the phenomenon of internal radioactivity offers a handy source of heat production in the innards of the planet.

Conventional geology seemed, then, to face a paradox — caught between the evidence for global contraction and equally strong evidence for expansion.

The most probable explanation of the paradox is simply this: that there have been alternating periods of surface expansion and contraction caused by periodic distortions of the planet's shape. In a real sense, the earth, over vast periods of time, has been pulsating. During times of crustal expansion (high rotational speed), the surface cracks and mantle material pours through the rifts, enlarging the ocean floors. In periods of contraction, the lithosphere is forced to fold and contract upon itself, mountains being built and continental slabs moved as the crust is compressed.

Key to the concept, obviously, is the constantly reoccurring nature of these changes, and the endless expansion/contraction cycle. The magnitude of the geoidal changes is less important than their frequency. The pulsation process, ever repeated over the geological eons, can account for almost any degree of crustal deformation.

As observed in Chapter 5, there is a complete pulsation cycle about every 100,000 years, each cycle including one expansion and one contraction phase. Every million years, Earth undergoes about ten expansions and ten contractions, easily accounting for the observed compression of the continents and the creation of the oceans over an expanse of hundreds of millions of years.

The process must be abetted somewhat by an absolute increase in the volume of the earth during periods of rapid rotation. The increasing spin velocity of the planet in these phases results in a decrease in Earth's internal pressure due to the greater centrifugal force, producing expansion of the mantle.

The mantle is rather uniform in composition, mostly made up of peridotite. However, at certain levels of depth, due to the pressure effects, the peridotite undergoes changes in it crystalline structure known as phase transitions.[1] These transitions are clearly revealed by seismic wave studies. The changes in crystalline structure produce marked changes in volume for any given mass of peridotite: the greater the pressure, the less the volume. So, reductions in pressure effected by increased centrifugal force would produce an increase in mantle volume and a net expansion of the planet.

These expansions and contractions of volume work in concert with the distortions of the planetary geoid to exacerbate crustal stretching and warping.

During compressional phases, both the continental lithosphere and the oceanic lithosphere are compressed and folded. That is, mountain ranges are produced on land and under the sea. The continental ones are familiar enough — we may live in their shadows or drive across them on weekends. But the sub-oceanic ranges were undetected until only a few decades ago. They consist of an almost endless series of parallel mountain chains on the ocean floor as one moves away from the rift system (fig. 23). These parallel ranges are a key clue because they cannot be explained by any current theory of continental drift, *but are precisely what would be expected under the rotational pulsation concept.* The alignment of these

---

1 Wyllie, Peter, "The Earth's Mantle," *Scientific American*, Mar 1975, p.55 ff.

mountain chains is practically conclusive proof of the validity of Geopulsation Theory.

Each new planetary expansion phase clearly tends to make the oceans wider than before as the rifts open. Each new contraction phase compress the continents and the ocean floor. The cycle works to steadily increase the area of the oceans and to constrict and thicken the continental blocs — up to a point. When resistance to further compression becomes great enough, an oceanic plate will be driven beneath a continental plate and into the upper mantle, a process known as subduction.

Plainly, the geopulsation model does not conform to the longstanding assumption that seafloor spreading and plate movements proceed through a steady, continuous process. A stop-and-go component is involved: alternating crustal contractions and expansions which, over very protracted time periods, produce the same long-term effects as the continuous model. So the perception of continual, persistent motion is actually illusory.

That presumed continuity, it should be emphasized, is only an assumption. There is no proof for it; the evidence is all the other way. Since the accordion-like pattern of mountain chains paralleling the rift system is plainly indicative of an episodic process, and could hardly be more opposed to the continuous model, there has to be cyclical component in the drift phenomenon.

Quoting from a perceptive analysis of the Atlantic ridge by Joe Cann, University of Newcastle on Tyne: "Recently geologists have been looking more and more closely at the processes that create ocean and mid-ocean ridges and find increasingly that episodic processes are significant...It seems that there is some form of tectono-magmatic cycling in the mid ocean ridge processes."[1] While such a cyclic sequence does not fit the accepted plate tectonics model, it dovetails neatly with Geopulsation Theory. (It should not be assumed that every crustal contraction produces another parallel seafloor mountain range since the compressive force might fold some continental sector or force a plate edge subduction.)

Such data are just some of the latest illustrating that every scrap of new evidence to emerge since the author's formation of the rotational pulsation concept in the '70s has confirmed it, while none contradict it. Considering the volume of new evidence — archeological, climatic, geological — that has surfaced in the interim, the chance that such concurrence is mere happenstance can be seen as negligible.

THE MECHANISM OF CREEP

It is easy to see how Geopulsation Theory accounts for sea floor spreading and continental compression. How it produces continental drift is only a little

---

1 Cann, Joe, "Feeling the pulse of the Ridge," *Nature*, Nov 10, 1988, p.108.

less evident. "Drift," of course, is not quite the right word. More descriptively, a kind of continental creep takes place in certain situations.

In some areas, mainly around the edges of the Pacific basin, the margins of the expanding oceanic lithosphere have been driven beneath the adjoining continental blocs. A prime example is seen along the west coast of South America where a deep submarine trench runs parallel to the great Andean mountain chain along the coast. In this zone, and others like it, the continental bloc, rather than folding further in a compressional phase, simply overrides the ocean floor. The continent is actually being rafted as a unit in a certain direction — in South America's case, westerly.

Fig. 20: The pattern of submarine mountain ridges running parallel to the great rift system provides the conclusive argument for Geopulsation Theory.

This ridge pattern is exactly what would be produced by alternating phases of planetary expansion and contraction. A contraction phase produces a ridge which is then moved away from the rift by an expansion phase accompanied by upwelling through the rift. The next contraction the produces another parallel ridge, and so on. The parallel ridge pattern is inexplicable in any other terms; the convection cell theory cannot begin to account for it. Only expansion/ contraction phases could produce such a pattern, and only variable planetary spin could produce such expansion/contraction alternations. (Map illustration from Debate About the Earth, Tacheuchi, et al, Freeman Cooper & Co., 1970.)

To delineate the process: In the higher velocity rotational phases (expansions), the oceanic rifts in the Atlantic, Pacific and Indian Oceans split open. Magma oozes into the rifts and solidifies. As the planet's rotation slows and it enters a contraction phase, something obviously has to give. Either a crustal plate has to fold somewhere or else part of the oceanic crust must be subducted back down into the asthensophere and upper mantle. In the case of South America, it is the subduction process that is taking place because it is easier for the continent to override the Pacific plate than to undergo further folding.

As the expansion and contraction cycles are repeated over and over again, the continental bloc that is South America impinges ever further on the Pacific basin while the Atlantic grows correspondingly wider and wider. The continent is ac- tually moving intermittently westward with each expansion/contraction cycle. Continental movement then, like mountain building, proceeds rather by fits and starts, occurring basically during the Earth's contraction phases.

Obviously, the Geopulsation concept requires that the drift phenomenon must be much less extensive in the high latitudes than in the lower since the de- gree of planetary distortion decreases with latitude. That this has recently been found to be exactly the case represents another confirmation of the theory. A study of Arctic and southwest Indian Ocean ridges, reported in 2003, showed that these high latitude ridges have been spreading at an ultra slow rate, only a fraction of the average.[1]

The continental creep that is taking place in the current geological era con- sists mostly of impingement on the Pacific Basin because it is on the margins of this basin that most of the present subduction trenches are located. These trench zones are notorious for their violent volcanic and earthquake activity — the famous Pacific "Ring of Fire." But even lesser trenches, such as the Caribbean, have demonstrated that they can be disastrously damaging in their seismic ef- fects. The subduction trenches are not static features, by any means, due to the migrations of the ridge–rift system. Their locations change over geological time as these massive cracks creep slowly across the face of our earth. The Red Sea, for

---

1 Dick, Henry J.B., Lin, Jian, & Schouten, Hans, "An ultra slow-spreading class of ocean ridge," Nature, Nov. 27, 2003. p. 413.

instance, is a comparatively recent extension of the Indian Ocean rift which has severed Arabia from Africa.

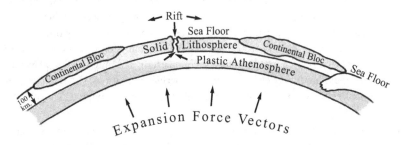

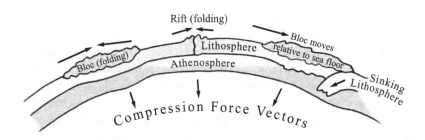

Fig.21. (a) During an expansion phase, the circumference of the earth tends to increase, separating the oceanic rifts which are filled in with material from the asthenosphere. This material solidifies to become a part of the ocean floor. (Vertical scale is much exaggerated.)

(b) During a contraction phase, the circumference of the earth tends to decrease, forcing the folding of weak zones of the lithosphere, including the continental blocs. In cases where the continental bloc is overriding the sea floor, the contraction produces additional override. The next expansion will create more sea floor and the succeeding contraction phase will further compress the tectonic plates and force more overrides.

Another presently active rift appears to be splitting East Africa away from the rest of the continent. And on the floor of the Indian Ocean, oceanographers have found the remnants of some now inactive rifts, such as the 90 Degree Ridge running south from the Bay of Bengal.

As the rifts migrate, they affect different sectors of the continental masses. And new subduction trenches are created on the margins of new plates. Over the eons long span of their activity, the rifts have changed their direction and number countless times. For instance, the direction of the main Pacific Rift was altered radically about 45 million years ago — a fact evident from the change in the direction of the Hawaiian seamount chain's drift starting at that time. The great Atlantic Rift system, scientists believe, opened up only about a hundred million years ago.

Attempting to trace all the past movements of the continental blocks, and fragments thereof, over the preceding thousands of millennia would be a formidable, maybe impossible, task. But it is not really necessary to do so. The relevant point is that all this continental creep is easily explainable via the Rotational Pulsation concept if we bear in mind the constant change and evolution of the rift system and the endless repetition of the expansion/contraction cycle.

It seems the Geopulsation Theory at last answers the old riddle about what happens when the irresistible force meets the immovable object: crustal compression and continental creep.

It might be noted that some magmatic extrusion from the rift systems can be expected even in the quieter phases of the rotational variation cycle. Even though the present rate of velocity change is relatively small, some extrusion is being seen along the North Atlantic rift and elsewhere. The degree of this activity is trifling compared to what happens during the periods of more rapid expansions and contraction. Still, we should remark on its cause.

The present day upwelling merely reflects the fact that crustal adjustments never cease entirely. The mantle, due to extreme internal viscosity, is always lagging the changes in rotational speed. The form of the earth is always "playing catch up." The present extrusions, depending on location and regional conditions, could be due to either small scale rift-splitting or slight compression which would force up magma between the crustal plates like toothpaste from a tube.

To sum up matters, Geopulsation embodies a solution to most of the major extant problems of geology. It resolves them easily, without deviation from established geophysical laws or known facts. It eliminates the need for those elongated and improbable convention cells in the Earth's mantle. Unlike other hypothesis, the force vectors are entirely adequate to accomplish the work of crustal folding and displacement. In the bargain, the theory also accounts for a number of other unexplained geophysical phenomena, both major and minor.

THIS NOT SO SOLID EARTH

The net impact of Geopulsation Theory is to exacerbate the picture of a world less stable and reliable than was imagined only a few years ago. Our planet is not as firm or as placid as we believed — or would like to believe. The once rock-solid Earth has given way under our feet with the discovery that the continents warp, twist and creep about the planet's surface — usually more drastically than now. What has been seen as one of the steadiest factors in our environment, the earth's

rotation, is not so steady after all. It varies with time, producing unsettling consequences that we are powerless to negate.

The continents will writhe and shiver more violently in the future than they
do today, and the Ice Ages will continue to come and go regardless of what tech-
no-man may or may not do. Whatever effects may result from the activities of our
species on this earth will pale before the colossal natural forces that rule the great
climatic cycles. More likely than not, we have already reached the peak point of
the present interglacial episode and the slow unstoppable onset of the next Ice
Age is only a few millennia away.

These prospects will seem discomfiting to many, particularly those who like
to think of the earth as a sort of benign mother that will be kind to us if only
we are kind to her. But such a world view is more than a little naïve. The fact is
Mother Earth is an erratic and often violent orb, subject to periodic spasms on a
scale far beyond what is recorded in written history. We humans subsist precari-
ously on the thin planetary skin, never very far removed from calamity — as some
of the peoples of Asia so recently discovered. The roots of cataclysm are deep, in-
trinsic and very nearly everlasting, an unavoidable product of the timeless forces
of geopulsation. Mankind as a species will survive the onslaughts of the coming
millennia, as we have in the past, only if our descendents prove to be as hardy and
adaptable as our ancestors.

In a geological timeframe, the apocalyptic view of the world is not so far off the
mark. It is only the present temporary state of relative planetary quietude and our
own short term chronological focus that make it possible to think otherwise.

Having traversed the shadowy maze that is prehistory, it can be seen that we
have come some distance. What has been uncovered along the way amounts to a
substantial rewrite of conventional geology, history, anthropology and archeology. The essential framework:

That the planet's precession cycle produces a periodic misalignment in the
rotational axis of Earth's core vis-à-vis the solid mantle/crust. An effect of this
misalignment is a corresponding cycle of variations in the earth's spin speed over
periods of about 100,000 years.

The rotational changes are responsible for both the Ice Ages and continental
drift. The key to "drift" is an ongoing expansion and contraction of Earth's crust
via spin speed deviations that alternately distend and compress the surface area.

The Pleistocene changes in sea level are more a cause than a result of glaciation. Produced by varying planetary rotation, these fluctuations have been so
pronounced that at times a near connection between Europe and America has
been created along the Atlantic ledge, allowing early maritime man to reach the
New World via point to point navigation, ca. 35,000 BP. Contrary to conventional belief, the first Americans were actually island-hopping Stone Age folk from

Europe. Gene flow from Asia later overlaid this primordial stock, creating what are now called the Native Americans.

Serendipitous aspects of Geopulsation Theory provide a geological foundation for both the existence and destruction of the island Atlantis and early Bronze Age colonization of an extended Azorean archipelago. During it long career, the Atlantean society — originally the Bell Beaker complex — made contact with the Americas and impacted the high cultures of the New World. But half the early tradition of European civilization — the far western half — was all but lost in the explosion of the Tore/Atlantis supervolcano and the devastating wars between the ancient East Mediterranean powers and those of the Atlantic.

The phenomenal persistence of the Atlantis tradition over the millennia, despite a steady drumbeat of official condemnation, is so remarkable that one is tempted to give weight to Jung's theories of racial memory — or to Plato's contention that all knowledge is really only recovered recollection. However that may be, it can no longer be doubted that the tale of Atlantis is, as the great Greek sage put it, "actual history."

While some of the revelations of our new prehistory will seem startling to the traditionally conditioned mind, scores of anthropological and archeological data dovetail in a chronologically consistent pattern to support the new perspective. And there appears to be nothing contradictory.

The fact that we have a single phenomenon, Geopulsation, that resolves at one stroke both of the key puzzles of geology — continental drift and the Ice Ages — makes it likely enough that the analysis is valid. The fact that this same phenomenon also unravels two of the biggest enigmas of human prehistory — the settlement of the Americas and the Atlantis Legend — makes the case even surer. The burden of proof, then, would now seem to rest with those who might wish to contest our conclusions.

DIAGRAMS A AND B

See diagrams on the next page. Dashed lines indicate the solid core spin axis, the angle of which varies through the precession cycle.

The diagrams show how the rotation of the earth is altered by differential rotation of the solid core vis-à-vis the mantle/crust. The core does not constantly spin on the same axis as the planet's solid shell (as commonly assumed) since the two precess at different rates. When (as in our own era) core and mantle precession are out of phase (A), a directional drag is transmitted through the liquid outer core retarding the rotation of Earth's shell. When the precessions are in phase (B) and all parts of the planet are spinning on the same plane, the earth's rotation accelerates since the directional drag disappears and the core has a slightly faster spin rate.

The present day alignment of the inner core spin axis cannot be directly determined but there are strong indicators that it does not coincide with that of the mantle/crust. Both the magnetic poles and the core's axis of anisotropy diverge about ten degrees from the geographic poles.

The anisotropic axis is thought to be related to the crystalline grain in the solid iron core which affects the velocity of seismic waves traveling through it, depending on their direction. The anisotropy itself is most likely linked to the core's spin, the implication being that the solid core's rotation axis is presently canted by about ten degrees from the main earth axis. Since the speed of earth's rotation now appears to be close to a minimum, this 10 degree misalignment must be near its max, though it may have been slightly more during peak deceleration phases, e.g., 25,000 years ago. (The hydraulic coupling between the earth's outer shell and inner core prevents any very much larger deviation.) It is plainly impossible that the relationship between the core axis and Earth's main axis is static, considering the gyroscopic, precessional, gravitational and hydraulic coupling effects involved.

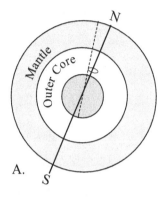
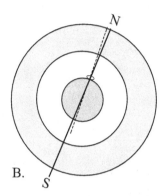

It is the core's anisotropy that has been used in ingenious efforts, first by Song and Richards, to ascertain the difference between core and mantle rotation. But the jury is still out on their estimate that the differential is only about one degree per year. There are recent indications, for instance, that the core's anisotropy is not uniform, a factor that could materially affect the calculation. (Other investigators, using the same technique, have found considerably larger and somewhat smaller variations.) More uncertainty is added by the fact that the computations are based on the assumption that the core rotates on the same axis as the planet's outer shell, which we have discovered not to be the case. Various other data suggest the differential is likely to be considerably larger than estimated, though present knowledge does not allow for highly specific interpretation. The 1 to 2% variations in the whole earth's rotation speed provide a rough indicator but are less than definitive due to various extraneous factors.

Just as the extent of crustal disruption was underestimated prior to the discovery of plate tectonics, so the extent of disturbances in the planet's core is being vastly underestimated today. Facts are usually more complicated that we'd like, and the old model of our planet's interior is clearly too simplistic. On the plus side, geophysicists should have plenty to investigate in the coming decades.

Crit. Then listen, Socrates, to a tale which, though strange, is certainly true, having been attested by Solon, who was the wisest of the seven sages. He was a relative and a dear friend of my great grandfather, Dropides, as he himself says in many passages of his poems; and he told the story to Critias, my grandfather, who remembered and repeated it to us. There were of old, he said, great and marvelous actions of the Athenian city, [21] which have passed into oblivion through lapse of time and the destruction of mankind, and one in particular, greater than all the rest. This we will now rehearse. It will be a fitting monument of our gratitude to you, and a hymn of praise true and worthy of the goddess, on this her day of festival.

Soc. Very good. And what is this ancient famous action of the Athenians, which Critias declared, on the authority of Solon, to be not a mere legend, but an actual fact?

Crit. I will tell an old-world story which I heard from an aged man; for Critias, at the time of telling it, was as he said, nearly ninety years of age, and I was about ten. Now the day was that day of the Apaturia which is called the Registration of Youth, at which, according to custom, our parents gave prizes for recitations, and the poems of several poets were recited by us boys, and many of us sang the poems of Solon, which at that time had not gone out of fashion. One of our tribe, either because he thought so or to please Critias, said that in his judgment Solon was not only the wisest of men but also the noblest of poets. The old man, as I very well remember, brightened up at hearing this and said, smiling: Yes, Amynander, if Solon had only, like other poets, made poetry the business of his life, and had completed the tale which he brought with him from Egypt, and had not been compelled, by reason of the factions and troubles which he found stirring in his own country when he came home, to attend to other matters, in my opinion he would have been as famous as Homer or Hesiod, or any poet.

And what was the tale about, Critias? said Amynander.

About the greatest action which the Athenians ever did, and which ought to have been the most famous, but, through the lapse of time and the destruction of the actors, it has not come down to us.

Tell us, said the other, the whole story, and how and from whom Solon heard this veritable tradition.

He replied: — In the Egyptian Delta, at the head of which the river Nile divides, there is a certain district which is called the district of Sais, and the great city of the district is also called Sais, and is the city from which King Amasis came. The citizens have a deity for their foundress; she is called in the Egyptian tongue Neith, and is asserted by them to be the same whom the Hellenes call Athene; they are great lovers of the Athenians, and say that they are in some way related to them. To this city came Solon, and was received there with great honour; *[22]* he asked the priests who were most skilful in such matters, about antiquity, and made the discovery that neither he nor any other Hellene knew anything worth mentioning about the times of old. On one occasion, wishing to draw them on to speak of antiquity, he began to tell about the most ancient things in our part of the world — about Phoroneus, who is called "the first man," and about Niobe; and after the Deluge, of the survival of Deucalion and Pyrrha; and he traced the genealogy of their descendants, and reckoning up the dates, tried to compute how many years ago the events of which he was speaking happened. Thereupon one of the priests, who was of a very great age, said: O Solon, Solon, you Hellenes are never anything but children, and there is not an old man among you. Solon in return asked him what he meant. I mean to say, he replied, that in mind you are all young; there is no old opinion handed down among you by ancient tradition, not any science which is hoary with age. And I will tell you why. There have been, and will be again, many destructions of mankind arising out of many causes; the greatest have been brought about by the agencies of fire and water, and other lesser ones by innumerable other causes. There is a story, which even you have preserved, that once upon a time Phaethon, the son of Helios, having yoked the steeds in his father's chariot, because he was not able to drive them in the path of his father, burnt up all that was upon the earth, and was himself destroyed by a thunderbolt. Now this has the form of a myth, but really signifies a declination of the bodies moving in the heavens around the earth, and a great conflagration of things upon the earth, which recurs after long intervals; at such times those who live upon the mountains and in dry and lofty places are more liable to destruction than those who dwell by rivers or on the seashore. And from this calamity the Nile, who is our never-failing savior, delivers and preserves us. When, on the other hand, the gods purge the earth with a deluge of water, the survivors in your country are herdsmen and shepherds who dwell on the mountains, but those who, like you, live in cities are carried by the river into the sea. Whereas in this land, neither then nor at any other time, does the water come down from above on the fields, having always a tendency to come up from below; for which reason the traditions preserved here are the most ancient.

The fact is, that wherever the extremity of winter frost or of summer sun does not prevent, mankind exist, sometimes in greater, *[23]* sometimes in lesser numbers. And whatever happened either in your country or in ours — or in any other region of which we are informed — if there were any actions noble or great or in any other way remarkable, they have all been written down by us of old, and are preserved in our temples. Whereas just when you and other nations are beginning to be provided with letters and the other requisites of civilized life, after the usual interval, the stream from heaven, like a pestilence, comes pouring down, and leaves only those of you who are destitute of letters and education; and so you have to begin all over again like children, and know nothing of what happened in ancient times, either among us or among yourselves. As for those genealogies of yours which you just now recounted to us, Solon, they are no bet-ter than the tales of children. In the first place you remember a single deluge only, but there were many previous ones; in the next place, you do not know that there formerly dwelt in your land the fairest and noblest race of men which ever lived, and that you and your whole city are descended from a small seed or remnant of them which survived. And this was unknown to you, because, for many genera-tions, the survivors of that destruction died, leaving no written word. For there was a time, Solon, before the great deluge of all, when the city which now is Ath-ens was first in war and in every way the best governed of all cities, and is said to have performed the noblest deeds and to have had the fairest constitution of any of which tradition tells, under the face of heaven.

Solon marveled at his words, and earnestly requested the priests to inform him exactly and in order about these former citizens. You are welcome to hear about them, Solon, said the priest, both for your own sake and for that of your city, and above all, for the sake of the goddess who is the common patron and parent and educator of both our cities. She founded your city a thousand years before ours, receiving from the Earth and Hephaestus the seed of your race, and afterwards she founded ours, of which the constitution is recorded in our sacred registers to be eight thousand years old.......

Many great and wonderful deeds are recorded of your state in our histories. But one of them exceeds all the rest in greatness and valour. For these histories tell of a mighty power which unprovoked made an expedition against the whole of Europe and Asia, and to which your city put an end. This power came forth out of the Atlantic Ocean, for in those days the Atlantic was navigable; and there was an island situated in front of the straits which are by you called the Pillars of Heracles; the island was larger than Libya and Asia put together *[25]*and was the way to other islands, and from these you might pass to the whole of the opposite continent which surrounded the true ocean; for this sea which is within the straits of Heracles is only a harbour, having a narrow entrance, but that other is a real sea, and the surrounding land may be most truly called a boundless continent. Now in this island of Atlantis there was a great and wonderful empire which had rule over the whole island and several others, and over parts of the continent, and, furthermore, the men of Atlantis had subjected the parts of Libya within the columns of Heracles as far as Egypt, and of Europe as far As Tyrrhenia. This vast power, gathered into one, endeavored to subdue at a blow our country and yours and the whole of the region within the straits; and then, Solon, your country shone forth, in the excellence of her virtue and strength, among all mankind. She was pre-eminent in courage and military skill, and was the leader of the Hellenes. And when the rest fell off from her, being compelled to stand alone, after having undergone the very extremity of danger, she defeated and triumphed over the invaders, and preserved from slavery those who were not yet subjugated, and generously liberated all the rest of us who dwell within the pillars. But afterwards there occurred violent earthquakes and floods; and in a single day and night of misfortune all your warlike men in a body sank into the earth, and the island of Atlantis in like manner disappeared in the depths of the sea. For which reason the sea in those parts is impassable and impenetrable, because there is a shoal of mud in the way; and this was caused by the subsidence of the island.

Let me begin by observing first of all that 9000 was the sum of years which had elapsed since the war that was said to have occurred between all those who dwelt outside the Pillars of Herakles and those who dwelt within them; this war I am now about to describe. Of the combatants on the one side, the city of Athens was reported to have been the ruler and to have directed the contest. The combatants on the other side were led by the kings of the island of Atlantis, which as I was saying once had an extent greater than that of Libya and Asia, and when afterwards sunk by an earthquake became an impassible barrier of mud to voyagers sailing from home hence to the ocean......

..Solon said the priests in their narrative of that war mentioned most of the names which are recorded prior to the time of Theseus, such as Cecrops, and Erechtheus, and Erichthonius and Erysichthon, and the names of the women in like manner......

I have before remarked in speaking of the allotments of the gods, that they distributed the whole earth into portions differing in extent and made for themselves temples and instituted sacrifices. And Poseidon, receiving for his lot the island of Atlantis, begat children by a mortal woman, and settled them in a part of the island, which I will describe. Looking towards the sea, but in the center of the whole island, there was a plain which is said to have been the fairest of all plains and very fertile. Near the plain again, and also in the center of the island at a distance of about fifty stadia [ca. 6 mi.], there was a mountain not very high on any side. There dwelt one of the earth-born natives of that country, named Euenor, and he had a wife named Leukippe, and they had an only daughter called Kleito. The maiden was growing up to womanhood, when her father and mother died; Poseidon fell in love with her and had intercourse with her, and breaking the ground inclosed the hill in which she dwelt all round, making alternate zones of sea and land larger and smaller encircling one another, two of land and three of water, which he turned as with a lathe out of the center of the island, equidistant in every way so that no man could get to the island, for ships and voyages were not yet heard of. He, being a god, easily effected special arrangements for the center island, bringing two streams of water under the earth, which he caused to ascend as springs, one of warm water and the other of cold and making every variety of food to spring up abundantly in the earth.

He also begat and reared five pairs of twin sons, dividing the island of Atlantis into ten portions(114); he gave to the first-born of the eldest pair his mother's dwelling and the surrounding allotment, which was the largest and best, and made him king over the rest; the others he made princes and gave them rule over many men and a large territory. And he named them all; the eldest, who was the king, he named Atlas, and from him the whole island and the ocean received the name of Atlantic. To his younger twin brother, who obtained as his lot the ex-tremity of the island towards the Pillars of Herakles, as far as the country which is still called the region of Gadeira in that part of the world, he gave the name which in the Hellenic language is Eumelos, in the language of the country which is named after him, Gadeiros. Of the second pair of twins he called one Ampheres and the other Euaimon. Of the third pair of twins he gave the name Mneseus to the elder and Autochthon to the one who had followed him. Of the fourth pair of twins he called the elder Elasippos and the younger Mestor. And of the fifth pair he gave the elder the name of Azaes and to the younger that of Diaprepes. All these and their descendants were the inhabitants and rulers of divers islands in the open sea; and also, as has been already said, they held sway in the other direc-tion over the country within the Pillars as far as Egypt and Tyrrhenia.

Now Atlas had a numerous and honorable family, and his eldest branch al-ways retained the kingdom, which the eldest son handed on to his eldest for many generations; and they had such an amount of wealth as was never before possessed by kings and potentates and is not likely ever to be again, and they were furnished with everything that they could have both in the city and country. For because of the greatness of their empire many things were brought to them from foreign countries, and the island itself provided much of what was required by them for the uses of life. In the first place they dug out of the earth whatever was to be found there, mineral as well as metal, and that which is only a name and was then something more than a name, orichalc, was dug out of the earth in many parts of the island, and except gold was then the most precious of metals. There was an abundance of wood for carpenter's work and sufficient maintenance for tame and wild animals.

Moreover there were a great number of elephants in the island,(115) and there was provision for animals of every kind, both for those that live in lakes and marshes and rivers, and also for those that live in mountains and on plains, and therefore for the animal that is the largest and most voracious of them all. Also whatever fragrant things there are in the earth, whether roots, or herbage, or woods, or distilling drops of flowers and fruits, grew and thrived in that land; and again, the cultivated fruit of the earth, both the dry edible fruit and other species of food that we call by general names of pulse, and the fruits having a hard rind, affording drinks and meats and ointments, and a good store of chestnuts and the like.....

And they arranged the whole country thus: First they bridged the zones of sea which surrounded the ancient metropolis, and made a passage into and out of the royal palace; and then they began to build the palace in the habitation of the god and their ancestors. This they continued to ornament in successive generations, every king surpassing the one who came before him to the utmost of his power, until they made the building a marvel to behold for size and beauty. And beginning from the sea they dug a canal of three plethra [i.e., 300 Greek feet] in width and one hundred feet in depth, and fifty stadia in length, which they carried through to the outermost zone, making a passage from the sea up to this, which became a harbor, and leaving an opening sufficient to enable the largest vessels to sail through. Moreover they divided the zones of land which parted the zones of sea, constructing bridges of such a width as would leave a passage for a single trireme to pass out of one into the other, and roofed them over; and there was a way underneath for the ships, for the banks of the zones were raised considerably above water. Now the largest of the zones into which a passage was cut from the sea was three stadia in breadth, and the zone of land which came next of equal breadth, but the next two, as well the zone of water as of land, were two stadia, and the one which surrounded the central island was a stadium only in width.

(116) The island in which the palace was situated had a diameter of five stadia. This and the zones and the bridge, which was a plethrum in width, they surrounded by a stone wall, on either side placing towers, and gates on the bridges where the sea passed in. The stone which was used in the work they quarried from underneath the central island and from underneath the outer and inner circles. One kind of stone was white, another black, and a third red, and as they quarried they at the same time hollowed out double docks within, having roofs formed of the native rock. Some of their buildings were simple, but in others they put together different stones which they intermingled for the sake of ornament, to be a natural source of delight. The entire circuit of the wall, which went around the outermost one, they covered with a coating of brass, and the third, which encompassed the citadel, flashed with the red light of orichalc. The palaces in the interior of the citadel were constructed in this wise: In the center was a

holy temple dedicated to Kleito and Poseidon, which remained inaccessible, and was surrounded by an enclosure of gold; this was the spot in which they originally begat the race of the ten princes, and thither they annually brought the fruits of the earth in their season from all the ten portions, and performed sacrifices to each of them. Here too was Poseidon's own temple of a stadium in length, and half a stadium in width, and of a proportionate height, having a sort of barbaric splendor. All the outside of the temple with the exception of the pinnacles they covered with silver, and the pinnacles with gold. In the interior of the temple the roof was of ivory adorned everywhere with gold and silver and orichalc; all the other parts of the walls and pillars and floor they lined with orichalc. In the temple they placed statues of gold....

(117) In the next place they used fountains both of cold and hot springs; these were very abundant, and both kinds wonderfully adapted to use by reason of the sweetness and excellence of their waters. They constructed buildings about them and planted suitable trees; there were the king's baths, and separated baths for private persons, also separate baths for women and others again for horses and cattle, and to each of them they gave as much adornment as was suitable for them. The water which ran off they carried, some to the grove of Poseidon, where were growing all manner of trees of wonderful height and beauty, owing to the excellence of the soil; the remainder was conveyed by aqueducts which passed over the bridges to the outer circles; and there were many temples built and dedicated to many gods; also gardens and places of exercise, some for men and some set apart for horses in both of the two islands formed by the zones, and in the center of the larger of the two, there was a race-course of a stadium in width and in length allowed to extend all around the island for horses to race in. Also there were guard-houses at intervals for the bodyguard, the more trusted of whom had their duties appointed to them in the lesser zone, which was nearer the Akropolis, while the most trusted of all had houses given them within the citadel and about the persons of the kings. The docks were full of triremes and naval stores and all things were quite ready for use.... Crossing the outer harbors, which were three in number, you would come to a wall which began at the sea and went all round: This was everywhere distant fifty stadia from the largest zone and harbor and enclosed the whole, meeting at the mouth of the channel towards the sea...

(118) The whole country was described as being very lofty and precipitous on the side of the sea, but the country immediately about the surrounding city was a level plain, itself surrounded by mountains which descended towards the sea; it was smooth and even, but of an oblong shape, extending in one direction 3000 stadia, and going up the country from the sea through the center of the island, 2000 stadia; this whole region of the island faces towards the south, and is sheltered from the north. The surrounding mountains are celebrated for their number and size and beauty...

I will now describe the plain, which had been cultivated during many ages by many generations of kings. It was rectangular, and for the most part straight and oblong, and what it wanted of the straight line followed the line of a surrounding ditch. The depth, width, and length of this ditch were incredible, and gave the impression that a work of such extent, in addition to so many others, could not have been artificial. Nevertheless, I must say what I was told. It was excavated to the depth of 100 feet, and its breadth was a stadium everywhere; it was carried round the whole of the plain, and was 10,000 stadia in length. It received the streams which came down from the mountains and, winding round the plain and touching with the city at various points, was there led off into the sea. From above likewise, straight canals 100 feet wide were cut in the plain, and again led off into the ditch towards the sea: these canals were at intervals of 100 stadia, and by them they brought down the wood from the mountains to the city and conveyed the fruits of the earth in ships, cutting transverse passages from one canal into another, and to the city....

As to the population, each of the lots in the plain had an appointed chief of men who were fit for military service, (119) and the size of the lots was to be a square ten stadia each way, and the total number of all the lots was 60,000. And of the inhabitants of the mountains and of the rest of the country there was a vast multitude having leaders to whom they were assigned according to their dwellings and villages. The leader was required to furnish for war the sixth portion of a war-chariot, so as to make up a total of 10,000 chariots; also two horses and riders upon them, and a light chariot without a seat accompanied by a fighting man on foot carrying a small shield and having a charioteer mounted to guide the horses; also he was bound to furnish two heavy-armed, two archers, two slingers, three stone-shooters, and three javelin-men who were skirmishers, and four sailors to make up the complement of 1200 ships....

Each of the ten kings had his own division and in his own city had the absolute control of the citizens and in many cases of the laws, punishing and slaying whomsoever he would. Now the relations of their governments to one another were well regulated by the injunctions of Poseidon as the law had handed them down. These were inscribed by the first men on a column of orichalc, which was situated in the middle of the island at the temple of Poseidon, whither the people were gathered together every fifth and sixth years alternately, thus giving equal honor to the odd and to the even number. And when they were gathered together they consulted about public affairs, and inquired if any one had transgressed in anything and passed judgment on him accordingly, and before they passed judgment they gave their pledges to one another thus: There were bulls who had the range of the temple of Poseidon, and the ten who were left alone in the temple, after they had offered prayers to the gods that they might take the sacrifices that were acceptable to them, hunted the bulls without weapons but with staves and nooses; and the bull they caught they led up to the column; the victim was then struck over the head by them and slain over the sacred inscription....

When therefore after offering sacrifice according to their customs they had burned the limbs of the bull, they mingled a cup and cast in a clot of blood for each of them; (120) the rest of the victim they took to the fire after having made a purification of the column all around. Then they drew from the cup in golden vessels and, pouring a libation on the fire, they swore that they would judge according to the laws on the column and would punish any one who had transgressed, and that for the future they would not if they could help transgress any of the inscriptions, and would not command or obey any ruler who commanded them to act otherwise than according to their father's laws. This was the prayer which each of them offered up for himself and for his family, at the same time drinking and dedicating the vessel in the temple of the god, and after spending some necessary time at supper, when darkness came on and the fire about the sacrifice was cool, all of them put on most beautiful dark-blue robes and, sitting on the ground at night near the embers of the sacrifices on which they had sworn and extinguishing all the fire about the temple, they received and gave judgment, if any of them had any accusation to bring against any one; and when they had given judgment, at daybreak they wrote down their sentences on a gold tablet, and deposited them as memorials with their robes....

Such was the vast power which the god settled in that place, and this he later directed against our land on the following pretext, as traditions tell: For many generations, as long as the divine nature lasted in them, they were obedient to the laws and well-affected towards their divine kindred; for they possessed true and in every way great spirits, practicing gentleness and wisdom in the various chances of life and in their intercourse with one another. They despised everything but virtue, not caring for their present state of life and thinking lightly of the possession of gold and other property, which seemed only a burden to them; neither were they intoxicated by luxury, nor did wealth deprive them of their self-control, (121) but they were sober and saw clearly that all these goods are increased by virtuous friendship with one another, and that by excessive zeal for them and honor of them the good of them is lost.... But when this divine portion began to fade away in them and became diluted too often with too much of the mortal admixture, and the human nature got the upper hand, then they, being unable to bear their fortune, became unseemly, and to him who had an eye to see they began to appear base, and had lost the fairest of their precious gifts......

BIBLIOGRAPHY

Albright, W.F. *The Archaeology of Palestine*: Pelican Books, 1960.

Anderson, Don L. "The Plastic Layer of the Earth." *Scientific American*, July 1962.

Bean, George E. Turkey's Southern Shore: An Archaeological Guide: Praeger, 1968.

Berlitz, Charles F. *Atlantis, the Eighth Continent*: Ballantine, 1985.

Bibby, Geoffrey. *Four Thousand Years Ago*: A.A. Knopf, 1961.

Bischoff, J.L. & Rosenbauer, R.J. "Uranium Series Dating of Human Skeletal Remains from the Del Mar and Sunnyvale Sites." *Science*, August 28, 1981.

Bramwell, James. *Lost Atlantis*: Newcastle Publishing Co., 1974.

Bray, W. & Trump, D. *The American Heritage Guide to Archaeology*: American Heritage Press, 1970.

Brennan, Louis. *No Stone Unturned*: Random House, 1959.

Canby, Thomas Y. "The Search for the First Americans." *National Geographic*, September, 1979.

Carson, Rachel. *The Sea Around Us*: Oxford University Press, 1961.

Carter, George F. "Mystery of the First Americans." *Science Digest*, January, 1961.

_____ *Pleistocene Man at San Diego*: John Hopkins Press, 1957.

Catlin, George. Letter and Notes on the Manners, Customs, and Condition of the North American Indians: Ross & Haines, Inc., 1965.

Clark, J. Grahame. *World Prehistory: an Outline*: Cambridge University Press, 1957.

Coe, Michael D. *America's First Civilization*: American Heritage Publishing Company, 1971.

Coon, Carleton S. *The Origin of Races*: A.A. Knopf, 1962.

Cottrell, Leonard. *The Concise Encyclopedia of Archaeology* (2nd Edition): Hawthorne Books, 1971.

Covey, Curt. "The Earth's Orbit and the Ice Ages." *Scientific American*, February, 1984.

Daniel, Glyn. The Megalith Builders of Western Europe: Pelican Books, 1963.

De Camp, L. Sprague, Lost Continents, Dover Publications.,1970

Donnelly, Ignatius. *Atlantis, the Antediluvian World*: Harper & Row, 1971.

Dyson, James L. *The World of Ice*: A.A. Knopf, 1962.

Escabar, et al. "The Dentition of the Queckchi Indians." *American Journal of Physical Anthropology*, November, 1977.

Fell, Barry. *America B.C.*: Quadrangle; New York Times Book Co., 1976.

Fiedel, Stuart J. *Prehistory of the Americas*: Cambridge University Press, 1993.

Goodman, Jeffrey. *American Genesis*: Summit Books, 1981.

Grabau, W. The Rhythm of the Ages: Earth History in the Light of the Pulsation and Polar Control Theories: Vetch, 1940.

Gray, John. *The Canaanites*: Praeger, 1964.

Greenman, E.F. "The Upper Paleolithic and the New World." *Current Anthropology*, February, 1963.

Guido, Margaret. *Sardinia*: Praeger, 1967.

_____. Sicily: an Archaeological Guide: Praeger, 1967.

Haag, W.G. "The Bering Strait Land Bridge." *Scientific American*, January, 1967.

Hapgood, Charles. *The Earth's Shifting Crust*: Pantheon Books, 1958.

Hawkes, Jacquetta. *Atlas of Ancient Archaeology*: McGraw Hill, 1974.

_____. *Dawn of the Gods*: Random House, 1968.

_____. *Prehistory* (Vol.I): A Mentor Book, 1965.

Hays, J.D., Imbrie, J. & Shackleton, N.J. "Variations in the Earth's Orbit: Pacemaker of the Ice Ages." *Science*, December 10, 1976.

Heyerdahl, Thor. *Early Man and the Ocean*: Vintage Books, 1980.

Homer. *The Iliad*: A Mentor Book.

_____. *The Odyssey*: The Encyclopaedia Brittanica Inc., 1964

Hooten, E.A. *Apes, Men, and Morons*: G.P. Putnam's Sons, 1937.

Hibben, Frank C. *The Lost Americans*: Lippencott, 1946.

Malaise, René. "Oceanic Bottom Investigations and their Bearing on Geology." *Geologiska Foreningens I Stockholm Forhandlingar*, Mars-Apr., 1957.

MacNeish, Richard S. "Early Man in the New World." *American Scientist*, May-June, 1976.

Mac Gowan, Kenneth. *Early Man in the New World*: Macmillan Co., NY, 1950.

Man Across the Sea, C.L. Riley, J.C. Kelley, C.W. Pennington, R.L. Rands, Eds., University of Texas Press, 1976.

McKendrick, Paul. *The Greek Stones Speak*: St. Martin's Press, NY, 1962.

McKern, Sharon and Thom. "Odyssey: the Peopling of the New World." *Mankind*, April, 1970.

Mellers, Paul, Ed. *The Emergence of Modern Humans*: Cornell University Press, 1990.

Menard, Henry. "The East Pacific Rise." *Scientific American*, December, 1961.

Meyer, K.E. "Was There a Pre-Columbian Melting Pot." *Life*, October, 1970.

Morison, Samuel E. *The European Discovery of America*: Oxford University Press, 1971.

Moscati, Sabatino. *Ancient Semitic Civilizations*: Putnam's Sons, 1957.

Oakley, Kenneth. *Frameworks for Dating Fossil Man*: Aldine Publishing Co., 1964.

Pallottino, Massiuco. *The Etruscans*: Indiana University Press, 1975.

Plato. *Critias*: Encyclopaedia Brittanica Inc., 1964.

___. *Timaeus*: Encyclopaedia Brittanica Inc., 1964.

Pomeroy, S.B., et al. *Ancient Greece*: Oxford University Press, 1999.

Raemsch, B.E. & Vernon, W.W. "Some Paleolithic Tools from Northeast North America." *Current Anthropology*, March, 1977.

Rosenberg, G.D. & Runcorn, S.K., Eds. *Growth Rhythms and the History of Earth's Rotation*: Wiley Co., London, 1975.

Renfrew, Colin. *Archaeology and Language*: Cambridge University Press, 1987.

Sandars, N.K. *The Sea Peoples*: Thames and Hudson, NY, 1985.

Savory, H.N. *Spain and Portugal: the Prehistory of the Iberian Peninsula*: Praeger, NY, 1968.

Service, Alastir & Bradbury, Jean. *Megaliths and their Mysteries*: Macmillan Publishing Co., NY, 1979.

Sutcliffe, Anthony. *On the Track of Ice Age Mammals*: Harvard University Press, 1985.

Snodgrass, Anthony M. *The Dark Ages of Greece*: Edinburgh University Press, 1971.

Soustelle, Jacque. *Mexico: Archaeologia Mundi*: World Publishing Co.

Stacy, F.D. "The Main Field." *Global Geophysics*, American Elsevier Publishing Co., 1970.

Stengel, Mark K. "The Diffusionists Have Landed." *Atlantic Monthly*, January, 2000.

Stephenson, F.R. "Historical Eclipses." *Scientific American*, October, 1982.

Strong, Donald E. *The Early Etruscans*: Putnam Co., NY, 1968.

Takeuchi, H., Uyeda, S. & Kanamore, H. *Debate About the Earth*: Freeman Cooper & Sons, San Francisco, 1970.

Trump, David H. *Central and Southern Italy Before Rome*: Thames and Hudson, NY, 1966.

_____. *The Prehistory of the Mediterranean*: Yale University Press, 1980.

Umbgrove, J.H.F. *The Pulse of the Earth*: Martinus Nijoff, 1947.

Veeh, H.H. & Chappell, J. "The Astronomical Theory of Climatic Change, support from New Guinea." *Science*, February 6, 1970.

Wells, John W. "Coral Growth and Geochronometry." *Nature*, March 9, 1963.

Wendt, Herbert. *In Search of Adam*: Houghton Mifflin, NY, 1966.

Whitehouse, Ruth D., Ed. *Dictionary of Archaeology*: Facts on File Publications, NY, 1986.

Winchester, Simon. *Krakatoa*: Harper Collins Pub., 2004

Wood, Michael. *In Search of the Trojan War*: Facts on File Publications, NY, 1986.

Wormington, H.S. *Ancient Man in North America*: Denver Museum of Natural History, 1957.

Wright, Karen. "First Americans." *Discovery*, February, 1999.

Wyllie, Peter. "The Earth's Mantle." *Scientific American*, March, 1975.

INDEX

A

Achaeans, 90, 96-97, 101, 126-127, 129-131, 135-136, 138-140
Alaska, 7-9, 18-19, 21, 57, 83
Arctic Ocean, 8, 38, 43, 45, 63, 70
Asthenosphere
, 35, 58-59, 98, 159, 170
Athens, x, 111-113, 130-131, 137-140, 181, 183, x
Atlantica, ix, 5-7, 34, 63, 69, 83, 149, ix
Atlantic Ridge, 57, 92-93, 95-96, 148, 161, 167
Atlantis, v-vi, x-xi, 1-2, 7, 35, 84-98, 100-113, 115-117, 119-121, 123, 126, 130-133, 135, 140, 142-143, 153, 155, 173, 179, 182-184, 189-190, v-vi, x-xi
Azores, x, 84, 87, 91-98, 100, 102-104, 106, 119-120, 144, 150-153, x

B

Bat Creek, 150
Beaker Folk, x, 116-121, 123, 126, 131, 141, 149, 151, 153, 173, x
Bering Strait, 7-10, 18, 22, 28-29, 62, 70, 81, 190
Beringia, 7, 10, 18-22, 25, 29, 81, 83
Bimini, 153
Bluefish Caves, 18
Bolling (interstadial), 10, 17, 81

Bronze Age, 77, 79-80, 91, 124, 126, 130, 133, 139, 143-144, 151-152, 154-155, 173
British Isles, 31, 87-90, 116-117

C

Cactus Hill, 11, 72
Canary Current, 144, 151-152
Canary Islands, 88
Carabelli's cusp, 26
Carter, George, 21-22, 67, 189
Catastrophism, 59-60
Catlin, George, 25, 74-75, 77, 189
Chandler, Seth, 54
Chassey, 151
Clark, J. Grahame, 31, 78, 189
Climap Project, 45, 62
Clovis, 10-12, 14, 18, 23, 29, 31, 66, 72
Continental drift, 2, 55, 57, 156-157, 159-163, 165-167, 172-173
Convection, 159-162, 169
Coon, Carleton, 23-24, 26, 189
Cordilleran (ice sheet), 17
Cotton, 145, 147-148
Crete, 84, 87, 90-91, 96, 101, 127-130, 134-138, 140

D

Denyens, 129, 133-135, 137, 141
Dillehay, Tom, 10, 13